Hitler vs. Roosevelt

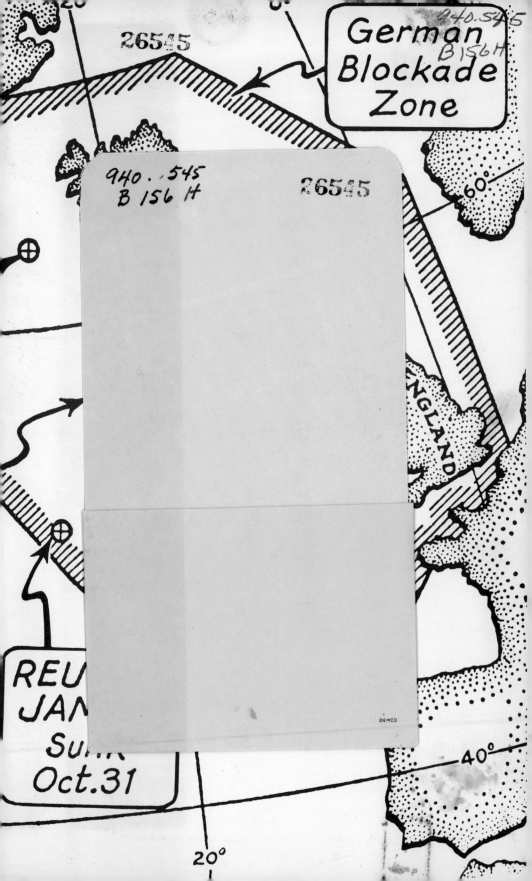

Hitler
vs.
Roosevelt

The Undeclared Naval War

Thomas A. Bailey
AND Paul B. Ryan

THE FREE PRESS
A Division of Macmillan Publishing Co., Inc.
NEW YORK

Collier Macmillan Publishers
LONDON

The Free Press
A Division of Macmillan Publishing Co., Inc.
866 Third Avenue, New York, N.Y. 10022

Collier Macmillan Canada, Ltd.

Library of Congress Catalog Card Number: 78-73023

Printed in the United States of America

printing number

1 2 3 4 5 6 7 8 9 10

Library of Congress Cataloging in Publication Data

Bailey, Thomas Andrew
    Hitler vs. Roosevelt : the undeclared naval war.

    Includes bibliographical references and index.
    1. World War, 1939-1945--Naval operations,
American. 2. World War, 1939-1945--Naval operations,
German. 3. World War, 1939-1945--Naval operations--
Submarine. 4. Roosevelt, Franklin Delano, Pres. U. S.,
1882-1945. 5. Hitler, Adolf, 1889-1945. I. Ryan,
Paul B., joint author. II. Title.
D773.B28 1979   940.54'5   78-73023
ISBN 0-02-901270-8

CONTENTS

LIST OF ILLUSTRATIONS

INSERT OF ILLUSTRATIONS

Eight Pages of Captioned Photographs following page 146

ILLUSTRATED MAPS

CARTOONS

OTHER ILLUSTRATIONS

PREFACE

A flood of books has poured from the presses since the 1930s regarding Hitler, Roosevelt, and World War II. These works have stressed such themes as diplomacy, war, grand strategy, propaganda, espionage, and the tyranny of National Socialism. Until now none has focused directly on the personalized feud between Roosevelt and Hitler that found vent in the German-American undeclared naval war of 1939–1941. This was a back-door clash that both sides more or less pretended did not exist; in fact, they rather hoped it would go away.

We believe that we have pieced together for the first time a complete account of all the friction points of any consequence in German-American relations that involved ships, ship incidents, or other naval matters within the framework of unfolding events. The list is a formidable one indeed. These affairs involved enforced forbearance on the part of Hitler and untiring persistence on the part of Roosevelt.

Both of the present authors retain vivid memories of these troubled times. The younger one, then a U.S. Navy career officer, served in surface ships in the Atlantic and in submarines in the Pacific. He was bombed at Pearl Harbor and participated in the Battle of Midway. His long-term connections with the U.S. Navy have enabled him to secure documentary materials in Washington not readily available to civilian historians. Together, we believe that we have uncovered about as much regarding the essentials of these incidents and episodes as ever will be known, thanks in large part to the captured German archives.

The older author, an academic historian, viewed the scene at the time from the ivory-tower detachment of Stanford University. He recalls reacting with anger to what appeared to be Roosevelt's determined efforts to drag the nation into an all-out shooting war. Especially galling was the President's radio speech misrepresenting the attack by the *U-652* on the U.S. destroyer *Greer*.

Yet to know all is to forgive all, as the saying goes, and we emerged from this study with a more sympathetic understanding of what Roosevelt was really trying to do. His major strategy, despite much deviousness in tactics, was to defend America by helping the British (and the Russians) survive Hitler's overwhelming assaults without involving the United States in a full-dress war. The Japanese attack at Pearl Harbor abruptly ended this dangerous gamesmanship.

For information of various kinds, much of it personal recollection of the times, we gratefully record our indebtedness to the following: Rear Admiral Frank M. Adamson USN (ret.); Dr. Dean Allard, Archivist of the U.S. Naval Historical Center, Washington, D.C.; Rear Admiral F. J. Boyle, USN (Ret.); Lieutenant Wayne M. Brown, USMC (Ret.); Frances L. Carey, U.S. Naval War College Library, Newport, Rhode Island; Rear Admiral Harold L. Challenger, USN (Ret.); Commander Henry W. Dusinberre, USN (Ret.); Director William R. Emerson, Franklin D. Roosevelt Library, Hyde Park, New York; Barbara Ennis, Bureau of Public Affairs, Department of State, Washington, D.C.; Captain Gordon Fowler, USN (Ret.); Vice Admiral Laurence H. Frost, USN (Ret.); Dr. Milton O. Gustafson, Chief, Diplomatic Branch, National Archives, Washington, D.C.; Agnes Hoover, U.S. Naval Historical Center, Washington, D.C.; Dr. Warren F. Kimball, History Department, Rutgers University; Dr. George H. Knoles, History Department, Stanford University; A. V. Krochalis, Naval Intelligence Command, Washington, D.C.; Barbara Lynch, Navy Department Library, Washington, D.C.; Dr. Maierhofer of the Bundesarchiv, Freiberg, Germany; Frederick Meigs, Navy Department Library, Washington, D.C.; Captain Paul A. Miller, of the Marine Corps Reserve; Dr. William J. Morgan, U.S. Naval Historical Center, Washington D.C.; Dr. Raymond O'Connor, History Department, University of Miami; Captain Fitzhugh Lee Palmer, USN (Ret.); Harry Rilley, Military Branch, National Archives, Washington,

D.C.; Gibson B. Smith, Military Archives Division, National Archives, Washington, D.C.; Rear Admiral Hubert E. Strange, USN (Ret.); Ronald E. Swerczek, National Archives (Diplomatic Branch), Washington, D.C.; Henry Vadnais, U.S. Naval Historical Center, Washington, D.C.; Captain Frank K. B. Wheeler, USN (Ret.); Rear Admiral W. J. Whiteside, USN (Ret.); Robert Wolfe, Chief, Modern Military Branch, National Archives, Washington, D.C.

We are also deeply indebted to the reference staff of the Hoover Institution, Stanford University, and also to the staff of the Stanford University Libraries, and to Dr. Stanley L. Sharp.

Dr. Gordon W. Prange, University of Maryland, has graciously granted us permission to quote freely from his invaluable collection, *Hitler's Words* (Washington, D.C., 1944). And Betty Jean Herring did a superb typing job.

THOMAS A. BAILEY, Byrne Professor of
American History, Emeritus
Stanford University, California

CAPTAIN PAUL B. RYAN, U.S.N. Ret.,
Research Associate, Hoover
Institution, Stanford, California

Hitler vs. Roosevelt

CHAPTER 1

THE DAY OF THE DICTATORS

The Peace Treaty [of Versailles] is intolerable. Its economic fulfillment necessarily means political slavery, and its political fulfillment means economic slavery. The abolition of this treaty, therefore, is a necessity.

Adolf Hitler, Munich,
April 20, 1923

Roots of the Hitler-Roosevelt Feud

Adolf Hitler was a child—a misbegotten child—of World War I. If this titanic conflict had not erupted, followed by the unpeaceful Peace of Versailles, he might well have lived out his impoverished days ranting in the beer halls of an unbombed Munich.

Hitler was also an unacknowledged offspring of Woodrow Wilson's humanitarianism and idealism. If the American President had not involved the United States in the war in 1917, Europe would have contrived to make a peace of exhaustion in its own way, as it had done for centuries past. If Wilson had not induced Germany to lay down its arms by the seductive promises of his Fourteen Points—promises tragically broken—Hitler would not have been

1

able to exploit the persistent theme of betrayal in his spectacular rise to power.

The Nazi Führer hated not only Wilson but also Franklin Roosevelt, whom he berated publicly as a "minion" of the idealistic President. Unquestionably, Roosevelt was a dedicated Wilsonian who had championed the Fourteen Points, as well as the Treaty of Versailles, with Wilson's League of Nations riveted in as the very first section.

No doubt the war experiences of Hitler and Roosevelt had a significant bearing on the form that their feud would take. Though an Austrian by birth and upbringing, Hitler volunteered for service in the German army early in the conflict, and served to the end of the war as a foot soldier on the Western Front. He was hospitalized for a thigh wound and again for temporary blindness from gas, and he won the coveted Iron Cross for bravery in combat. But he did not rise above the rank of corporal. Ironically, the future leader (Führer) of the German armies was given low marks for leadership by his superiors.[1] One point to remember in this context is that by background and training Hitler was a land-warfare man. He might have won World War II if he had fully recognized the importance of the crucial Battle of the Atlantic and had diverted sufficient resources from tanks to building a few dozen more submarines.

In 1918 Hitler's front-line unit had not tangled with the American doughboys, but the future Führer must have been aware that the coming of the Yanks in force coincided with the reversal of the last-gasp German drive in the spring of 1918. This recollection probably had something to do with Hitler's determination to lean over backward to avoid provoking the Americans intolerably before the Japanese attacked Pearl Harbor in December 1941.

Franklin Roosevelt, by contrast, was sea-minded. An avid amateur sailor, he had gained valuable experience during World War I as Assistant Secretary of the Navy, and became something of an expert on anti-submarine warfare. This expertise later served him in good stead during World War II, when he was President. Like Theodore Roosevelt and many other patriotic Americans, F.D.R. was eager to get into action in France in 1917–1918, but his superiors believed that he could serve more usefully by continuing as Assistant Secretary of the Navy.

On an inspection tour in 1918 Roosevelt contrived to cross the Atlantic in a zigzagging American destroyer past convoys of Allied merchant ships; he came close enough to the front lines in France to undergo firing; and he visited the destruction at Belleau Wood and

Verdun, where the U.S. Marines and the French had done some of their bloodiest fighting. In 1936, as President, he proclaimed on radio his detestation of war: "I have seen war. I have seen war on land and sea. I have seen blood running from the wounded. I have seen men coughing out their gassed lungs. I have seen the dead in the mud. I have seen cities destroyed. I have seen two hundred limping, exhausted men come out of line—the survivors of a regiment of one thousand that went forward forty-eight hours before. I have seen children starving. I have seen the agony of mothers and wives. I hate war."[2]

Roosevelt's reaction is entirely believable and may have had a bearing on his continued reluctance to get into an all-out shooting conflict in 1940–1941.

By contrast, Hitler had delivered numerous rabble-rousing speeches blasting the negotiators of the Armistice that had ended the shooting on November 11, 1918. In the so-called pre-Armistice contract, the victorious Allies, with two reservations, had promised the Germans a "soft" peace treaty based on Wilson's hope-giving Fourteen Points. But after the fallen foe was disarmed, the vengeful Allies did not deliver on their promises. Most of the Fourteen Points were blunted, bent, broken, overridden, or ignored.

Hitler, the impassioned orator, tirelessly exploited this "betrayal" by the victors during his rise from political obscurity. The facts are that German soil had not been invaded in the west and that the Germans did not feel really beaten. Thus the myth was born that the Jews and the Bolsheviks had stabbed Germany fatally in the back, and the resulting atmosphere was made to order for a demagogue of Hitler's stripe. Tragically, the democratic, new Weimar Republic in Germany was forced to live in this stifling atmosphere of betrayal—and it died in 1933.

As for the Treaty of Versailles itself, Hitler had repeatedly and publicly condemned specific articles. Germany was forced to accept the "guilt" of having brought on the war, but few Germans, including Hitler, believed that they were solely to blame. Point V of the Fourteen held out assurances that Germany could retain her colonies. Yet they were taken over by enemies, like Britain and France, who already had vast overseas holdings.

The unkept promises or grievances growing out of the Fourteen Points and the Treaty of Versailles thus provided an ascending Hitler with convenient ammunition. The back-breaking reparations burden became intolerable, as he repeatedly pointed out. Disarmament for Germany was demanded, but the victors remained armed.

Self-determination had been extolled by Wilson, but the Germans of
Austria, Czechoslovakia, and Poland were denied union with Germany. Ironically, Hitler became a more avid preacher of self-determination than Wilson had ever been. And the League of Nations to
preserve the peace turned into a League of Victors, with Germany
left outside the gates for seven years.

A dramatic move to preserve peace by outlawing war came
with the naive Kellogg-Briand peace pact of 1928, sponsored by the
United States and France. This agreement was ratified by sixty-two
nations, including Germany. The signatories pledged themselves
never to wage war except in self-defense. Such was the explosive international atmosphere when Hitler clawed his way to the chancel-
lorship early in 1933, in the teeth of a majority vote at the polls in
1932 against his own Nazi party. This was the last free general election that an undivided Germany was to enjoy.

Debts and the Depression

Franklin Delano Roosevelt, master politician and America's premier
orator, assumed the presidential mantle on March 4, 1933. For more
than the three years since the stock market crash of 1929 the United
States had been wallowing in the Great Depression, and Roosevelt
had won his election by condemning Hoover and promising to deal
boldly and effectively with the economic disaster. There can be no
doubt about his boldness, only about his effectiveness. Roosevelt was
an offspring of the Great Depression in the sense that he probably
would not have gained the White House in 1932 if the prosperity of
the Roaring Twenties had continued throughout the Hoover years.

On January 30, 1933, one month and five days prior to Roosevelt's inauguration, Adolf Hitler became Chancellor of Germany,
and from this vantage point gradually grasped supreme power.
Foremost German orator and politician, the new Führer, like Roosevelt, was a product of the Great Depression. He almost certainly
would not have attained dictatorial power when he did, if at all, had
the Depression not struck Germany with devastating force. In his
amazing ascent Hitler milked from the massive German unemployment and related miseries a maximum of political advantage.

In numerous hypnotic speeches, Chancellor Hitler blamed the
current depression on the Treaty of Versailles, with its shearing
away of Germany's colonies, with its confiscation of much of the nation's merchant shipping, and with its other economic burdens.
Prominent among Hitler's targets were the Americans, especially

the "big Jewish firms," whose number and influence he grossly exaggerated.[3] The unpleasant truth is that Washington's policy regarding German reparations and the Allied war debts, all intercon-
nected, did much to worsen, if not cause, the depression in Europe.

During World War I and shortly after the Armistice, the
United States had loaned some $10 billion to her Associates for the
purchase of arms and other war material. These outlays came first in
the United States in the form of credits advanced. Little money, including gold, crossed the Atlantic. Business in the United States
prospered, American workers took home fat pay envelopes, and the
Treasury raked in excess profits taxes and other benefits.

Britain, France, and Italy, in that order, were the heaviest bor-
rowers, and with the dawn of peace they were forced to face up to
the problem of repayment. One difficulty was that the victors were
counting on reparations from Germany to discharge all or much of
their indebtedness to the United States. If Washington would only
cancel these outstanding debts, then the ex-Allies could presumably
reduce the reparations burden on Germany—a burden that became
even more onerous when the Great Depression descended like a suf-
focating smog. During the 1920s American ("Jewish") bankers in-
vested hundreds of millions of dollars in Germany, and these sums
provided the foreign exchange that greatly assisted the borrowing
nations in financing the installments on their debt to the United
States. To a substantial degree the Americans were really paying
themselves by the roundabout route of Germany, France, and Britain. Ironically, American investments in German heavy industry
and other enterprises played a significant role in strengthening
Hitler's overwhelming war machine. He was not as appreciative as
he could have been, for in March 1936 he publicly condemned foreign credits as forcing Germany to expand her exports artificially
and at a loss to herself.[4]

In 1924 Germany's reparations payments had been temporarily
scaled down under the Dawes Plan, named after an American
banker, Charles Gates Dawes. When the installments proved too
heavy, the Young Plan, promoted by an American lawyer-industri-
alist, Owen D. Young, provide for much smaller installments but
over the definite span of fifty-eight and one-half years. Put into operation in 1930, this scheme aroused the fury of a then emerging politician, Adolf Hitler, partly because it would confine to fiscal bondage
generations yet unborn. After he had gained supreme power in 1933,
Hitler openly repudiated the remaining reparations payments.
Oddly enough, he found himself in the strange company of Ger-

many's ex-foes, which had defaulted on their debts to the United States—permanently, as events turned out. Uncle Sam was left holding the sack, but he and his alleged "Jewish bankers" remained high on Hitler's hate list.

Aggression in Two Hemispheres

The depressing decade of the 1930s experienced repeated and wholesale aggressions by the dictators. New acts of violence eclipsed the earlier but relatively minor defiance of the League of Nations when Poland had seized the city of Vilna in 1920, and when Italy had infuriated the Greeks by occupying the tiny island of Corfu in 1923. Increasingly, international commitments and international law were being flouted.

Large-scale defiance of the Kellogg-Briand peace pact first came in 1929, not from Hitler but from the Soviet Union, which did not joint the League of Nations until 1934. After persisting friction with the Chinese over a sphere of interest in China's Manchuria, the Soviets launched a full-scale invasion and speedily brought their adversary to terms. Secretary of State Stimson, the moralistic voice of Washington, undertook to remind Moscow of its treaty obligations to keep the peace. He received a stinging rebuke for attempting to preach restraint to a nation that the United States did not even formally recognize. This alarming incident further advertised the vulnerability of China, the weakness of the Kellogg-Briand Pact, and the futility of attempting to check an armed aggressor with the wrist-slap of world indignation.

China's feebleness increasingly tempted overcrowded Japan, which, more than Hitler, was pressingly concerned with additional living space. In September 1931 the warlords of Japan launched a carefully planned and precisely executed occupation of Manchuria, China's enormous northern province. The attack was touched off by a minor explosion on a key railroad, obviously "planted." After the Chinese forces were routed, Tokyo transformed Manchuria into the puppet state of Manchukuo under a hand-picked government. The war-bent Tokyo regime remembered how Nippon had been forced by the Great Powers to disgorge China's Shantung in 1919. Accordingly, the warlords chose to strike while Europe and America were bogged down in the Great Depression.

The Japanese seizure of Manchuria was a flagrant violation of three solemn international commitments. One was a formal obligation not to engage in aggressive warfare, both as a member of the League of Nations and as a signatory of the Kellogg-Briand Pact. Additionally, Tokyo had flouted its commitment under the Nine Power Treaty, signed at Washington in 1922, "To respect the sovereignty, the independence, and the territorial and administrative integrity of China." Japan stood self-condemned as an international outlaw.

By resolute and united action, the depression-ridden members of the League of Nations might conceivably have forced Japan into line. As weapons, they could have used either economic boycotts or military and naval forces. But the European powers, notably Britain and France, shied away from the prospect of going it alone without the active support of the nonmember United States. President Herbert Hoover, a peaceful Quaker and a noninterventionist, would have nothing to do with ironfisted measures. Accordingly, his Secretary of State, Henry L. Stimson, struck back with a light tap on the wrist. He declared, in the overpraised Hoover-Stimson nonrecognition doctrine, that the United States would not recognize any territorial or other changes brought about by force.

An investigative commission, sent out by the League of Nations, published its report in September 1932. Although finding some extenuating circumstances, the investigation condemned the Japanese invasion of Manchuria. But instead of driving Japan out of the invaded area, this rebuke drove the Japanese out of the League of Nations by the route of resignation. Thus, the birth cries of the puppet state of Manchukuo could be later recognized as the preliminary death rattle of the League of Nations. In a broad sense the League fell apart, collective security perished, and World War II began in 1931 on the windswept plains of Manchuria.

Japan thus made off with ill-gotten gains, despite international law and multinational disapproval. This object lesson in banditry was not lost on dictators Mussolini and Hitler when they turned to international outlawry in pursuit of their territorial ambitions. On October 14, 1933, Chancellor Hitler, after some seven months in office, abruptly withdrew Germany from the General Disarmament Conference, and for good measure from the League of Nations as well. He was not about to be bothered by any paper restraints, no matter how feeble they might be.

The Outlook

Hitler Rearms the Reich

Chancellor Hitler and his Nazis continued to capture the headlines. The overwhelming Saar plebiscite of January 1935, as authorized by the Treaty of Versailles, resulted in that coal-rich area's being formally taken from French custody and returned to Germany, effective March 7. This completely legal restoration marked the first postwar territorial expansion of Germany.

Emboldened by these assertive moves, Hitler became more aggressive. On March 16, 1935, nine days after the Saar transfer, he took full advantage of the deepening disagreements among the ex-Allies—Britain, France, and Italy. He boldly denounced and thus negated the arms limitation clauses of the Treaty of Versailles. Yet his unilateral course was not completely surprising, because a bitter and defiant Germany had been secretly rearming or scheming to do so ever since the signing of the peace pact at Versailles in 1919.

Yet Hitler had potentially menacing neighbors on both sides—France, Poland, and Czechoslovakia—all with relatively strong armies. There was a certain fairness in allowing the Germans to build up a substantial defensive force. For these reasons Hitler's unilateral denunciation of the relevant restrictive clauses of the Treaty of Versailles did not arouse as much condemnation as he probably expected. The most disturbing new element was his introduction of peacetime conscription, which, we should note, also prevailed in such powerful potential foes as France, Italy, and Russia.

Allied spokesmen, including Winston Churchill, claimed that Germany could not legally and unilaterally denounce a treaty in such a way as to "endanger the peace of Europe."[5] But the Germans had a rather persuasive reply. They pointed out that the Treaty of Versailles was accepted under duress (as are all victors' treaties) and that in domestic law any agreement signed at the point of a gun is invalid. Additionally, the victors had not fulfilled their part of the pre-Armistice agreement to disarm. But the question of who was right in this dispute now seems somewhat irrelevant. The Germans could have added that by 1935, if not before, international compacts were again becoming "scraps of paper," 1914 vintage.

The British, unlike the French, were not burdened by conscription because of the intervening English Channel. Surprisingly, they acquiesced in Hitler's rearmament by negotiating a startling naval limitation treaty with Germany in June 1935. By its terms the Germans would be entitled to build up to one-third of Britain's naval tonnage, including as much as 60 percent of their rival's submarine strength. On its face, this did not seem like a menacing amount, but it constituted, according to Winston Churchill, more than the German shipyards would be able to produce before 1939, when Hitler actually launched World War II.[6]

In return for permission to construct these U-boats, the Germans agreed to abide by the humane rules of submarine warfare as embodied in the London Naval Treaty of 1930. Many Britons at the time feared that Hitler would not honor these restrictions, as indeed

he did not. As for the French, they were understandably upset by
this seemingly unnecessary naval surrender by London, and their
subsequent feeling of betrayal further weakened their common front
against a resurgent Germany.

The Rome-Berlin Axis

The spotlight next shifted to Benito Mussolini, the posturing "saw-
dust Caesar" of Italy. Taking full advantage of the cross-purposes of
Britain and France, he launched an invasion of primitive Ethiopia
in October 1935.

Italy had fared badly in the scramble for African colonies during the period from the 1890s to the end of the Peace Conference of
Paris in 1919. Mussolini himself could never forget the disgrace
flowing from the wiping out of an entire Italian army by the Ethio-
pians at Adowa in 1896. To be sure, Italy was still a member of the
League of Nations, pledged to conciliation or arbitration before
going to war, but Mussolini could well remember how ineffectual
the League had been in trying to halt the Japanese thrust into
Manchuria in 1931–1932.

The League of Nations, meeting in Geneva, promptly branded
Italy the aggressor and voted sanctions in the form of economic embargoes. But the League shied away from including oil, the one com-
modity that would have brought Mussolini's war machine to a
creaking halt. The British conspicuously held back. A wave of paci-
fism had been sweeping the British Isles, and the fear prevailed that
the Italian navy might cripple the fighting ships of Britain in the
constricted Mediterranean. An important but unpredictable factor
was the United States, which as a non–League member might reap
a fortune by supplying Italy with the desperately needed oil.

Several by-products of Mussolini's ironfisted conquest of Ethiopia must be emphasized. It further demonstrated what Japan's invasion of Manchuria had widely advertised, namely, that the
League was contemptible as an instrument for restraining a powerful aggressor, partly because of the non-adherence of the United
States. Not only did the League suffer a staggering blow but the
brutal invasion of Ethiopia was also accompanied by such atrocities
on both sides as to demonstrate further that international law was
largely a dead letter as far as the aggressors were concerned. The law
of the jungle was the wave of the future.

Hitler's turn now came to make a sensational move. Encouraged by the continuing timidity of the ex-Allies in not protecting Ethiopia, he daringly occupied the demilitarized Rhineland with German troops on March 7, 1936. This was a flagrant violation of the near-defunct Treaty of Versailles and of the Locarno Pacts of 1925, which Hitler had the forethought to denounce formally in advance. The most puzzling aspect of this alarming stroke is that the French plainly had the power to eject the Germans. Hitler's generals pleaded with their Führer not to take such a desperate gamble, so weak was the German army and so strong was the French, but he plunged ahead in the expectation of pulling back if he met any resistance. To his great relief, the coup went off peacefully, amid great rejoicing by Germans both in the Rhineland and elsewhere in Germany. The shortsightedness of the French is difficult to explain. Yet one may note that close cooperation with the British seemed unlikely, and the hope lingered that Hitler might yet calm down if appeased in this fashion.

The Belgians, alarmed by the German occupation of the Rhineland, committed a comparable act of folly. On October 14, 1936, Belgium formally denounced its military alliance with France and resumed complete liberty of action as a neutral state—a status that she had "enjoyed" before the Germans invaded in 1914. Hitler responded with a solemn guarantee of neutrality, which of course went out the window when he brutally attacked Belgium without warning in the spring of 1940.

Mussolini's Ethiopian gamble had naturally drawn him closer to his fellow dictator, Adolf Hitler. The new union was concluded on November 1, 1936, when the jut-jawed Italian proclaimed the Rome-Berlin Axis—an accord that was further strengthened by the Italo-German military alliance of May 22, 1939. Japan was later included, on September 27, 1940, and the dictatorial aggressors of the have-nations were henceforth banded together in a formidable coalition. Its members, fortunately for the democratic world, did not always march to the same drummer.

Neutrality by Act of Congress

In the United States the Ethiopian crisis of 1935–1936 had the further side effect of propelling through Congress a hastily drafted neutrality bill, that of 1935. This measure was the fruition of a neutrality neurosis that had developed out of the events since the ending of World War I in 1918. First there had been disillusionment over the collapse of Wilsonian idealism; then growing disenchantment with the recent Allies; and then the unseemly quarrel with them over war debts, so intimately tied in with German reparations. In 1934–1935 a flood of lurid books and articles poured from the American press, describing the fantastic profits that the "merchants of death" had made from selling munitions to the Allies. Following a Senate investigation the ill-founded belief took hold that American munitions manufacturers and bankers had dragged the United States into the war to protect their profits and loans. Overlooked or underemphasized was Wilson's inflexible stand for a free sea and his subsequent clash with the German U-boats.

Such near hysteria helped to push through Congress the (First) Neutrality Act of 1935, as well as its revision of 1936, known as the Second Neutrality Act. The United States thus legislated herself out of war by forbidding the sale or transport of munitions to nations that found themselves in armed conflict. No distinction whatever was made between aggressors and victims, between dictators and democracies, between wrong and right, between decency and indecency. The Third Neutrality Act (1937) modified this straitjacket concept somewhat. Thereafter, commodities that could be made into munitions, such as copper and lead, might be sold on a "cash and carry" basis for two years. But foreign purchasers would have to pay for these cargoes with cash and haul them away in their own ships.

By 1937 it was painfully evident that if war convulsed Europe again, Hitler and Mussolini, either or both, would be the aggressors. They would not be able to send merchant ships to America, with or without cash, in the teeth of the British and French surface navies. On the other hand, Britain, France, and the other democracies would be able to purchase arms in the United States—if only they could raise the cash.

The accusation has often been voiced that Hitler started World War II in part because he realized that his enemies could not obtain arms from the United States after the shooting began. The truth is that the democracies could secure unlimited quantities of oil, copper, and other sinews of war if they could manage to penetrate any German blockade that might be established. When the Führer attacked Poland in 1939 he could not have been worrying much about faraway America, where arms manufacturing was still in painfully low gear. He was in fact concerned about his own munitions, for he had on hand only a limited supply for heavy fighting. He was confidently counting on the German blitzkrieg in Poland, and he succeeded overwhelmingly.

The Dress-Rehearsal Spanish War

The trio of dictators—Hitler, Mussolini, and Stalin—showed their contempt for the obligations of neutrality by participating actively and openly in the viciously fought Spanish Civil War, 1936–1939, involving Loyalists versus rebels. The conflict claimed an estimated 700,000 lives, considerably more than America's great Civil War of 1861–1865.

The popularly elected Loyalist or Republican (Popular Front) government in Madrid, heavily infiltrated with radicals, was initially attacked by right-wing insurgents. These were conservative and Catholic, and they found a tough-minded leader in Francisco Franco, aided substantially by Moorish mercenaries. Many of these troops were ferried across the narrow Mediterranean by transport planes of Hitler's air force. Dictator Franco ultimately triumphed after this bloodbath, ignored Hitler's appeals to join him in battle, sat out World War II, and ruled with an iron hand for thirty-seven autocratic years.

Britain and France, heading the democratic nations of Europe, sought to "localize" the Spanish conflict, largely because their own peoples were so sharply divided between the right and the left. One attempt at neutrality was the Non-Intervention Committee, sitting in Nyon, near Geneva, and representing more than a score of nations, including Germany and Italy.[7] Hitler and Mussolini, soon to be united in the Axis alliance, openly flouted this solemn commitment and the general obligations of neutrality. Mussolini ordered to Spain an estimated 50,000–75,000 uniformed "volunteers," some of whom were transparently disguised as "medical units."

All told, Hitler provided Franco with aircraft and tank units, supported by technicians, totaling some 10,000 so-called volunteers. The Germany "pocket battleship" *Deutschland,* at anchor in the rebel harbor of Ibiza, came under attack from a Loyalist airplane. She suffered some damage and the loss of twenty-two men killed, plus more than eighty wounded. An outraged Hitler, instead of using ordinary diplomatic channels for a protest, dispatched a fleet of five warships to the harbor of Almeria. The subsequent bombardment virtually destroyed about thirty-five buildings and took nineteen lives.[8]

The month before, on April 26, 1937, without obvious provocation, waves of German bombers attacked and systematically destroyed the Spanish Basque town of Guernica. The fleeing survivors were machine gunned for a total of some 1,600 killed and 900 wounded. By the admission of Marshal Goering in 1946 the Germans regarded this action as a testing ground for the bombing of cities in the forthcoming world war.[9]

Outrageously vexatious were "pirate" submarines in the Mediterranean. They began to chase, shell, and torpedo dozens of merchant ships, including British and Russian, many of them carrying munitions and other war supplies to the Loyalist regime in Madrid. These "phantom" undersea craft were generally believed to be of Italian nationality; Count Ciano, then Italian Foreign Minister, specificially named one of them in his diary.[10] The British and the French took the initiative in setting up a nine-power Mediterranean patrol with some forty destroyers and a comparable number of aircraft. Initially this force proved rather effective. The Italians at first spurned it, but ultimately they were permitted to patrol a specified area themselves—a classic case of the fox's being authorized to guard the hen coop. Some sinkings continued, the victims mostly ships carrying supplies to the Loyalists.

President Roosevelt, responding to America's neutrality fixation regarding the Spanish bloodbath, recommended that Congress extend the existing neutrality legislation of 1936 to civil wars, as well as to international conflicts. In normal times the Communist-infiltrated Loyalist government in Madrid would have been entitled to purchase shipments of arms from the United States. But these were not normal times, and Congress approved the requested ban with only one dissenting vote. The legislators thereby demonstrated that the American people were as shortsighted as the nearby but warfearing British and French governments. More than a half million human beings, as well as a democratically elected government, perished in Franco's Spain. The law-flouting dictators were thus spurred along the downhill road to the atomic Armageddon of 1945.

CHAPTER 2

HITLER LAUNCHES
A GLOBAL WAR

*You [Hitler] have repeatedly asserted that you and the German people have no desire
for war. If this is true there need be no war.*

Roosevelt's appeal to Hitler,
April 14, 1939

Spotlights on China and Austria

As Europe pulled out of the postwar chaos, Japan continued to view
with keen interest the spectacular rise of the dictators in Europe. In
November 1936 the Japanese strengthened their Manchurian flank
against the Soviet Union by entering into an anti-Comintern (anti-
Communist) pact with Hitler's Germany. Thus protected, Japan's
warlords launched a large-scale invasion of China, beginning in July
1937 and continuing inconclusively to the atomic holocaust of August 1945.

In keeping with the new spirit of the times, the China incident
flared forth without the usual formality of a declaration of war. It
continued in open defiance of the Kellogg-Briand Pact of 1928 and
the Nine Power Treaty signed at Washington in 1922. The attack
was not in a violation of the League of Nations Covenant, for Japan

had formally withdrawn from that organization in 1933. But the assault on China was a stunning setback for those trusting souls who still clung to their faith in the sanctity of international law and treaties.

A vigilant Hitler meantime had never taken covetous eyes off his native Austria, a little, German-speaking country that he had long envisaged as an essential part of a Greater Germany. After softening up the Vienna government by infiltrating it with Nazi agents and propaganda, he bullied Austria's leaders into partial submission. Then he moved in suddenly with clanking tanks and took over that "orphaned" nation in March 1938, to the frenzied cheers of newly Nazified Austrians. This act of aggression forced Austria to violate the Treaty of Saint Germain, which she had concluded with the victorious Allies in 1919 and which barred any future union with Germany. Hitler regarded his coup, with some justification, as a partial fulfillment of Woodrow Wilson's dream of self-determination. Yet if the Führer was right in principle he was wrong in practice.

American public opinion had meanwhile grown increasingly distrustful of Hitler's antics. The large Jewish community in the United States naturally deplored the policy of persecuting the Jews that Hitler had launched, starting tragically on April 1, 1933, two months after becoming Chancellor. One reaction in the United States was the tearing down of the swastika emblem from the palatial German liner *Bremen* in New York harbor (July 26, 1935). Some months later Mayor La Guardia delivered a speech in New York in which he referred to Hitler as "that brown-shirted fanatic." For their part President Roosevelt and prominent members of his administration made clear their displeasure in commenting on the brutal persecutions by Hitler's gangsters.

The Czech Crisis

Late in September 1938 the most dangerous confrontation yet to rock postwar Europe came to a head. The crucial issue was Hitler's demand for the German-populated Sudetenland of Czechoslovakia. This tiny democracy had gained these strategic border expanses in the peace settlement of 1919–1920, contrary to a strict application of the Wilsonian principle of self-determination. A major objective was to make the patchwork western frontiers of Czechoslovakia more defensible.

Hitler's clever scheme was to infiltrate and soften up the Sudetenland with Nazi agents or spokesmen, as he already had done in Austria. Then he would annex the disputed territory even at the cost of war. Some of his generals warned him that the army was not yet ready for combat on such a scale, because the Czechs had a well-trained and well-equipped military force, as well as supposedly formidable mountain defenses. Yet Hitler seemed fanatically determined to fight, beginning on October 1, 1938.

Additional prearranged "incidents" in the Sudetenland by Nazis or pro-Nazis flared forth. Prime Minister Chamberlain of Great Britain so far humbled himself, on September 15, 1938, as to fly to Hitler's "eagle's nest" at Berchtesgaden to plead for an amicable solution. A war-bent Hitler laid down harsh terms. Chamberlain then flew back to London and secured the timorous acquiescence of France, plus the grudging consent of the Czechs. He next returned to Germany to bend the knee to Hitler, on September 27. This time the Führer, in a towering rage, raised his demands; he evidently was determined to have the glory of war before winter came, even after his main adversaries had capitulated. On the same day the British government issued orders to mobilize the Royal Navy.

A day earlier, September 26, 1938, Roosevelt had cabled a personal message to Hitler pleading for a peaceful solution of the Sudeten dispute. He also addressed the same appeal to Paris, London, and Prague. His fear was that the imminent war would suck in Germany and Italy on one side, with Britain, France, and Czechoslovakia on the other. Roosevelt pointed out that a general conflict would adversely affect the social and economic structure of the nations involved, including indirectly the United States. The parties concerned were bound by the Kellogg-Briand Pact of 1928 to keep the peace by resorting to negotiation, conciliation, and arbitration. Roosevelt concluded, "On behalf of the 130 millions of people of the United States of America and for the sake of humanity everywhere I most earnestly appeal to you not to break off negotiations looking to a peaceful, fair, and constructive settlement of the questions at issue."[1]

Hitler Rebuffs Roosevelt

Three brief but sympathetic responses, dated the same day, promptly arrived in Washington from London, Paris, and Prague. About five times longer than the longest of these was Hitler's reply, dated the next day, September 27, 1938. It was a diabolically clever attempt to shift responsibility for the Czech crisis onto shoulders other than his own.

At the outset Hitler reminded Roosevelt that Germany had laid down its arms in 1918 in "the firm confidence" that peace would be based on Wilson's Fourteen Points. But "Never in history has the confidence of a people been more shamefully betrayed than it was then." The principle of self-determination had been flagrantly flouted by awarding three and one-half million Germans to Austria, rather than to Germany, where they belonged. Attempts of the Czechs to Czechify these Germanic foreigners had produced disorders of various kinds, as a result of which "214,000 Sudeten Germans" had been forced to flee to Germany, leaving "countless dead, thousands of injured, ten thousands of persons arrested and imprisoned, and desolated villages." (Hitler did not add that many of these alleged disorders had been stirred up by his own agents.)

The Führer concluded his unyielding response to Roosevelt by saying that the Czech government had already agreed to the separation of the Sudetenland from Czechoslovakia. All that remained was for this promise to be carried out: "It does not rest with the German Government, but with the Czechoslovak Government alone, to decide whether it wants peace or war."[2]

On September 27, 1938, the date of Hitler's defiant answer, Roosevelt responded with a renewed appeal that was slightly longer than his first. He repeated his earnest plea for continued negotiations. But, evidently with an eye to American isolationists, F.D.R. added that the United States would "assume no obligations in the conduct of the present negotiations."[3] Additionally, the President made contact with Mussolini, who then informed his German ally, Hitler, on the telephone.

Precisely what effect Roosevelt's intercession had cannot be determined. But a triumph of sorts was achieved when the Führer grudgingly consented to a four-power conference at Munich, Germany. There, on September 29, 1938, the mutilation of Czechoslovakia was formalized by Hitler, Mussolini, Prime Minister Chamberlain of Great Britain, and Premier Daladier of France. The French, unlike the British, were bound by a specific treaty to defend the luckless little nation if she dared to resist an invasion by Hitler's forces. The Brisish in such an event were obligated by their membership in the semi-defunct League of Nations. But we shall never know what would have happened if a Czech-German war had erupted, for the Czechs, lacking firm French and British support, knuckled under.

Two conspicuously empty chairs at Munich told their own tragic story. One of them should have been occupied by the victim, Czechoslovakia; the other, presumably by a Soviet representative. Stalin was completely snubbed, although he had a vital interest in preventing the aggrandizement of Hitler, his anti-Bolshevik arch-enemy. He later indicated that he would have come to the aid of Czechoslovakia, if the Western allies had only honored their defense commitments. Yet the sole feasible route for Soviet armies was through Romania and Poland, two nations that deeply feared and distrusted the Russians. Stalin would later use his vacant chair at Munich as another convenient excuse for concluding the Soviet-Nazi Nonaggression Pact in August 1939, thereby unleashing the dogs of World War II.[4]

The Munich Aftermath

The narrow escape from war at Munich brought the Western world immense relief, accompanied by widespread rejoicing. The British and French, not fully aware of Germany's overall military unreadiness, had been unduly impressed by Hitler's powerful air force, yet they had bought a year's time for preparation by selling out France's ally, Czechoslovakia. The "appeasers" salved their consciences to some degree by the assurance that transferring Czech Germans to Germany was genuine self-determination.

Naively, the democracies placed too much faith in Hitler's word. He had promised a Berlin audience three days before the Munich accord that "when this problem is solved there is for Germany no further territorial problem in Europe." (This pledge is commonly translated as "The Sudetenland is the last territorial claim I have to make in Europe.") Hitler added that he would then "have no further interest in the Czech State. . . . We want no Czechs!"[5]

But the word "Munich" immediately became a synonym for "appeasement"—that is, "surrender on the installment plan," or giving a dictator one more juicy morsel in the desperate hope that it would appease rather than whet his appetite for more. Henceforth "Munich" became a dirty word that was repeatedly employed to block even reasonable compromises. It was in fact a compromise, but a one-sided compromise: the democracies sold out the Sudetenland in return for a promise (not kept) that Hitler would take no

Hitler's pledge at the time of Munich, September 1938. *Fitzpatrick in the St. Louis Post-Dispatch*

more territory in Europe. So it was that the Munich nightmare became one of the most lasting heritages of Hitlerism. It epitomized the spirit of give and take, with the democracies giving and the dictators taking.

The demoralized British and French dearly purchased a year of grace by the Munich capitulation. But they did not use this time to maximum advantage, and from September 1938 to September 1939 Hitler's army and air force grew even more menacing.* Winston

---

* Thus, Germany began the war in 1939 with 57 submarines of all types, only 26 of them suitable for extended war patrols; at the peak, in May 1943, the number had risen to 219 operable U-boats.

Churchill believed that Britain, though badly unprepared, should have fought at the time of Munich, when Czechoslovakia seemed capable of putting up a stout resistance.[6] But by September 1, 1939, when Hitler finally started World War II in Poland, the British had developed radar and had cracked the top German code through the ingenious device known as "Enigma," which spawned the intelligence system known as "Ultra."[7] They enjoyed the priceless advantage of knowing when and where the attacking Nazi bombers were coming.

The year of delay actually gave the British and French a much better moral case. There was admittedly some force in Hitler's demand for Wilsonian self-determination for the Germans of the Sudetenland. But by seizing what was left of Czechoslovakia in March 1939, he fully revealed that he was not only a power-mad dictator but a barefaced liar and treaty breaker to boot.

Appeasement without Peace

The bad taste left by Hitler's ruthless grab of the Sudetenland was further embittered by his vicious anti-Semitism. Attacks on an unprecedented scale broke out against the German Jews on November 9, 1938, following the assassination of a German diplomat in Paris by a young Jew whose parents had been deported to Poland. With at least the tacit encouragement of Hitler, widespread riots erupted against Jews and Jewish shops on the Crystal Night of November 8, so called from the multitude of smashed windows. Official German estimates, probably underestimates, included the destruction, often by burning, of 814 shops, 171 homes, and 191 synagogues. In all thirty-six Jews were killed and about an equal number seriously injured.[8]

An America already profoundly disturbed by the Munich sellout recoiled in horror. President Roosevelt publicly declared, "I myself could scarcely believe that such things could occur in a twentieth-century civilization."[9] The United States Ambassador to Germany, Hugh R. Wilson, was temporarily summoned to Washington, ostensibly to provide information but obviously as a protest against the continued persecutions of Jews. The Berlin government tried to protest against Secretary of the Interior Ickes's condemnation of Hitler as a "brutal dictator." But the State Department bluntly refused to receive the complaint on the ground that Ickes had faithfully represented the views of "99½ percent" of the American people.[10]

At the time of the Munich sellout many apprehensive Europeans had questioned not only Hitler's willingness to honor his plighted word but also his commitment to self-determination. All doubts were erased on March 15, 1939, nearly six months after Munich, when German troops occupied much of former Czechoslovakia. The next day Slovakia was placed under a German "protectorate," and Hungary was allowed to annex Ruthenia. Gone was Hitler's promise at the time of Munich that he wanted "no Czechs"; gone were his assurances that he was merely seeking self-determination for Germans. Gone was any faith that the weak-kneed appeasement at Munich would put an end to Hitler's expansionist appetite. On March 20, 1939, the United States recalled the American Ambassador in Berlin as a publicized protest against the dismemberment of Czechoslovakia; henceforth both Washington and Berlin were represented only by Chargés d'affaires.

The next day (March 21, 1939) Hitler demanded and secured from Lithuania, under threat of imminent seizure by the German navy, the tiny Baltic district of Memel. This area had been shorn off from Germany under the Treaty of Versailles and was inhabited primarily by Germans. Next on the Führer's grab list was the Polish corridor, capped by the German-inhabited free city of Danzig. On March 28, 1939, Hitler denounced Germany's nonaggression pact with Poland, dating back to 1934, and three days later Britain and France gave their futile pledge to support Poland in the event of an attack.

Roosevelt's Appeal to Hitler

The spirit of conquest was in the air—and contagious. On April 7, 1939, Mussolini's legions invaded and overran Albania, after slight resistance, thus adding to the new Roman empire a long-coveted vassal. On the same day dictator Franco of Spain, seeking to bolster his position, joined Germany, Italy, and Japan in adhering to the anti-Soviet, anti-Comintern pact. He thus became a kind of junior partner with his twin benefactors, Hitler and Mussolini, whose illicit aid had boosteed him to power.

Midway in that same month, April 15, 1939, President Roosevelt bluntly cabled Hitler and Mussolini for pledges that they would not attack thirty-one specifically named nations, including a justifiably nervous Poland and all the rest of Europe, plus the Near East. In the interests of humanity and world peace, Roosevelt hoped that

Hitler would give assurances of nonaggression for "ten years at least—a quarter of a century, if we dare look that far ahead."[11]

Roosevelt had labored earnestly with the State Department in preparing this sweeping appeal, but it was not one of his greatest state papers. Read in the cold light of today, it seems not only somewhat disjointed and sophomoric but naively presumptuous. Hitler was most unlikely to honor the proposed pledge, even if given, especially in view of his record of flouting formal international agreements and his avowed commitment to the Big Lie. Poland was at that time the only obvious object of Hitler's aggressive designs, and to drag in all these other countries, ranging from Ireland to Iran, was so extravagant as to be regarded in Germany as insulting. Yet Roosevelt's lengthy list included many nations that were ultimately attacked by the Fuhrer, ranging all the way from Denmark, Norway, the Netherlands, France, and Luxembourg in the west to Yugoslavia, Greece, and Russia in the east.

Hitler's Insulting Response

An annoyed Fuhrer might have ignored Roosevelt's appeal completely or fired off a tart cablegram advising the President not to stick his aristocratic nose into other people's business. Instead, he chose to appear before the puppet Reichstag, after a preparation of two weeks, to deliver (April 28, 1939) one of the longest of his important public declamations—more than two hours in length and stretching over forty-eight closely printed pages.[12] (The official printed version takes about three hours to read aloud.) William L. Shirer, the perceptive American newspaper correspondent who was present, ranks the speech as the greatest of all Hitler's oratorical efforts. Its appeal lay in its sophistry, sarcasm, and dramatic references to past injustices and present prejudices. The orator was repeatedly and noisily applauded, especially when he evoked uproarious laughter by reading off, in exaggerated and sarcastic tones, each of the thirty-one names on Roosevelt's undiscriminating grab list. Hitler omitted Poland, probably intentionally and slyly.[13]

The Fuhrer began by referring to the "curious contents" of Roosevelt's unorthodox appeal for peace, and to the discourteous ploy of releasing the cablegram to the press before the addressee had received it. He would therefore reply publicly, in person and on nationwide radio, so that the press could inform the President on a tit-for-tat basis. Hitler then thanked Providence for having raised him, "an unknown soldier of the Great War," to a position of power. He could thus lead his "dearly loved people" in shaking off the shackles of the foul Treaty of Versailles, drafted by "madmen" and "criminals," and in extricating the Reich from the morass of the Great Depression. He next went on to demonstrate how he had become an apostle of peace by causing the Reich, without war, to patch up its differences with France and England that had grown out of the iniquitous Treaty of Versailles. He then proceeded to demonstrate how he was fully justified in seeking, and winning, (Wilsonian) self-determination for the four million Germans of Czechoslovakia and the seven and a half million of his countrymen in Austria. As for the Poles, Hitler blamed them angrily for the current international friction, and justified Germany's claim to German-inhabited Danzig and to a German-controlled route through the Polish corridor. He fully endorsed the recent action of Mussolini in seizing Albania, which further fulfilled Italy's right to more living space.

Hitler claimed that a peace-loving Germany had not fought a war since 1918. (He did not mention the 10,000 or so Germans in the Spanish Civil War or the threats of war that had netted him Czechoslovakia.) He needled Roosevelt, the man of peace, for heading a nation that had refused to join Wilson's pacifistic League of Nations. The United States, he asserted, was thrusting its meddlesome nose into the affairs of Europe, although under the umbrella of the Monroe Doctrine Roosevelt would not permit Europe to interfere in the affairs of the Americas. Hitler would not presume to tell the Americans what to do, as Roosevelt was telling him, because the President "would probably rightly consider such a presumption tactless." Alluding to tariff barriers erected by the United States, and with barbed reference to Wilson's relevant Point III, Hitler declared, "It would be a noble act if President Franklin Roosevelt were to redeem the promises made by President Woodrow Wilson."

In concluding, Hitler noted that he had become Chancellor in 1933, almost simultaneously with the President's inauguration. He had led his people out of the wilderness of depression. (He might have added, but this was painfully obvious, that Roosevelt had failed to do likewise.) The American leader, heading a rich and unbeaten country that enjoyed ample living space, had the easier task. Yet, by contrast, Hitler modestly claimed that he had "conquered chaos" in Germany. He had brought back "stolen" provinces, gathered together the German people, and had put the "whole of 7,000,-000 unemployed" to useful work. He had built the "mighty roads" (autobahns), dug canals, and erected gigantic new factories. He did not add that the autobahns had been constructed partly for military communication and transportation, that thousands of unemployed younger men had been taken into the armed forces, and that many factory workers were engaged in rearming Germany by piling up munitions of war.

The Führer further declared that he was willing to enter into peace guarantees with the thirty-one nations named, but they would have to take the initiative and negotiate on a basis of absolute reciprocity. Yet elsewhere in his speech he had rattled the saber by announcing his denunciation of the Anglo-German naval limitation agreement of 1935 and by reaffirming his termination of the Polish-German nonagression treaty of 1934. Both England and Poland had contrived to give Germany offense, and Poland, Hitler charged, had already broken her side of the bargain.

Hitler concluded his masterpiece of political polemic by pointing out that a rich America could afford to concern herself with the problems of the entire world. But Providence had placed him in a sphere that was "unfortunately much smaller, although for me it is more precious than anything else, for it is limited to my people." Undoubtedly he had restored prosperity to Germany, and with it an amazing degree of hope and national self-respect. But this he had done before plunging Poland, and much of the rest of the world, into war.

Roosevelt was indignant at this scorching, point-by-point rejoinder, under twenty-one specific heads, but he kept his silence. The more rabid American isolationists believed that the Führer had humiliated the President, and they rejoiced to have such a devastating statement of the German point of view. Senator Gerald Nye, a leading isolationist, remarked simply and unsympathetically, "He asked for it."[14] But Roosevelt probably counted on arousing both world opinion and American opinion to the dangers posed by the dictators, and Hitler's refusal to give unqualified assurances to all the thirty-one possible victims may have served the purpose of "smoking him out."

The Hitler-Stalin Bombshell

During the four months that followed Hitler's blast at Roosevelt, events moved inexorably toward the terrifying climax. On July 26, 1939, the United States gave the stipulated two years' notice of the termination of her trade treaty of 1911 with Tokyo. This was a severe blow to Germany's ally under the three-power Axis pact, because it meant that the United States was preparing to embargo shipments of oil and other critical supplies to Japan. That final step was taken exactly two years later, in July 1941, thus driving the Japanese to the mad attack at Pearl Harbor.

Stalin meanwhile had been growing increasingly apprehensive of an attack by Hitler, who had never made any secret of his consuming hatred of Bolshevism and its Jewish prophets, namely Marx and Trotsky. The Führer had long been preaching, with some plausibility, the need for living space. Next-door Russia, with her vast agricultural expanses, offered the most desirable living room within relatively easy reach. Stalin's defensive armies needed time to recover their strength following the bloody purge of allegedly pro-German officers in 1937. Certain conservative spokesmen in the West, conspicuously in Britain, were openly saying that Hitler should be turned against Stalin, for then the two bloody-handed menaces could bleed each other to death on the windswept steppes of Russia. After that, the rest of the world could sleep in peace.

A surprise move came from Russia on April 16, 1939, almost simultaneously with Roosevelt's appeal to Hitler regarding the Führer's thirty-one possible victims. Moscow approached the London government looking toward some kind of defensive alliance with Great Britain and France.[15] But Britain and France had already pledged their support to Poland on March 30, and the Poles, hating the Russians fully as much as they did the Germans, would have no part of an Anglo-Russian pact.

A two-faced and fearful Stalin next entered into secret negotiations with Hitler in his search for guarantees against aggression. The British, blissfully unaware of their peril, dispatched a military commission to Moscow to conduct further negotiations. But London gave the distinct impression that it did not really mean business. It sent only second-drawer men and they embarked on a slow ship, instead of a fast airplane, and they consumed more than a week in reaching Moscow. When they arrived at their destination the concessions that the British offered the Soviets for a treaty of guarantee did not go far enough to be persuasive. So it was that behind the backs of the Britons the scheming Stalin and Hitler arranged for the signing of the Ribbentrop-Molotov five-year Nonagression Pact, August 23, 1939. After the war Ribbentrop was hanged as a criminal; Molotov, on the winning side, was not even tried.

The Nazi-Communist pact was the diplomatic bombshell of the century. Stalin, fully aware of the loose talk in the West about sick-ing Hitler onto him, had cleverly reversed the tables. He was now turning Hitler onto Poland and then onto the "impregnable" French Maginot Line, evidently in the hope that Germany, France, and Britain would again bleed themselves to exhaustion. The Sphinx of the Kremlin could then stab Hitler in the back or wait to bestride a prostrate Europe like a veritable colossus. As events turned out, he bought less than two years' time because the Western Front collapsed in the spring of 1941 under Hitler's blitzkrieg.

The Hitler-Stalin Nonaggression Pact of August 23, 1939, was preceded on August 19 by a seven-year Russo-German commercial agreement. Germany would grant Moscow a credit of 200 million marks, and the Soviets would ship to Germany the immense quantities of grain, oil, and metals that Hitler urgently needed. This backdoor arrangement, over which much bickering subsequently developed, gave promise that the British "hunger blockade," unlike that of 1914–1919, would not be effective in the new world war.

The Hitler-Stalin pacts, aside from alarming the governments of Britain, France, and Poland, had other rippling effects. Communists the world over, including the United States, had been branding rumors of such a Russo-German alliance as barefaced lies. Caught off balance while condemning Hitler and Nazism, they were forced to reverse themselves in midair and acclaim Communism's newfound ally.

The Japanese, Hitler's partners in the Anti-Communist Pact of 1936, were dumbfounded. The sudden switch not only freed Hitler's armies to attack Poland but also gave the Russians a freer hand to stab the Japanese in the back in eastern Asia. This naked exposure of Hitler as a double-dealing ally may have had something to do with Japan's ultimate decision to fight the kind of war in Asia that would be of little help to Hitler, especially after he had turned and attacked Stalin in June 1941.

The Führer Leads to War

Hitler was now free to launch his furious attack on the hated Poles and restore to the Reich the Germans of Danzig and the Polish corridor—Germans who had been slaughtered, he charged, by "the tens of thousands."[16] (Hitler never explained that such figures were grossly exaggerated by the Nazi press, and that many of the incidents had been fomented or fabricated by Nazi agents.) In his forthcoming radio broadcast proclaiming the outbreak of war with

Poland he was to claim that he had made fair offers of settlement
and that the Poles had attacked first. To make these charges convincing, Hitler had given orders to secure 150 Polish army uniforms
and put them on German soldiers. These men were to arrange to
leave behind them the bloodied body of a condemned man, drugged
and then shot in such a fashion as to provide evidence of an unsuc-
cessful attack on German soil.[17] Faithful to the gospel of *Mein Kampf,*
Hitler was using the barefaced lie to the end.*

Prime Minister Chamberlain of Great Britain, the once ac-
claimed "hero" of Munich, broadcast a message directly to the German people. It came the day after Britain honored its pledge to
Poland and declared war on Germany. Referring to Hitler, the British leader reminded his hearers: "He gave his word that he would
respect the Locarno Treaty; he broke it. He gave his word that he
neither wished nor intended to annex Austria; he broke it. He declared that he would not incorporate the Czechs in the Reich; he did
so. He gave his word after Munich that he had no further territorial
demands in Europe; he broke it. He gave his word that he wanted no
Polish provinces; he broke it. He has sworn to you for years that he
was the mortal enemy of Bolshevism; he is now its ally. Can you
wonder his word is, for us, not worth the paper it is written on?"[18]

The Hitler-Stalin commercial agreement and also the Nazi-Soviet Nonaggression Pact were accompanied by a secret protocol. Not
published until 1948, the document divided Poland into roughly
equal German and Russian spheres, preliminary to a "permanent"
division. Additionally, Lithuania, adjoining Germany, was to be in
the German sphere, while Finland, Estonia, and Latvia were reserved for the Russian sphere.[19] After the fall of France in 1940, Stalin violated this agreement by absorbing Lithuania. He thus
generated friction that contributed to the final break with Hitler in
June 1941.

On the night of September 3, 1939, the day on which Britain
and France declared war, the golden-voiced Roosevelt broadcast by
radio an intimate "fireside chat" to the American people. Using
John Donne's familiar metaphor that "no man is an island," the
President noted that when peace is broken anywhere, peace is in
danger everywhere. (He might have added that an attack on hu-

---

* Using captured Polish documents, Nazi propagandists in the United States
launched a formidable campaign in 1940. They accused the United States of encouraging the Poles to resist with assurances (unauthorized) of American support. See *Documents on German Foreign Policy,* IX, pp. 45, 48–49.

manity anywhere is an attack on humanity everywhere.) "This nation will remain a neutral nation," he vowed, "but I cannot ask that every American remain neutral in thought as well" (as Woodrow Wilson had urged in 1914). "Even a neutral," Roosevelt continued, with an obvious thrust at Hitler, "cannot be asked to close his mind or conscience." The President ended with strong assurances: "I have said not once but many times that I have seen war and that I hate war. I say that again and again."

"I hope the United States will keep out of this war. I believe that it will. And I give you assurances that every effort of your government will be directed toward that end."

"As long as it remains within my power to prevent, there will be no blackout of peace in the United States."[20]

As will become painfully apparent, these promises, like so many of Roosevelt's assurances, could not be kept or at any rate were not fully kept. The force of unforeseen circumstances was too strong. The President would have been on safer ground had he said "keep out of this *declared* war," for he did succeed in doing so until the United States was attacked at Pearl Harbor.

Roosevelt was often forced to follow rather than lead public opinion from 1939 to 1941, largely because of its contradictory desires. A Gallup poll in October 1939, a month after Hitler had attacked Poland, revealed that 84 percent of the American people who had an opinion on this question wanted the Allies to win. Only 2 percent favored Nazi Germany.[21] In April 1945, when American troops were invading Hitler's Europe, another poll showed that eight out of ten respondents believed that until Pearl Harbor the President should have been trying to keep the country out of conflict.[22] These clashing statistics do much to explain the difficulties confronting Roosevelt's leadership.

As for the German-Americans, when World War I had erupted in 1914 there were about nine million inhabitants of the United States who either had been born in Germany or could claim at least one parent born in Germany. Such a hyphenated multitude had been a vexatious problem to Wilson as he tried to steer a neutral course. But a quarter of a century later most of these Germanophiles were dead or they and their descendants had become to some degree Americanized. Even the scant 2 percent of Americans of 1939 who wanted Germany to win could not have been entirely German.

The German-American Bund organized in small groups of brown shirts, sporting swastikas and shouting "Heil Hitler." But their noisy exhibitionism was an embarrassment to the Nazi cause. In the United States most of these bundists existed as outcasts, and they consisted of relatively recent emigrants from Germany who to some extent had been mesmerized by the Führer.[23] As a result, they did not present Roosevelt with a major problem.[24]

CHAPTER 3

ROOSEVELT'S UNNEUTRAL NEUTRALITY

I regret that Congress passed that Act [Neutrality Act]. I regret equally that I signed that Act. . . . I seek a greater consistency through the repeal of the embargo provisions, and a return to international law.

Roosevelt's appeal to Congress,
September 21, 1939

Roosevelt Plays Favorites

President Roosevelt had long realized that the supposedly impartial Neutrality Act of 1937 favored the aggressors over the democracies. This self-denying statute permitted all countries to purchase American arms in time of peace, but once a conflict had broken out an embargo would be clamped down on the warring nations. Anticipating hostilities after Munich, both France and Britain hastened to place large orders for airplanes and other materiel, all of which had to be held up once fighting began in Europe. Roosevelt had never really favored such straitjacket neutrality legislation; he much preferred a scheme under which he could withhold arms from the aggressor while sending them to the victim. The legislation that Congress had passed was neutrality, but, once war erupted, it was the kind of neutrality that worked against the democracies and hence the national interest. At least, this was the view of the President and other pro-Ally internationalists.

When the European war finally exploded, Roosevelt dutifully urged the American people to be neutral in deed, if not thought. He then proceeded to do just about all that he could to favor the embattled democracies against Hitler. The Neutrality Act of 1937 could not become operative unless the President officially proclaimed the existence of a war, so he held off until September 5, 1939, four days after Hitler invaded Poland.[1] Roosevelt evidently reasoned that a brief delay would give the British and the French a slight advantage in getting some of their purchased aircraft and other munitions out of the country on the statutory "cash-and-carry" basis. He even had hoped that he would be able to seize German merchant ships in American harbors after hostilities broke out, but the U.S. Attorney General advised F.D.R. that such action would be construed by Berlin as an act of war.[2]

Roosevelt's detaining of the *Bremen,* the queen of Germany's passenger fleet, outraged patriotic Germans at home and abroad. On August 29, 1939, about three days before Hitler invaded Poland, this palatial liner was to sail from New York while there was yet time to escape capture or destruction by alerted British warships. American port authorities ostensibly feared that the vessel might be converted at sea into an armed raider. As a result, they combed the ship from stem to stern for two days allegedly looking for hidden guns, mounted or unmounted. The searchers even engaged in a meticulous, one-by-one recount of the life preservers. Roosevelt's confidential exchange of letters with the Treasury Department at this time reveals that he personally gave orders to delay for a few days the departure of the *Bremen.*[3]

At his White House press conference on August 29, 1939, Roosevelt was asked whether he was "aware of what is going on with the *Bremen?*" He readily admitted that he was and then proceeded to provide some self-serving historical background. His professed fear was that the German liner would get to sea, mount guns, and then become a commerce raider like the Confederate *Alabama* in the American Civil War. (This ship had left the British port of Liverpool in 1862, had received her arms "on the high seas," and then, along with other Confederate raiders, had ravaged Yankee commerce to the tune of about $15 million in damages eventually paid by Great Britain to the United States.)[4]

This was one of the more conspicuous times when Roosevelt twisted history during the so-called neutrality period to make a point. The *Bremen* and the *Alabama* were not even remotely analogous. The *Alabama* was built as a warship, not as a passenger ship, more than a year after war had broken out between North and South. She was not armed on the high seas but at the friendly Portuguese Azores by two accompanying British ships. In 1939 British destroyers were waiting near the three-mile line outside New York harbor, and if war with Britain had then broken out the *Bremen* almost certainly would not have put to sea. So great was her consumption of oil that she could not conceivably have operated successfully as an armed merchant cruiser.

Outwardly Roosevelt's delaying of the *Bremen* conformed to the strict letter of neutrality because the crack British liner *Aquitania* and the French *Normandie,* among others, were carefully searched during the same week. But this was a classic case of the unfairness that arises from treating unequals as equals. There was little chance that the Allied ships would be captured by German U-boats or surface raiders, yet the odds seemed to be heavily against the *Bremen*'s threading her way through the British blockade. There was no possibility whatever that the large Allied passenger ships would be converted into commerce raiders because Germany had little or no high-seas commerce to raid and because armed ships of the British navy were ready, even eager, to do their job.

The *Bremen,* recently released, was plowing the Atlantic about four days later, when Britain and France officially entered the war, September 3, 1939. Warned by radio, the liner escaped the British blockading fleet by detouring far north of the normal shipping lanes, and by finally putting into the Arctic Russian port of Murmansk. There she was assured of a friendly reception by Stalin, Hitler's co-conspirator in the fateful Nonaggression Pact of the preceding month. In December 1939, escorted by German warplanes, the *Bremen* made a dangerous but successful dash to the north German port of Bremerhaven, where she played no further role in the war, other than being bombed in 1945 and left a total loss. The anti-Jewish leader of the pro-German bund in the United States had not been slow to condemn the anti-Nazi and pro-Jewish "President Rosenfeld." The commander of the *Bremen,* on reaching his haven in Germany, castigated the Americans for having deliberately delayed his ship in New York harbor.[5]

Roosevelt Urges Unneutrality

As we have noted, under the Neutrality Act of 1937 the warring powers could not buy armaments but only the raw materials for weaponry, such as iron, steel, aluminum, and oil. These supplies had to be carried away by the purchasers in non-American ships and paid for without American credit—the memorable "cash-and-carry" principle. This restriction on selling raw materials expired in two years, on May 1, 1939, four months before Hitler assaulted Poland. As a result, American merchant ships, laden with nonexplosive contraband of war, were free to sail into the danger zones, where some of these carriers would inevitably be sunk. Grave complications would inevitably arise, as in 1914–1917, and the United States probably would be dragged into the war.

During the anxious weeks before and after Hitler's furious lunge into Poland, Roosevelt tried to persuade Congress to amend the neutrality legislation so as to permit the democracies to buy American weapons, including high explosives. To offset this step toward war, he would require American merchant ships, whatever they were legally carrying, to avoid the European combat zones. But the isolationists were extremely vocal throughout the country and in Congress, and these suggestions were either ignored or spurned.

The outbreak of war in Europe jolted a lethargic Congress into action. The American people, overwhelmingly pro-Ally, wanted to send arms to the embattled democracies, but they did not want to endanger American ships or passengers in foreign ships. Roosevelt called Congress into a special joint session, beginning September 21, 1939, and then appeared before both houses to present his recommendations.[6] He declared that the neutrality legislation of the 1930s, which he now regretted having signed, had so far changed the "historic foreign policy" of the republic as to militate against "peaceful relations" abroad. From earliest times, "with one notable exception," the nation's neutrality policy had "been based on international law." Actually, that policy still was so based, for the Neutrality Acts of 1935, 1936, and 1937 had not abandoned international law; they had only registered a determination not to assert all possible rights under it.

Roosevelt then went on to read to Congress a politician's version of American history. Prior to 1935, he declared, the nation's one deviation from a neutrality based on international law had come in the years just prior to the War of 1812. At that time the Congress had passed the self-crucifying Embargo and the Non-Intercourse Act, both designed to bring Britain to terms by cutting off trade with her. That policy, Roosevelt declared, had turned out to be a "disastrous failure" because "it was the major cause of bringing us into active participation in European wars in our own War of 1812. It is merely reciting history to recall to you that one of the results of the policy of embargo and non-intercourse was the burning in 1814 of part of this Capitol in which we are assembled to-day."

The speaker was making history, not "reciting" it, because he was misrepresenting the facts, whether knowingly or not. The President's obvious purpose was to strike fear into the hearts of Congress and thus achieve his ends. The truth is that the Embargo and the Non-Intercourse Act did not drag America into the War of 1812; on the contrary, they probably came within a narrow margin of keeping the nation out of that conflict. The prolonged economic warfare of the United States under President Madison almost succeeded in bringing England to peaceful terms. Under extreme pressure from British shippers, the London government essentially had yielded to American demands for a peaceful settlement two days prior to the declaration of war by Congress, not by the British. A few more days of patience and there might have been no armed conflict, only a continuing undeclared war, fought mostly with economic weapons. America was too weak to use other devices with any real hope of success.

Roosevelt also misrepresented facts—and not for the last time—when he indicated that President Madison's embargo measures were an unwise departure from international law. Indeed, he referred several times to the need for a "return to international law." But F.D.R. made it clear that this supposed "return" would favor the democracies against the aggressors. Actually, an embargo, whether on cotton or cartridges, may be instituted in the United States by an act of Congress and hence by domestic law. It has little relevance to international law. An independent nation, whatever its motives or the consequences, has a sovereign right to prohibit exports from its domain, and some have done so, often for purposes of conserving guns and ammunition for home use. But Roosevelt was misusing both history and international law to achieve a partial repeal that he deemed in the national interest, unneutral though his recommendation might have been.

Unneutral Aid to the Democracies

Following Roosevelt's earnest appeal came a windy six-week debate in Congress, during which the interventionists and the noninterventionists (isolationists) battered one another verbally. Finally, the so-called Neutrality Act of November 4, 1939, passed by a vote of 243 to 181 in the House and 63 to 30 in the Senate. The official tally seems to have squared roughly with the public opinion polls.[7] The new legislation, which followed Roosevelt's major recommendations, was a clear compromise. The isolationists permitted foreign purchasers of munitions to take them away in their own ships on a cash-and-carry basis. But this part of the "neutrality" legislation meant that only the sea-controlling democracies, not Hitler, could receive them. To balance this unneutral concession to the American interventionists, the 1939 Neutrality Act set up European danger zones extending far out to sea from the waters of the belligerents. Into these prohibited areas no American merchant ships could legally sail. If this restriction had existed in 1917, President Wilson might never have become involved in war with Germany. From November 1939 to November 1941, or as long as this prohibition existed, no American merchant ship was sunk by a German submarine in the announced combat zones for the simple reason that none could legally sail there. The profits of American shippers naturally dropped.

The preamble of the Neutrality Act of 1939 emphatically declared that the United States, while imposing certain "restrictions" on American nationals, "expressly reserves all the rights and privileges to which it and its nationals are entitled under the law of nations."[8] Such a specific disclaimer contradicted the interventionists, including Roosevelt, who had appealed for a "return" to international law as the way to keep the country out of war. A citizen has a perfect right to witness a riot as a bystander but he also has a perfect right to exercise prudence and stay home.

The *New York Herald-Tribune* (October 25, 1939) conducted a poll of fourteen leading international lawyers on the modification of the Neutrality Act of 1937. One query was whether a repeal of the arms embargo would violate America's obligations as a neutral under international law. The response was ten "no," three "yes," and one "undecided." As for the legality of the cash-and-carry restrictions imposed on the belligerents who transported raw materi-

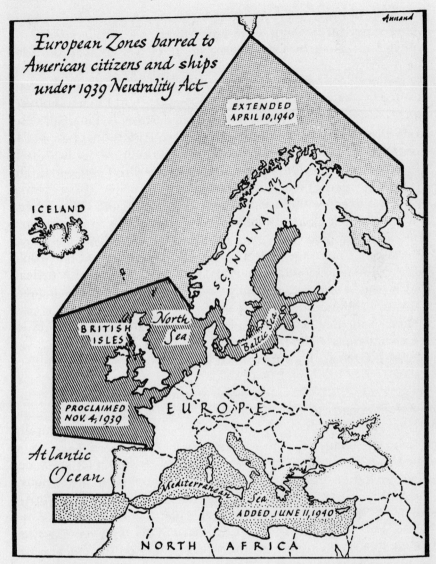

European Zones barred to American citizens and ships under 1939 Neutrality Act

EXTENDED
APRIL 10, 1940

ICELAND

SCANDINAVIA

North Sea

Baltic Sea

BRITISH ISLES

EUROPE

PROCLAIMED NOV. 4, 1939

Atlantic Ocean

Mediterranean Sea

ADDED JUNE 11, 1940

NORTH AFRICA

From Thomas A. Bailey, A Diplomatic History of the American People, *9th ed.*, Prentice-Hall, copyright © 1974

als, twelve voted approval and two were undecided. (International lawyers resemble justices on the Supreme Court; they tend to vote their biases and seldom are in complete agreement on hard cases.)

Paradoxically, the so-called Neutrality Act of 1939, like its predecessor, contained one other unneutral clause, even though it was rooted in the Monroe Doctrine and the traditional Pan-American policy of the United States. The proviso prohibiting the transportation of arms and passengers to belligerent nations in United States ships did not apply "to any American republic engaged in war against a non-American state or states [Germany?], provided the American republic is not cooperating with a non-American state [Germany?] or states in such war. . . ."[9] In other words, if any one of the lawless powers—Germany, Italy, and Japan—should attack Brazil or Argentina, citizens of the United States could legally ship arms directly to their hemispheric brothers. Hitler was again put on notice, although he probably was too preoccupied to take heed. Certainly the German (Nazi) press showed little interest in the pending revision of the Neutrality Act.[10]

Thus Roosevelt, in pursuance of "peace" and "neutrality," pushed through Congress the revised act of 1939. The exclusion of American shipping from the European danger zones promoted "storm-cellar neutrality." But such a restriction had the incidental effect of immensely aiding the German U-boat blockade of Britain, and in this sense it unneutrally favored Germany. Still, the cash-and-carry shipment of munitions was an important unneutral concession to the democracies. Roosevelt's ultimate decision to convoy these materials led not to "peace" but to an undeclared shooting war with German U-boats in the North Atlantic.

The Pan-American Chastity Belt

A path-breaking step toward insulating the western hemisphere against belligerent activity came in the autumn of 1939. Responding to an invitation from the host country, the foreign ministers of all the American republics approved the Declaration of Panama (October 3, 1939). This agreement established a "security zone," or "safety belt," around the Americas south of Canada, ranging from 300 to about 1,000 miles out to sea, depending on the indentations of the hemispheric coastline. The belligerents were formally warned to refrain from naval action within that vast area.

The so-called security zone contravened belligerent rights under international law, at least in the opinion of many legal experts. It was also an unenforceable edict that would almost certainly do nothing to strengthen the rights of neutrals. To prevent British cruisers from attacking German raiders, the American neutrals would have to get into the fight themselves, and such intervention would hardly be the type of neutrality envisaged by the safety belt, jokingly referred to as the "Chastity Belt."

The Hemispheric Safety Belt 1939

From Thomas A. Bailey, A Diplomatic History of the American People, *9th ed.*, Prentice-Hall, *copyright © 1974*

The most conspicuous defiance of the newly proclaimed security zone came December 13–17, 1939. Three British cruisers in South American waters engaged in a desperate, sixteen-hour, running fight with the larger and heavier gunned "pocket battleship" *Admiral Graf Spee.* The German vessel, heavily damaged, took refuge in the neutral Uruguayan harbor of Montevideo. Unable to make adequate repairs within the time limit set by the Uruguayan government, the German commander, under radio orders from Hitler, scuttled his ship. He then committed suicide.

Provoked by this spectacular invasion of their waters, the twenty-one American republics dispatched a joint protest to Britain,

France, and Germany against violations of the safety zone by belligerent activity. Roosevelt himself, for the sake of the record, reluctantly complained of British operations against German ships within the Pan-American security zone, and Winston Churchill, again First Lord of the Admiralty, undertook to reply.[11] He pointed out that the destruction of German raiders in American waters operated to the advantage of the American republics. Much of their seaborne commerce, especially foodstuffs from South America, was being shipped to Britain and France, and virtually none to blockaded Germany. Under international law German raiders could seize or sink, by lawful procedures, all enemy shipping of any description and all neutral vessels carrying contraband to their enemy. By this time the two camps of belligerents regarded as contraband about every essential item, including foodstuffs.

Inevitably the presence of British patrols served the best interests of both Great Britain and the American republics. The record shows that the *Admiral Graf Spee,* after three months in the South Atlantic, had destroyed nine British cargo vessels totaling 50,000 tons. In these operations, quite in contrast with the submarine warfare that finally developed, the German raider sank her victims *with* warning and *with* adequate provision for the safety of passengers and crew. German U-boats had no room for a considerable number of survivors, but the *Admiral Graf Spee,* like other German surface raiders, made a practice of either taking aboard passengers and crew or transferring them to other vessels. The *Altmark,* a German armed merchantman, served as a supplier or "mother ship," as well as a prison ship for survivors of the sinkings. The *Altmark* and her prisoners will appear again spectacularly in connection with a British violation of Norwegian neutrality.

Clearly the presence of British patrols was something of a boon to the American republics. The *Admiral Graf Spee,* as we have seen, had destroyed various ships that either had carried or were carrying Latin American exports of food. Churchill might have reminded Roosevelt that the hemispheric safety zone was more hurtful to Hitler than to Britain. But this grim truth must have been obvious to Roosevelt, although perhaps not so clear to the Latin American nations that had collectively midwifed the neutrality belt. At any rate, the Germans were so fully aware of what was going on that Hitler could nurse one more grievance against the United States. The British, for their part, attempted to intercept enemy ships "as far away as possible from the American coasts."[12]

"Plain English" Naval Patrols

The memorable Declaration of Panama, as noted, staked out a clearly defined security zone. In so doing it sanctioned and nominally expanded the jurisdiction of the embryonic "neutrality patrol" authorized by President Roosevelt on September 5, a month earlier. The United States at first patrolled an area roughly 200 or 300 miles out to sea and ranging southward along the Atlantic coast from Canada to and including the Caribbean and the Gulf of Mexico. Participating were many U.S. Navy ships, whose chief duty was to report on and to track the movements of belligerent warships, including submarines. Presumably, the basic purpose was to defend and neutralize the waters of the western hemisphere, as envisaged by the Declaration of Panama. But there was also the veiled threat that warships of the United States would intervene in naval engagements, provided that they had enough strength present.

This sweeping extension of the area to be covered by the neutrality patrol obviously was more favorable to the British and the French than to the Germans. The two Allies had vastly more commerce that was vulnerable to attacking raiders like the *Admiral Graf Spee*. Roosevelt himself was especially concerned about German submarines and the surface ships that might supply these raiders with oil and provisions. On October 9, 1939, a week after the security zone was announced, he addressed a portentous directive to the Acting Secretary of the Navy: "Planes or Navy or Coast Guard ships *may* report the sighting of any submarine or suspicious surface ships in *plain English* [italics added] to Force Commander or Department." Also the American warship or airplane was to "remain in contact as long as possible."[13]

The "plain English" requirement had an obvious purpose that was hardly neutral. It meant that nearby British patrols were to be instantly alerted so that they could move in promptly for the kill. Roosevelt's directive ended with the words "loss of contact with surface ships cannot be tolerated." Nor was the reference to submarines evenhanded; only German or Italian U-boats would be prowling these waters.

The Allies controlled the surface of the sea in the eastern Atlantic, and this priceless advantage meant that the Germans probably would dispatch submarines to American waters, as they ultimately did with a vengeance after Japan attacked Pearl Harbor. As a partial safeguard against such incursions, Roosevelt further showed his concern about U-boats by issuing a proclamation on October 18, 1939. Invoking the then existing Neutrality Act of 1937, he placed severe restrictions on foreign submarines seeking to enter the territorial waters of the United States. He was acting, he declared, "to maintain peace between the United States and foreign states, to protect the commercial interests of the United States and its citizens, and to promote the security of the United States. . . ."[14] Specifically, no submarines of any belligerent nation could henceforth enter the ports or territorial waters of the United States, except those compelled by force majeure, that is, by a breakdown of machinery, combat damage, or other misfortunes. In arriving, such submersibles were to operate solely on the surface, with proper flags flying, and they were to depart the same way.

At this early stage of the war the Germans had better uses nearer home for their relatively few U-boats. But they must have perceived that Roosevelt's proclamation, though ostensibly neutral, was aimed at them more than at the Allies, and doubtless was so intended. To this extent it was one more German grievance against so-called American neutrality. The equal application of the law to unequals can easily result in inequality.

"Protecting" the *Columbus*

Shortly after Hitler plunged into Poland, anxiety deepened in Germany regarding the fate of German steamships, most of which had been caught in foreign harbors, including those of Latin America. Some eighty-five of these vessels were trapped in the western hemisphere, about thirty-two of which eventually made their way back to Germany.

Rumors rapidly spread that these merchantmen would be used as mother ships, or suppliers, for Hitler's submarines operating in American waters. In Mexican ports alone nine German merchant vessels, including two passenger liners, lay at anchor. Allied patrols suspected that they were preparing to make a dash for home at the earliest opportunity.

One of these vessels was the *Columbus,* a splendid liner of 32,000 tons (bigger even than the sunken *Lusitania* of 1915), the third largest passenger ship under the German flag. When war broke out the *Columbus* had already departed New York on a Caribbean pleasure cruise with about 725 passengers, most of them Americans. After some rebuffs, the captain dumped his alarmed guests at Havana, Cuba, and then sought refuge at the Mexican port of Vera Cruz, where there was a German "colony." His presence and activities provided some foundation for rumors that at night he was supplying nearby German submarines with fuel and food.

After waiting about two months, the *Columbus* undertook a dash for home. The liner was trailed by a succession of American destroyers and cruisers of the neutrality patrol, which radioed her position to Washington in such a way as to advise nearby British patrols to place themselves in a position to intercept the *Columbus*. Presumably, the British warships would wait until their prey had passed the outer edge of the safety zone promulgated at Panama.

Much doubt existed on all sides as to the precise function of the American patrols. The British feared that within the security zone U.S. warships might attempt to rob them of their victims, in which case ugly incidents would occur. The captain of the *Columbus,* almost incredibly, regarded the trailing Americans as his protectors, for his radio receiver was evidently not monitoring the same radio frequency on which U.S. warships were broadcasting position reports in plain English. There is even evidence that German representatives in Washington had appealed in advance for units of the U.S. Navy to protect the *Columbus* until she escaped from the Gulf of Mexico.[15] The captain of the *Columbus* kept in touch with his pursuing American "guardians," and when one of them dropped out he would signal, "God speed; a safe return; and Merry Christmas."[16]

The escaping *Columbus* had the misfortune to encounter the British destroyer *Hyperion,* possibly alerted by the nearby "escorting" U.S. cruiser *Tuscaloosa.* The luckless Germans were about 350 miles off the coast of New Jersey, but were they outside the ambiguously defined security zone? The American captain of the *Tuscaloosa* said "no" but the German captain said "yes." A glance at the map shows that the Germans were wrong by about 100 miles.

In any event, the security zone was evidently not violated because, strictly speaking, the British destroyer did not engage in belligerent action. She merely fired two blank shells (nonexplosive) with the apparent intention of halting the liner and determining her identity, as belligerent ships were privileged to do on the high seas under international law. The response of the Germans was to scuttle and set fire to their own ship, as carefully preplanned. They were the ones who destroyed the vessel; the British did not, although that probably was their intent, even with the more powerful U.S. *Tusca-loosa* standing by, theoretically to protect the neutrality of the security zone.

The *Tuscaloosa* picked up the more than 500 survivors from their lifeboats, treated them royally, and landed them in New York. The rescued captain and his crew were most grateful; the German chargé in Washington even called at the State Department to express gratitude for the rescue.[17] Evidently, Berlin did not suspect until later that the "friendly" Americans had done their best to doom the *Columbus*.

Washington classified the surviving crew of the *Columbus* (two had been lost at sea) as "distressed seamen," and they were given sanctuary in the United States for sixty days. There was no reasonably safe way to transport this large body of men back to Germany through the British blockade, although a few of them later attempted to return by way of Japan, then neutral. After various delays, the bulk of detainees were transported to a former CCC camp (Civilian Conservation Corps) at Fort Stanton, New Mexico. Among other amenities, the camp provided a post exchange, a theater, and a hospital. These "abused" men became bona fide prisoners after December 11, 1941, when Hitler declared war. Obviously, these survivors were far better off in warm New Mexico than in the icy vastnesses of the Russian front.[18]

"Shadowing" the *Columbus*

Additional light is thrown on the *Columbus* episode by a memorandum prepared by Captain Frank K. B. Wheeler, a retired U.S. Navy officer who had served in the *Jouett,* one of the four destroyers patrolling the waters off the Mexican port of Vera Cruz.[19] One of Wheeler's duties was to act as communications officer, and as such he was privy to all radio messages sent and received by the ship. The Chief of Naval Operations in Washington, Roosevelt's subordinate, had ordered the U.S. patrols to identify and trail any Axis ships, reporting all information regarding them directly to headquarters. The President, with pins on a White House chart, was known to be taking a keen interest in these operations.

The *Jouett's* commander had received ambiguous orders to steam close to the harbor of Vera Cruz so as to determine the exact location of the *Columbus*. Yet he was enjoined to make every effort not to be recognized. In his zeal to confirm the presence of the liner, he deliberately violated Mexico's territorial waters, where the destroyer was sighted by Mexican gunboats. The Washington authorities, acting in what they presumably regarded as the national interest, instructed the *Jouett's* skipper to omit any mention of the incident in his log so as to conceal this incursion. When the *Columbus* finally emerged, the *Jouett* trailed her for several days. The destroyer's radio sent to Washington the position of the *Columbus* every hour and then every half hour in "administrative code," so simple that "any school boy could break it." After reaching the Key West area, the *Jouett* turned over the trailing to other warships, with the dramatic results already described.

Captain Wheeler concludes: "It is of interest that during the four or five days we trailed the *Columbus,* the German captain of the ship was most polite in signaling to us of imminent course and speed changes. At night he used a wake light to make it easier for us. Otherwise, his ship was completely darkened. He exchanged pleasantries by signal and thanked us when, near Key West, we turned her over to another escort ship and took our departure. It was clear to us that the purpose of our position-reports was to allow British naval ships to track the *Columbus*. The British ships were within direction finder (DF) range during our transit of the Gulf of Mexico."

The unsuspecting German captain evidently welcomed such protection as American warships could give him against potential British and French foes while inside the security zone. His objective appears to have been to remain within the closed area until he had reached such northerly latitudes that he could take full advantage of increasing darkness and wintry weather to make a successful dash for Germany.

A rather troublesome question arises. If the American neutrality patrol trailed German merchant ships to protect them against British warships, why did not American destroyers extend the same courtesy to British merchant ships that might fall prey to German raiders? One possible explanation is that there were too many British merchant ships and too few German raiders. But the correct answer appears to be that the U.S. Navy, under the direction of President Roosevelt, was pursuing a pro-Ally neutrality that fell far short of being evenhanded. One should note that the *Columbus* left Vera Cruz on December 14, 1939, the day after the ill-starred *Admiral Graf Spee* encountered the three British cruisers off the Río de la Plata, well within the security zone. The British showed no respect whatever for imaginary lines in the face of so formidable and destructive an adversary.

Betraying More German Ships

By an odd coincidence, on the same day that the *Columbus* was scuttled, a distressing fate, but a happier one, befell the German freighter *Arauca*. On December 14, 1939, this 4,354–ton ship left Vera Cruz with a valuable cargo of sisal, phosphates, hides, and other materials useful for the German war machine. Pursued by radioing U.S. warships, she sailed rather close to the Gulf coast and then the Atlantic coast of Florida. Off Oakland, Florida, she received a solid warning shot from an approaching British destroyer, and barely managed to reach United States territorial waters and the protection of American destroyers. In this case the British flagrantly violated the Declaration of Panama security zone.[20]

The *Arauca,* anchored at Port Everglades, did not venture out again under the German flag because for a while the British cruiser maintained a vigilant watch. The crew was interned and, after a prolonged delay, by August 1941 the ship had been taken over by the U.S. Maritime Commission for trade in nitrates with Chile.[21]

Hitler's subordinates took careful note of American involvement in such incidents, although no formal protests appear to have been lodged at the time. But we should note that Hitler, in his memorable war-declaring speech to "the robots of the Reichstag," referred specifically to these disagreeable affairs.[22] Ticking off the names of a half dozen merchant ships, he blamed the United States for unneutral collusion with the British. He charged bluntly that "American cruisers in the Security Zone handed over the German ship *Columbus* to the British." This was an exaggeration, although it contained more truth than he perhaps realized.

In this same speech, Hitler further charged that United States forces "cooperated to prevent the attempted escape of the German steamer *Arauca.*" He also declared that some five weeks later the U.S. cruiser *Trenton* (January 27, 1940) contravened international law by advising "enemy naval forces of the movements of the German steamers *Arauca, La Plata* and *Mangoni.*" Hitler further asserted that in November 1940 Roosevelt had ordered the German steamers *Phrygia, Idarwald,* and *Rhein* to be "shadowed" (*verfolgen*) so that they were compelled to "scuttle themselves" to avoid falling into enemy hands.[23]

These last three vessels had left the Mexican port of Tampico late in 1940 without attracting much attention, although two

United States destroyers were reported to be off that harbor when they departed. The *Idarwald* appears to have set fire to herself but the flames were extinguished by the boarding party from a British warship. The *Phrygia* and the *Rhein* were reportedly scuttled to avoid seizure by the enemy.[24]

In his flaming speech declaring war in 1941, Hitler expressed particular concern over the fate of the German sailors on these ships that had been seized or sequestered. The crew of the *Columbus* probably was in his mind because this liner was the largest of the ships that had fallen into British hands through the presumed connivance of the Americans. He emphatically charged the Americans with having treated the distressed German seamen "in a most inhuman manner." Contrary to "international law" (as he interpreted it), they had been assigned specific residences and their travel had been restricted.[25] Hitler did not add that these detainees were up to that time lodged in reasonably pleasant camps or surroundings, and that they had the good fortune to sit out a war that cost the lives of several million able-bodied Germans. He might have reasonably concluded that the pro-British President Roosevelt at no time felt an urge to send them back to fight for Hitler's Reich.

CHAPTER 4

U-BOAT WARFARE BEGINS

This nation will remain a neutral nation, but I cannot ask that every American remain neutral in thought as well. . . . Even a neutral cannot be asked to close his mind or his conscience.

Roosevelt's fireside chat,
September 3, 1939

Submarines under Restraints

Many Americans, especially isolationists, predicted that World War II would be a rough carbon copy of World War I. The German armies would bleed to death in their futile assaults on France's mighty Maginot Line. Simultaneously, Britain's strangling naval blockade would bring hunger, even starvation, to the German masses. In the end Hitler would be forced to surrender, while America stood on the sidelines, not only secure but also raking in golden profits from the sale of supplies and arms to the Western democracies.

This comforting scenario proved to be a daydream. The British blockade, though fairly tight, did not strangle Germany, as in World War I. Hitler had a back-door access to the grain, oil, and other supplies of the Soviet Union, thanks to his commercial pact of August 1939 with Stalin. The Germans did not batter their heads against the "impregnable" Maginot Line, but instead executed a devastating end run that brought them swarming into France by a detour from the north through Belgium. The French dropped out of the war, Mussolini thrust a dagger into his neighbor's back, and the British were left in desperate isolation.

A chilling fear struck many American hearts that Hitler might capture the British fleet and then combine it and Europe's naval facilities with his own. The United States would then be in peril of invasion, sooner or later, perhaps by way of Latin America. In this panic atmosphere President Roosevelt was able to take the necessary liberties with international law and neutral obligations to bail out Britain. He continued this unconventional course even after the Hitlerian menace had become less threatening, especially after the Führer, repeating Napoleon's fatal blunder, plunged into the bottomless trap of Russia in June 1941.

At the outset World War II seemed to be taking off from the low level at which World War I had ended, at least as regards naval warfare and international law. On September 3, 1939, in the evening of the day on which Great Britain declared war on Nazi Germany, the British passenger liner *Athenia* was torpedoed by a U-boat without warning. She sank northwest of the British Isles with heavy loss of lives; more than a score of the dead were Americans. The grave implications of this attack for the United States will be noted later.

Despite this tragic incident, Hitler's policy at the outset of the conflict was not to sink passenger liners. The U-boat commander had blundered when he torpedoed the *Athenia*. The next day, September 4, 1939, the following message was radioed from Germany to all U-boats: "By order of the Führer, on no account are operations to be carried out against passenger steamers, even when under escort."[1] This was a remarkable concession, for even under prewar international law a passenger ship *under armed escort* forfeited all immunity from attack without warning.

To the surprise of many, in 1936 Hitler's Germany had voluntarily subscribed to the Protocol of London regarding submarine warfare. Its precise terms were:

(1) In their action with regard to merchant ships, submarines must conform to the rules of International Law to which surface vessels are subject.

(2) In particular, *except in the case of persistent refusal to stop* on being duly summoned, or of *active resistance* to visit or search, a warship, whether surface vessel or submarine, may not sink or render incapable of navigation a merchant vessel without having first

placed passengers, crew, and ship's papers in a place of safety. For this purpose the ship's boats are not regarded as a place of safety *unless the safety of the passengers and crew is assured, in the existing sea and weather conditions, by the proximity of land, or the presence of another vessel which is in a position to take them on board.* [Italics added][2]

The mystery remains why Hitler should have agreed in 1936, without arm-twisting, to restrict so lethal a weapon as the submarine while he was building up a formidable fleet of these craft. Given what we now know of him, he may have regarded the Protocol of London as a sleeping pill. It could deaden British awareness of their concession the year earlier, when in the Anglo-German Naval Agreement of 1935, Germany had agreed that she would not build beyond 45 percent of British submarine strength. In exceptional circumstances the Germans might exceed this limitation.[3] The Führer had only a cynical regard for truth and binding treaty commitments, and he could easily toss this agreement overboard if war broke out.

Hitler remembered, though not as vividly as he should have, that the U-boat had come perilously close to knocking England out of the war in 1917–1918. He also knew that submarines could be built more easily and inexpensively than battleships—"more bang for the buck" as American strategists were wont to say in a later context. The advantages of the relatively cheap U-boat were especially clear to a Germany that had been deprived of her naval arm by the Treaty of Versailles and was only now on the way to building up a powerful fleet. The most rational explanation of Hitler's conduct is that he neither wanted nor anticipated a war with the British, for whom he had considerable respect. He reckoned that Britain would not be so foolish as to honor her empty commitment to support Poland in 1939, and this view was bolstered by his recollection of how the British and the French had sold out Czechoslovakia at Munich in 1938.

U-Boat Sinkings Escalate

Hitler was unpleasantly surprised when both the British and the French stood behind Poland—rather far behind—by reluctantly declaring war after a delay of three days, on September 3, 1939. After he had speedily crushed the overmatched Polish armies with his mechanized might, he had counted on Britain and France to call it quits, as he formally proposed that they do. But they further jolted him by flatly rejecting one more bitter dose of appeasement. Hitler even issued orders to his U-boat commanders to go easy on British and French shipping, especially that of France, in the early weeks of the war. Perhaps his enemies would continue to remain inactive if he did not prod them into action. But once Poland was flattened and Germany's peace feelers had been spurned by both Britain and France, Hitler sanctioned orders to attack enemy passenger ships under escort (October 29, 1939) and then passenger ships that were armed (November 17, 1939).[4]

As the great conflict lengthened, these early restrictions on U-boats gradually went overboard so far as the Germans were concerned. Their surface raiders generally observed the time-honored rules by taking on board passengers and crews for liberation at a convenient port or by otherwise making reasonable provisions for their safety. But as the war ground on the Germans learned again what they had once learned in World War I. U-boats simply could not conduct commerce-destroying warfare with acceptable safety and maximum effectiveness, that is, if they surfaced, gave the conventional warning, visited and searched the target vessel, and then placed the passengers and crew in a position of safety.

Hitler's naval officers, notably Admiral Karl Dönitz, were not reluctant to give their reasons for all-out war. They claimed that the British foes did not abide by the spirit or even the letter of the London anti-submarine declaration of 1936, which outlawed "active resistance" by the victim. Winston Churchill, again First Lord of the Admiralty, began arming all merchant ships after the outbreak of war in 1939 and issued orders for active resistance.[5] Merchant vessels were equipped with radios for broadcasting the presence of the U-boat and hence subjecting it to possible sinking by oncoming destroyers, thus engaging in a form of active resistance. Merchant ships likewise were believed to be under orders to ram or attempt to ram the fragile submarine if a favorable opportunity presented itself, as in World War I. Orders or not, some tried to do so and a few succeeded.

During World War I, the British had destroyed a considerable number of U-boats with Q-ships, that is, innocent appearing vessels serving as decoys equipped with masked guns. A number of such craft were available early in World War II, but they scored no successes whatever and were soon abandoned. The German U-boat commanders quickly learned that they had better fire their torpedoes first and ask questions afterward, despite the paper shackles of the anti-submarine London Protocol of 1936.

Blockades and Counterblockades

Broadly speaking, World War II began where World War I had ended—after nearly a twenty-year armistice. This generalization is particularly true with respect to naval warfare and neutral rights.

In 1914 Great Britain had proclaimed an unorthodox if not illegal long-range blockade of Germany, allegedly in retaliation for an earlier sowing of contact mines in the open sea. When World War II burst forth in September 1939, the British soon reestablished their long-range blockade. This time it was put into operation without the fanfare that had accompanied London's announcement of November 4, 1914, when Great Britain had given notice of an intention to mine the North Sea. Such a blocking off of the open seas was in itself a drastic departure from international law. As in 1915, the Germans retaliated in November 1939 by proclaiming an illegal "paper blockade" of the British Isles, to be enforced chiefly by U-boats.

In still other respects the warriors of World War II copied the improved techniques of the earlier conflict. The system of shepherding a large convoy of merchant ships by warships was adopted at the outset. From the outbreak of war Winston Churchill made strenuous efforts to mount weapons, including anti-aircraft guns, on British merchant ships. Obviously, the orthodox procedures of visit and search could not be conducted against Allied shipping by German aircraft. Hence bombing went on mercilessly without any effort to abide by the unworkable requirements of international law.

As in 1914–1918, the flourishing German merchant marine, confronted with Britain's maritime mastery, virtually vanished from the high seas. The British captured some 15 usable German ships, and by the end of September 1939, 325 German vessels totaling 750,000 tons were helplessly and hopelessly interned in foreign ports.[6]

On September 26, 1939, twenty-three days after Britain declared war on Germany, Winston Churchill spoke in the House of Commons about the naval situation with considerable optimism. He announced that he was energetically arming British merchant ships and providing them with trained gunners. Old guns from World War I, which farsightedly had been saved, were being reconditioned and mounted. With all British merchantmen armed or about to be armed, the German submarines would have to attack submerged, and this limitation, Churchill noted, was to the advantage of the British. A U-boat commander, unable to fire his deck gun, would have to expend his few torpedoes, which would often miss and which would soon be depleted.

Churchill further observed that several of the German U-boats had chivalrously given "good warning" and had helped the orphaned crews to safety. This kind of sportsmanship soon became rare or nonexistent, largely because Britain's defensive-offensive measures made a gentlemanly submarine war impossible.

On this same occasion Churchill also informed Parliament that losses of merchant ships to submarines had dropped sharply during the first three weeks of the conflict. But he warned that "war is full of unpleasant surprises," for he was fully aware that the Germans were feverishly building more submarines and that grim days lay ahead.[7] The U-boat Battle of the Atlantic, and with it the war, was almost lost several years later, early in 1943, when radar-equipped U-boats, using "wolf pack" techniques, sank ninety-six ships in twenty days.

The Illegal British Blockade

As in 1914–1918, the European neutrals (notably Denmark, Sweden, Norway, and the Netherlands) protested bitterly but vainly against the interruption of their valuable commerce with Germany by the long-range British blockade. In November 1939, the Germans planted magnetic floating mines in British waters—Hitler's first lethal secret weapon— and they sank a reported twenty-nine ships in twelve days before effective counter-measures could be perfected. The Berlin government, in typical Nazi fashion, charged that the British had themselves planted the magnetic mines.

As a reprisal, the British announced that after December 4, 1939, they would seize on neutral ships all exports from Germany, even such noncontraband items as children's dolls. The nations most affected protested against this unlawful interference with their innocent business, notably Belgium, Denmark, Italy, the Netherlands, Norway, Sweden, and Japan. The Washington government, with its obvious anti-Hitler bias, remonstrated only mildly and reserved "all its rights" with reference to possible future action.[8]

Britain's crackdown on German exports evidently violated international law as established by the Declaration of Paris in 1856.

But the blow came as a reprisal, which could only be justified legally as an illegal act designed to counter what was regarded as another illegal act, in this case the sowing of magnetic mines. Yet even a reprisal could not properly be directed at neutrals.

As the conflict grew in fury Washington lodged increasingly fewer complaints with the British, quite in contrast with American practice in World War I. The basic explanation is that on November 4, 1939, two months after Britain and France had declared war on Hitler, America's new Neutrality Act became law, thus establishing forbidden war zones around the British Isles. Prior to this self-exclusion of U.S. shipping, the British had removed contraband cargo from about a half dozen American merchant ships that had been stopped on the high seas. As during World War I, Washington protested to London against such operations, including the examining of sealed mail on American vessels. But such objections were few and mild. The British did not take them too seriously: they knew that the United States was overwhelmingly on their side in a war against Adolf Hitler, now branded in democratic countries as Public Enemy Number One.[9]

Berryman in the Washington Evening Star, *1940; used with permission*

Torpedoing the *Athenia*

We return now to the *Athenia,* the victim of an external explosion on September 3, 1939, ten hours after Britain had declared war on Germany. Tragedy struck about 200 miles northwest of Scotland, as twilight was setting in and when visibility was not at its best. The truth about the assailant was not confirmed until after the war, notably at the Nuremberg trial of major war criminals. But at the time of the disaster the assumption was strong that the deed had been done by a U-boat. A floating mine was regarded in some quarters as a possibility, but in that case the explosion most probably would have occurred at or near the bow of the steamer, rather than on the port side amidships.

The *Athenia* was a passenger ship of 13,581 gross tons, owned and operated under the British flag. Sailing from Liverpool for Montreal, she was jammed with some 1,400 passengers, many of them clamoring to escape the theater of war and anticipated attacks by German aircraft with gas bombs. These luckless souls must have thought they were home free when Scotland's western isles faded from view. Out of 112 Americans on board, 28 lost their lives.[10]

At first glance this tragedy resembled that of the *Lusitania* of 1915, also a British passenger liner, which had helped to set Wilson on the fateful course that led to war with Germany in 1917. Yet the loss of American life on the *Athenia* was only 28, as compared with 128 on the *Lusitania.* Even so, the figure was shocking enough.

The *Athenia* was clearly sunk without warning of any kind. The *Lusitania,* on the other hand, though not warned conventionally, had been warned by the proclaimed U-boat zone, by a belated advertisement in American newspapers, and by the numerous torpedoings that had occurred or were occurring while the luxurious liner was sailing from New York to Liverpool.[11]

In the case of the British *Lusitania,* Berlin not only admitted the torpedoing but also attempted to justify it on the ground that the giant steamer was not just an "ordinary unarmed merchant vessel." The government in Washington had strong suspicions about the *Athenia,* especially after gathering affidavits from many survivors.[12] Secretary Hull concluded that the attacker was a submarine of unknown nationality; yet he did not stipulate a U-boat, although that was the obvious inference. But mere suspicions were not solid foundations for a formal diplomatic protest. At that time the prudent course seemed to be for Washington to look the other way and leave to the British the responsibility for protesting the loss of one of their ships.*

Within a few days German spokesmen and newspapers were publicly conjecturing that the *Athenia* had fallen victim to exploding boilers, to a mine, or even to a British submarine. The Germans obviously were not loath to see the British appear before the world in a bad light. Mouthpieces for the pro-German American Bund charged Winston Churchill, First Lord of the Admiralty, with having arranged for the torpedoing. Coincidentally, back in 1915 unofficial German apologists had also accused Churchill, then on his first stint as First Lord of the Admiralty, of having deliberately exposed the *Lusitania.*

The Nazi naval officials, under instructions from Hitler, promptly disclaimed any responsibility for the *Athenia*'s destruction, for Berlin did not welcome another *Lusitania* crisis with the United States, especially so early in the war. At the time of this disclaimer, we should note, the Berlin government was acting in good faith. It was responding to assurances from the Naval High Command that no U-boats were then known to be patrolling far enough west to encounter the *Athenia.* On the day following the torpedoing, as earlier observed, instructions from Hitler were radioed to U-boat commanders forbidding them to attack passenger ships "even when under escort." In conformity with long-existing international law, we remember, any ship of any nationality under armed escort was subject to attack without warning.

These few words from Hitler say much. He wanted to make sure that his inexperienced U-boat commanders, especially at this early stage in the war, understood and followed the strict orders that the *U-30* had already received. The Führer obviously leaned over backward when he added "even when under escort." He evidently remembered that the German U-boat had brought an aroused United States into World War I, with disastrous consequences for the cause of the then Corporal Adolf Hitler.

Hitler's Specious Cover-up

The naked truth is that the *Athenia* was mortally wounded by a torpedo fired from the submarine *U-30*. German commanders were

*A Gallup poll of September 1939 found that of those respondents with opinions, 60 percent believed that Germans had sunk the *Athenia* and 9 percent thought not. *Public Opinion Quarterly* IV, 100.

then under strict orders not to sink unescorted and unresisting enemy merchant vessels without proper provision for the safety of passengers and crews. All this was in accord with the London Protocol, as approved by Germany in 1936. Oberleutnant Lemp, commanding the *U-30*, did not return to Germany until September 27, 1939, twenty-four days after the torpedoing. At the time of the sinking he was immediately apprised of his blunder by British radio, but he could not report back to Germany until he had reached his home port. Strict radio silence had to be observed so as to reduce the chance of detection.

Lemp was visibly distressed when he met Admiral Dönitz, commander of submarines, at the dock. The erring officer explained his obvious disregard of orders by saying that he had mistakenly regarded the *Athenia* as an armed merchant cruiser, which he had been instructed, so he claimed, to be hunting. There was some plausibility in this explanation, for the evening twilight had reduced visibility and rendered identification of ships more difficult.

In a sworn statement admitted as evidence at the Nuremberg trials, Admiral Dönitz declared that his instructions had never specified any particular type of ship, such as an armed merchant cruiser. Yet the German Naval High Command considered a court-martial of Lemp unnecessary, for they were "satisfied that he had acted in good faith." Dönitz finally concluded that although Lemp "had taken reasonable care, he still had not taken sufficient precautions to establish fully the identity of the ship before attacking. . . ." Previous orders had required U-boat commanders to treat merchant vessels "according to prize law. . . ." As a result, Dönitz placed Lemp temporarily "under cabin arrest" because he "felt certain that a court-martial could only acquit him and would entail unnecessary publicity."[13]

Lemp may not have fully comprehended his orders or he may not have grasped the technicalities of prize law, as partly spelled out in the legalistic language of the London Protocol of 1936. Although night was falling, the visibility was not so bad that he could not have taken a more careful look at his victim before discharging the fatal torpedo. As a young and inexperienced commander early in the war, he may have been overzealous, even "trigger happy," in his ambition to score the first "kill" and become one of the U-boat aces of this war. At all events, the responsibility and blame were his.

An elaborate cover-up followed Lemp's return. With un-Germanlike inefficiency, a page in the log of the *U-30* was substituted (with a different quality of paper and differently numbered pages) to eliminate any reference to the torpedoing of the *Athenia*. Hitler ordered Propaganda Minister Goebbels to charge that Churchill had deliberately blown up the *Athenia* with some kind of time bomb. On October 23, 1939, nearly a month after Lemp's return, the chief Nazi newspaper, *Voelkischer Beobachter,* reported a fiery speech the day before by Goebbels. The blistering headlines could be summarized in these few words in English, "Archmurderer Churchill Sinks *Athenia.*" By a curious coincidence, as we have observed, in 1915 many Germans (but not the Berlin government) had accused Churchill of deliberately sinking the *Lusitania* with the objective of dragging the United States into World War I against Germany.[14]

Hitler's devious handling of the *Athenia* affair, with its tragic loss of twenty-eight Americans, is puzzling, for he clearly did not want another *Lusitania* to plague him. He could have announced that Lemp had violated his orders; that passenger ships, as was true, were not to be sunk (even under convoy); and that the culprit had been reprimanded and punished. All this was the truth, and it might have had some appeal to Americans reared in the Washingtonian tradition of the cherry tree and the hatchet. Whether or not many people would have believed Hitler can only be surmised. For when a notorious liar tells unpalatable truths about himself, he is likely to carry some conviction. But such a forthright course evidently did not appeal to the Führer, a true believer in the strategy of deception.

Hitler no doubt coveted the image of an infallible leader, with a faultless war machine, and he would look ridiculous by contradicting himself in public. Besides, here was an opportunity for the practitioner of the Big Lie to smear both Churchill and the British. No doubt the Führer could convince most Germans and probably many German-Americans of Germany's innocence. From his viewpoint a trumped-up tale would be more useful than the embarrassing truth.

As far as America was concerned, the *Athenia* case was the first in a long series of nasty episodes in the undeclared naval war between the United States and Hitler. Washington lodged no official protest, primarily because there was no hard evidence on which to base one, only suspicions.

The *Athenia* Aftermath

Whatever caused Lemp to fire the deadly torpedo at the *Athenia*, the results were more far-reaching than he, Hitler, or anyone else could have supposed.

Prime Minister Chamberlain bluntly accused the Germans of having "virtually opened the war" on a no-holds-barred basis. Not only had Germany violated international law before the conflict was ten hours old, but also Hitler had evidently served dramatic notice that he would not be bound by the humanitarian safeguards established in 1936 when Berlin had adhered to the London Protocol.

The ill-starred U-boat commander had seemingly proclaimed that Hitler was about to wage anew the unrestricted submarine warfare that had prevailed at the end of World War I. Such was not the case, but the British were certainly justified in drawing the obvious conclusion from this tragic initial blow. They forthwith adopted the policy of attacking U-boats on sight, thus making difficult if not impossible the time-honored visit-and-search type of cruiser warfare. The British also took immediate steps to resurrect the convoy system that had saved their skins in World War I.

President Roosevelt responded promptly to the *Athenia* disaster with condemnatory statements, and though pledged to neutrality, he quickly inaugurated warlike measures. On September 5, 1939, only hours after the liner sank, he ordered the beginnings of the wide-ranging neutrality patrol with American warships. He also arranged for 40 of 110 overage destroyers to be brought out of mothballs and reconditioned, including the yet to be famous *Greer*. Fifty of these obsolescent ships were later sent to Britain in the dramatic destroyers-for-bases deal of 1940, but they were perilously late in arriving. All fifty might never have arrived if the reconditioning had not begun at this early date.

On September 8, 1939, as survivors of the *Athenia* tragedy were being transported to New York, Roosevelt formally proclaimed a limited national emergency. His avowed aim was to employ greater presidential powers to safeguard neutrality and to strengthen the national defense.[15] On September 13, 1939, two days before the first *Athenia* survivors landed in America, Roosevelt summoned Congress into extraordinary session. He did not say so but his main purpose was to wring from that body a modification of the Neutrality Act of 1937 so as to be able to send more arms to the embattled democracies. The President had uppermost in mind helping them to resist the Nazis, the predators who had supposedly sunk the *Athenia* with malice aforethought, and who had acted in clear violation of the international law they had officially endorsed some three years earlier when agreeing to the London Protocol.

CHAPTER 5

SCANDINAVIAN SIDESHOWS

Force and military aggression are once more on the march against small nations, in this instance through the invasion of Denmark and Norway.

Franklin Roosevelt, statement on the Nazi invasion of Denmark and Norway, April 13, 1940

Seizing the *City of Flint*

A controversial new chapter in Roosevelt's undeclared naval war with Hitler opened on October 9, 1939, when a raiding German pocket battleship, the *Deutschland,* encountered an unarmed steamer, *City of Flint.* By a curious coincidence this American ship had been involved a month earlier with the *Athenia,* the first significant sinking in the war between Britain and Germany. As one of the nearest rescue ships of any size in the vicinity, the *City of Flint* had picked up many survivors and landed them at New York.

On her return voyage the *City of Flint* was stopped in the mid-Atlantic, in this instance by the *Deutschland,* while en route from New York to belligerent Britain. The mixed cargo of the freighter consisted of what was then generally regarded as contraband of war, including oil and flour. Accordingly, the Germans seized the vessel, as they were entitled to do under international law. They then put on board a prize crew of three officers and about eighteen men, together with nearly forty prisoner-seamen who had been rescued when the *Deutschland* sank a British steamer a few days earlier.

The evident intention of the German captors was to sail the American vessel on a roundabout course through the British blockade of the North Sea to a German port. There a prize court would determine the legality of the seizure and the fate of the ship, cargo, and crew. We should note that in this case adequate provision was made for the safety of human life, in compliance with the procedures established by international law. Yet one should note that the U-boats, with their small crews and severely limited space, were simply unable to wage war with maximum effectiveness if they operated under the ancient rules.

The unlucky *City of Flint,* now flying the German flag, was next heard of when she put into Tromsö, a port in the Arctic reaches of Norway. This harbor is about as far north as Russia's most important northerly harbor, Murmansk. Why the German captors should have gone so far out of their way remains something of a mystery, but the answer seems to be that the captured American ship did not have the proper navigational charts to guide her through the dangerous coastal waters of Norway. German ships loaded with Swedish ore from the more southerly Norwegian port of Narvik were managing to navigate the length of Norway by sailing dangerously just inside the three-mile limit of that nation's territorial waters. There they could count on immunity from British seizures.

At Tromsö the Norwegians permitted the *City of Flint* to take on water, in accordance with international law, but demanded the release of the American captives. Norway regarded the holding of Americans prisoner in a neutral port as a violation of the Hague Conventions of 1899 and 1907. More important, the Norwegian government refused to provide navigational charts for Norway's territorial waters southward. Rebuffed, the fugitive ship headed for Murmansk, where the German commander could confidently assume that the Russians, as partners in the recent Hitler-Stalin Nonaggression Pact of 1939, would be more hospitable.

The Odyssey of a Captured Prize

The *City of Flint* reached her Russian refuge on October 23, 1939. On the next day Secretary of State Hull cabled Ambassador Steinhardt in Moscow to protest that under international law a prize ship was permitted to enter a neutral port only under emergency conditions. These included unseaworthiness, stress of weather, or a lack of fuel and provisions. As soon as these unfavorable conditions ceased to exist, Hull properly argued, the offending ship was required to leave. If it remained, the neutral nation (Russia) was required to restore the American captain and crew to their ship forthwith and at the same time to intern the capturing German crew. Secretary Hull further instructed the American Ambassador to inform the Soviet Foreign Office that such energetic action should be taken at once; otherwise the Moscow government would violate the neutrality that it had announced in a note to Washington some weeks earlier.[1]

Aroused by this whole affair, Hull was especially anxious to discover the whereabouts and condition of the captured American crew. When the Soviets failed to supply the requested information, he suggested that Ambassador Steinhardt instruct a member of his Moscow staff to fly to Murmansk. The Ambassador was also to hint delicately to the Soviet Foreign Office that in the future Russian ships in American ports might expect the same kind of unfriendly treatment that they were meting out in this case.

Steinhardt promptly bestirred himself, but to his great annoyance the suspicious Soviets thwarted his attempts to reach the imprisoned American crew by telephone. Nor was he allowed to charter an airplane that would carry a member of the Embassy to Murmansk for an on-site inquiry. After several days of agonizing delay, the Moscow government announced (October 26, 1939) that the controversial freighter would be released, providing that she left Murmansk at once. Secretary Hull rightly feared that the prize crew would still be in control when the ship left Murmansk. He cabled Steinhardt to inform the Soviet Foreign Office that reports of such a release of the vessel had caused "considerable surprise" in Washington.

Hull's worst fears were realized when the *City of Flint* sailed from Murmansk with the German prize crew still in charge. The irate Secretary cabled Steinhardt that the conduct of Moscow in this controversy had caused "astonishment." He therefore requested an explanation for he suspected that his pressure on Moscow had been offset by counterpressures from Berlin. Stalin was then provoking a crisis with neighboring Finland so that he could put more strategic territory between himself and Nazi Germany. He was obviously eager to remain on good terms with Hitler, the distrusted and mismated partner whom he had recently acquired. In the case of the

City of Flint the Soviets were prepared, as nominal neutrals, to circumvent international law by permitting a major belligerent to use their ports as a base of commerce-destroying operations.

Ambassador Steinhardt in Moscow, barred from making contact with the American captain and crew, suffered from extreme frustration, as did all the other Americans involved. In his dispatches to Washington he referred to the "close collaboration" between Russia and Germany and to the evident fear of "German armed might." He concluded that the Soviet Union, as a silent partner of Hitler, would rather risk offending the far-off United States than nearby Germany.[2] Secretary Hull himself believed that the true explanation of Soviet obstructionism lay in Moscow, where Russia was acting in "collusion with Germany."[3] The captain of the *City of Flint* complained, in his affidavit cabled to Washington, that his impression of the Russians was "very bad," especially in denying him any contact with the United States Ambassador in Moscow.[4]

After a delay of several more days, the Soviet Foreign Office replied with what Hull regarded as a series of "specious explanations." Included were references to damaged machinery that was not damaged and to alleged "unseaworthiness" brought about by the lack of proper navigational charts. Ambassador Steinhardt conceded that the Soviet explanation contained distortions and inaccuracies, yet he believed that this response was the best that he could wring from Moscow at the time. He therefore recommended that no further complaints be lodged. Yet he had learned that the German captors had managed to secure from the obliging Russians various charts, including those for navigating Norway's territorial waters.[5]

The *City of Flint* Comes Home

The controversial *City of Flint* next sailed southward and put into the Norwegian port of Haugesund on the pretext that there was a sick American seaman aboard. This time the embarrassed hosts screwed up their courage, braved Hitler's wrath, and did what Moscow had declined to do. They honored their neutral obligations when they released the ship to her American captain and interned the German prize crew. One would want no better evidence that international law was on the side of the Americans, whatever the pretexts offered by either Berlin or Moscow.[6]

Vigorous protests from Berlin to the Norwegian government proved unavailing, and Hitler deferred revenge until the following spring, when he barely beat the British to the punch by overrunning Norway. The much-traveled *City of Flint,* finally sailing from the Norwegian port of Narvik, reached Chesapeake Bay safely in January 1940.[7] Hitler had agreed with his naval officers that the ship should be allowed to go home unmolested, partly because the United States was setting up her own closed-zone areas around the British Isles.[8] In this way the Americans became indirect partners in enforcing the German blockade.

Congress meanwhile had been taking heed of these curious events. On November 4, 1939, it passed the revised Neutrality Act, which established the forbidden danger zones for American shipping. By meaningful coincidence this was the same day that Moscow presented its hollow excuses for not living up to its neutral obligations regarding the *City of Flint.* There can be little doubt that the extraordinary odyssey of this ordinary freighter did much to strengthen the hands and voices of those congressmen who supported the revised law.[9] Obviously, if American ships avoided the proscribed areas, they had an excellent chance of not being seized, interned, or sunk in European waters.

Thus the *City of Flint* passed into history as yet another chapter in the gradually crystallizing conflict between Roosevelt and Hitler. In this case the Führer, together with his nervous accomplice in the Kremlin, was the offending party. But one must say on behalf of the Germans that, in this instance at least, they had tried to play by the rules of the game. They captured the freighter, instead of sinking her; they saved the officers and crew, instead of abandoning them. The captors were well within their rights when they headed for a German port and its prize court, but not when they sought to retain their prize and its imprisoned American personnel in neutral ports.

Fighting in Finland

After Hitler had crushed Poland in September 1939, he put out feelers for peace in the vain hope that Britain and France would withdraw from the war. After the resulting rebuff, the wintry period of the "phony war" set in, so called by the bored journalists who had no more fireworks to report. The prolonged inaction arose partly from the deployment of German armies from Poland to the Franco-Belgian frontier, preparatory to Hitler's planned assault on France in the forthcoming spring of 1940.

Fireworks of an unexpected sort erupted on November 30, 1939, when the clumsy Russian colossus suddenly assaulted plucky little Finland. This "Winter War," which lasted about three and one-half months, presented paradoxes. It not only violated the now-battered Kellogg-Briand Peace Pact but was also fought without a formal declaration of hostilities on either side—an omission now made fashionable by dictators. But Moscow at least had the grace first to denounce the nonaggression pact of 1932 with its victim.

The American people retained a special interest in Finland, which after World War I had achieved freedom from Russia in accordance with Wilsonian self-determination. The Finns had also received a loan of some $8 million from the United States for rehabilitation, and they had faithfully kept up their payments while the war-weary ex-Allies were defaulting on theirs.

Stalin had good reason for regretting the loss of Finland, now a proud and efficient democracy. Her southeastern borders lay within artillery range of Leningrad, the second most important city in the Soviet Union. Much heavy industry was concentrated there. If Hitler could extend his sway over southern Finland, either by treaty or by terror, he would gain a lethal strategic advantage. Obviously neither Stalin nor Hitler trusted each other, despite their solemn partnership in the ill-starred Nonaggression Pact of 1939.

The stouthearted and self-respecting Finns rejected Moscow's offer to swap some less valuable territory for the strategic area in question. Stalin's response was to attack his tiny but underrated neighbor, and although his troops suffered heavy initial losses to white-clad Finns on skis, the overwhelming might of the Soviets ultimately prevailed. Treaty-breaking Russia was expelled from the League of Nations by unanimous vote, but Stalin, the aggressor, like Hitler the aggressor, got what he wanted. One more nail was driven into the coffin of collective security, international law, the sanctity of treaties, and the elemental principles of humanity.

American sympathies, usually with the underdog, went out to the embattled Finns. Stalin seemed to be emulating Hitler's rape of Poland when he attacked Finland without warning, and then proceeded to bomb civilian centers and spray the fleeing citizenry with machine gun bullets. President Roosevelt issued a ringing denunciation, December 1, 1939. "It is tragic," he pointedly declared, "to see the policy of force spreading, and to realize that wanton disregard for law is still on the march." All peace-loving people "will unanimously condemn this new resort to military force as the arbiter of international differences." Clearly Roosevelt was referring also to the bad example already set by Adolf Hitler. On the next day the President issued an appeal for a moral embargo on the sale of aircraft to belligerents who bombed civilians.[10]

Despite such expressions of sympathy, a roar of dissent was voiced by American Communists and their sympathizers. They slavishly followed the Moscow line that unoffending Russia was being attacked by Finland—a bear by a rabbit. Moreover, a cautious United States was still in the grip of the neutrality psychosis. Earlier in the same November of 1939, Congress had passed the revised Neutrality Act, which permitted belligerents to buy munitions only on a cash and carry basis. Yet Finland had no usable seaport through which to import such weapons, and the timid Congress, after lengthy debate, appropriated some $10 million for agricultural and other civilian supplies for the fighting Finns. The story was one of too little, too late, and too useless.

Dictators on the Loose

The democratic Scandinavian countries, notably Sweden and Norway, extended sympathy to their embattled Finnish neighbors, while helping them with military supplies and volunteers. But such aid was limited because both Sweden and Norway were vulnerable to attack by either Stalin or Hitler or both, and these two dictators were bound together by parchment pacts and by the joint rape of Poland. With one eye on the Swedish iron mines that were supplying Hitler, the British and the French took steps to assemble an army of some 100,000 men, but too late in the game to save the Finns. Besides, the Norwegians and the Swedes, after drawing stern warnings from Berlin, were unwilling to arouse both Hitler and Stalin by permitting the unneutral passage of foreign troops across their territories.

Europe's dictators, notably Stalin and Hitler, resembled one another in their bullying tactics, but under the skin the affinity weakened. In Spain, Franco permitted some "volunteers" to go to Finland, for he well remembered that Russian Communists had fought side by side with his Loyalist foes in the recent Civil War. Mussolini, also anti-Communist, likewise allowed some "volunteers" to leave for Finland, but Hitler stopped Italian aircraft at his borders. At this stage the Führer and Stalin, faithful to the spirit of the Nonaggression Pact of 1939, were still "loyal" partners in aggression.

Finland's heroic but futile resistance was only indirectly related to Roosevelt's undeclared naval war with Hitler. But it does much to explain the puzzling conduct of Russia and the hesitancy of Norway in connection with the *City of Flint*. Finland was a showcase democracy, and in a broad sense an attack by dictator Stalin, with the acquiescence of dictator Hitler, was an attack on all democracies, including the United States. In February 1940, at the height of the Finnish war, the House of Representatives came within three votes of severing diplomatic relations with the U.S.S.R. by denying funds for the upkeep of the United States Embassy in Moscow. By a curious turn of the wheel, the next year the United States became a quasi-ally of Russia under the lend-lease program.

On February 10, 1940, about a month before the Finnish war formally ended, President Roosevelt addressed the Communist tinged American Youth Congress in Washington. Toward his conclusion, and with pointed reference to the Russo-Finnish conflict, he declared, "The Soviet Union, as everybody who has the courage to face the fact knows, is run by a dictatorship as absolute as any other dictatorship in the world. It has allied itself with another dictatorship [obviously Hitler's] and it has invaded a neighbor so infinitesimally small that it could do no conceivable possible harm to the Soviet Union. . . ." From the youthful audience, heavily infiltrated with Communists or their sympathizers, came a chorus of boos. This speech, which bracketed Hitler with Stalin as twin devils, was a new salvo in Roosevelt's verbal war against the Führer.[11]

The Capture of the *Altmark*

While the *City of Flint* was anchored at the Russian port of Murmansk, in October 1939, the American crew could observe a number of interned German passenger ships. Towering among them was the queenly *Bremen*. Her successful dash homeward the next month was proof that a hasty passage through Norwegian territorial waters by much smaller ships was feasible.

Norway's nervous neutrality was further highlighted by a dramatic incident, in February 1940, involving an auxiliary ship of the German navy, the *Altmark*. She had recently been serving in South Atlantic waters as a 12,000-ton mother ship for the raiding pocket battleship, *Admiral Graf Spee*. This powerful warship had been operating openly in South American waters in defiance of the Panama safety belt and United States patrols. All told, the *Admiral Graf*

Spee had seized and destroyed nine British merchant ships. The captured crews, numbering 299 men, had been transferred to the *Altmark,* which undertook to return to Germany by a circuitous northern course. She then turned southward through the long and narrow strip of Norway's territorial waters.[12]

Armed Norwegian patrols stopped the *Altmark* in a fjord not far from Bergen, and after two "searches" reported that she was unarmed and held no prisoners. Hence she could proceed unmolested to her German destination. The Norwegians, already under Hitler's gun, evidently wanted to see no evil in this vessel, for their examination had been blindly superficial. The British government knew that the *Altmark* had scores of prisoners aboard, and the Foreign Office interpreted international law to mean that Germany was violating Norwegian neutrality by using a warship to convey prisoners of war through neutral waters to further captivity.[13]

A frustrated Winston Churchill finally decided to seize the German ship and to shoot it out, if necessary, with the Norwegian escort ships. But Norway wisely chose not to resist. The British destroyer *Cossack* came alongside the *Altmark,* sent over a boarding party, and released the 299 prisoners (February 16, 1940). In the sharp hand-to-hand fighting four Germans were killed and five wounded. The victors also found on the *Altmark* four machine guns and two "pom-poms" (automatic anti-aircraft guns). Clearly the two searches by the Norwegian patrols for prisoners and arms had been far from exhaustive. How does one hide or keep quiet 299 men?

Britain's Royal Navy thus engaged in a counterviolation of neutrality against nut-crackered Norway, which for her part had been timorously remiss in living up to neutral obligations. The British seizure could find justification in international law, as London interpreted it, and such outraged protests as Norway made were doubtless voiced with one eye on the Germans. Even before this time an observer did not need much acumen to note that the law of nations had been substantially shelved for the duration of the war—for belligerents and neutrals alike.

Nazis in Norway

Stalin's assault on Finland had exposed the Scandinavian countries to greater jeopardy. The Russians did not relish the sending of needed supplied and genuine volunteers to the Finns from Sweden and Norway. Hitler felt uneasy about his crucial supply of iron ore from Sweden; in ice-bound winter months it had to be shipped southward through Norwegian territorial waters. These supplies could be legitimately seized as contraband by the British navy on the high seas, but not within Norway's three-mile limit.

Such shipments of iron ore under the very noses of the Royal Navy finally proved intolerable to the British. They tried to persuade Norway to stem the flow, but the Norwegian officials were loath to bring down the wrath of Hitler on their heads. In desperation, the British finally decided to violate Norwegian neutrality in a manner already made routine by Hitler and other aggressors.

On April 8, 1940, the London government informed both Norway and the shipping world that the Royal Navy had just laid mines in three areas of Norway's territorial waters, but not near the entrance to harbors or normal traffic lanes. The British pointed out that Hitler had so far disregarded neutral rights, including those of torpedoed Norwegian ships, as to make international law both meaningless and dangerous.[14]

As if to confirm Britain's accusations, Hitler launched a lightning attack on Norway the next day, April 9, 1940, by land, sea, and air. The assault was conducted on such a large scale and with such Germanic efficiency as to demonstrate that the blow had long been in the planning. The British promptly mounted a counterattack against Hitler's invaders; it attained some initial success but quickly collapsed.

Hitler proceeded to take over Norway and establish a puppet government. By such strong-arm methods he not only insured his supply of iron ore but also secured priceless air and naval bases for deadly operations in the North Atlantic. Henceforth he could be counted on to make conditions increasingly hazardous, both for the Royal Navy and for merchant ships bringing critical supplies to insular Britain.

Hitler Overruns Denmark

On the same day that Hitler assaulted Norway, April 9, 1940, his troops engulfed Denmark, which was able to offer only token resistance. The Nazi pretext for invading both Norway and Denmark was the desire to "protect" them from the British. As in the case of Norway, the clockwork occupation had obviously been planned months in advance, and it violated a nonaggression pact that Berlin had taken the initiative in negotiating with Denmark less than a year earlier. At that time Norway, Sweden, and Finland had spurned such a dubious safeguard. Their fears were fully justified when Hitler demonstrated that his plighted word was worth nothing—except to lull his victims to sleep.

Denmark was easy pickings, and that nation proved useful to Hitler largely because her inland waters and coastal bases afforded added protection to the ore ships coming from Norway and Sweden. As an added bonus, the butter, cheese, and eggs of Denmark that were flowing to the British Isles could be diverted to German stomachs.

How did Roosevelt respond to these barefaced assaults on two virtually helpless nations, one of which had the paper shield of a nonaggression pact? He not only publicly expressed outrage at this attack on weak neutrals, but he also translated his words into deeds. Invoking legislation already on the books, he froze Norwegian and Danish assets under the jurisdiction of the United States. This stroke meant that stocks, credits, bank deposits, and other forms of wealth would be retained under American trusteeship until they could be restored to their rightful owners. The sum involved was an estimated $267 million.[15] There seemed to be no point in equity or law in rewarding the aggressor for his aggression.[16]

Hitler was angered by these officious freezings. He was roughly in the position of a bank robber who had blown open the vault and then found that the funds were locked up elsewhere in a foreign bank. Later, in his bitter war-declaring speech of December 11, 1941, Hitler charged that Roosevelt ordered "the blocking of Norwegian and Danish assets under the lying pretext of placing them beyond German reach, although he knows perfectly well that the Danish Government in its financial administration is not in any way being interfered with, let alone controlled, by Germany."[17] Hitler made no mention whatever of Norwegian finances.

Reaching for Greenland

Gigantic and snow-clad Greenland, then under Danish sovereignty, turned out to be a major windfall for the United States and Great Britain, under circumstances to be described later. Roosevelt announced in a press conference (April 18, 1940) that most Americans regarded Greenland as "inside the Monroe Doctrine."[18] The implication was that this huge land mass was a part of the western hemisphere and hence vital to the security of all the American nations.

The windfall thus came under the protective blanket of the venerable and elastic Monroe Doctrine, which in effect had raised a warning hand against further colonization by European powers. Hitler, to his great annoyance, would receive more such reminders from the western hemisphere.

Roosevelt further responded to Hitler's extension of the war into Norway and Denmark. On April 10, 1940, the day after the Germans struck, he issued a presidential proclamation further implementing the Neutrality Act of 1939 by more than doubling the original combat area, or danger zone, around the British Isles.[19] The additional boundaries extended far to the north and west of the Norwegian coast and then embraced more waters of the Arctic Ocean by ranging about 200 miles east of the Russian port of Murmansk. Thereafter American ships could not lawfully enter these expanses, with the result that henceforth the United States was imposing a self-denying embargo against Norway, Sweden, and Finland. Denmark had already been embargoed in a similar fashion by Roosevelt's original war zone of November 4, 1939.

So it was that the freedom-loving democracies of Denmark and Norway slipped down the dictatorial drain. On March 12, 1940, a battered but courageous little Finland signed a peace treaty ceding, among other territories, her part of the Karelian Isthmus and the land bordering Lake Ladoga. The defeated victim was not absorbed, but the shadow of the hammer and sickle remained ominously present. Democracy, including that of the United States, was more definitely and desperately on the defensive.

CHAPTER 6

HITLER'S BLITZ
IN THE WEST

We stand ready not only to spend millions for defense but to give our service and even our lives for the maintenance of our American liberties.

Roosevelt's message to Congress,
May 16, 1940

Low Blows in the Low Countries

A month after Germany's twin victories over Norway and Denmark, Hitler unleashed his armed fury against Holland, Luxembourg, and Belgium. In none of these five attacks did Berlin bother with a conventional declaration of war. The Dutch, as too-close neighbors, had tried to avoid provocation by not mobilizing their modest armies, but to no avail. Belgium likewise had bent over backward to avoid offending Hitler. In 1936 she had severed all military connections with France, to the subsequent hurt of both, and had announced that she would pursue a policy of strict neutrality. The next year Hitler, as if to reassure the lone-wolf Belgians, pledged his word to respect this little nation's sovereignty unless she participated in military action against Germany.

When the crunch came, the Führer struck the Belgians with unrestrained force, using the pretext that the British and the French
were about to use Belgium and her two neighbors as a springboard
for invading the Reich.[1] Holland, Belgium, and Luxembourg were
all overrun in eighteen days, but only after some stubborn but futile
resistance. The neutrality of tiny Luxembourg had been guaranteed
by the Great Powers, including Germany, but she had the misfortune to lie in the path of Hitler's drive toward France.

On the first day of the three-pronged attack, May 10, 1940,
Roosevelt froze the financial assets in the United States of these
newest victims of Hitler's aggression. As in the cases of Denmark,
Norway, and (later) France, such freezings were an economic blow
directed at Nazi Germany, and hence were regarded there as a
brand of intolerable economic warfare that would be held against
the United States on the day of reckoning. Hitler did not overlook
these grievances in his lengthy speech of December 11, 1941, announcing his declaration of war on the United States.[2]

The President's Appeal to Arm

Roosevelt reacted vigorously against the menace of Axis dictatorship
in yet other areas. He appeared before Congress on May 16, 1940, to
deliver a special message asking for huge additional appropriations
for elemental defense.[3] He pointed out that "the American people
must recast their thinking about national protection." A new approach was necessitated by the speed of motorized armies; by para-
chute troops; by the staging of long-range bombing forays; and by
the employment of traitorous "fifth-columnists." Roosevelt went so
far as to resort to scare tactics when he pointed out the ever closer
distances of various overseas strategic points. The Germans admittedly had no long-range bombers capable of bombing New York
and returning, but Roosevelt did present rather disquieting data on
the distances of possible air bases. If the British island of Bermuda,
for example, fell into "hostile hands," the captor would need "less
than three hours for modern bombers to reach our shores." Clearly,
Hitler's stunning attack in western Europe had changed the overall
face of the war.

Continuing this appeal for preparedness, Roosevelt warned that
supposed "impregnable fortifications no longer exist." The most
effective defense for the United States required the manufacture
of massive amounts of modern armaments "to attack the aggres-

sor on his route before he can establish strong bases [Greenland?] within the territory of American vital interests." Unfortunately, "one belligerent power [Germany not mentioned] not only has many more planes than all its opponents combined, but also appears to have a weekly production capacity at the moment that is far greater than that of its opponents." Obviously America's own defense required an immense effort in aircraft production. Roosevelt then stated his desire to see the "nation geared up to the ability to turn out at least 50,000 planes a year." Isolationists hooted at such a preposterous figure, but ultimately American productive capacity greatly exceeded this goal.

On May 31, 1940, while the British army defending France was being driven into the sea at Dunkirk, Roosevelt sent an emergency message to Congress.[4] Referring to the new and frightening dangers that had suddenly arisen, he declared that only the most modern defenses would be effective against the new kind of destruction that had been loosed in the world. He therefore pleaded that additional appropriations be voted for the national defense. Congress responded with an outpouring, large for those days, amounting to more than $1.75 billion. Against whom was the United States preparing to defend herself at this time with such belated but gigantic efforts? Hitler and his fellow Nazis were fully aware that in American eyes they were World Enemy Number One.

France's Fall and Monroe's Revival

With France collapsing, Benito Mussolini deemed the time opportune to come into the fray from the rear on the side of his Axis partner. On June 10, 1940, Italy formally declared war on France and Great Britain, thus adding about 100 submarines to the German total of some 55. Roosevelt, outraged by this jackal-like attack, promptly extended the forbidden zone for U.S. shipping to the Mediterranean area (June 11). Speaking at commencement exercises at the University of Virginia, he angrily declared, "On this tenth day of June, 1940, the hand that held the dagger has struck it into the back of its neighbor." Foreshadowing later lend-lease aid against Hitler, he went on to say, "We will extend to the opponents of force the material resources of this nation; and, at the same time, we will harness and speed up the use of those resources in order that we ourselves in the Americas may have equipment and training equal to the task of any emergency and every defense."[5]

This ungentlemanly reference to a dagger in the back of a falling France was shocking to politicians who coveted the votes of Italian-Americans, as well as to those citizens who revered diplomacy of the old school. Such language was never used, least of all in public, by the head of a state. But Hitler and his fellow gangsters had discarded the manners and methods of the old school as they tossed treaties, international law, and plighted national faith upon the garbage heap of history.

Hitler's speedy crushing of France spurred Roosevelt into freezing all French financial assets under American jurisdiction, amounting in all to about $1.6 billion. Again, this blow could have been directed at none other than Hitler's Germany, and Hitler so recognized it in his speech declaring war in 1941.[6] Fear was felt in the United States for the fate of European colonial possessions in the western hemisphere; they might well be used by the conquerors for bases from which to harass American shipping or even to invade the United States. Aside from those holdings of Britain, yet unconquered, Washington was particularly worried about French and Dutch Guiana in South America, as well as the Caribbean islands of Guadeloupe and Martinique (French) and Curaçao (Dutch).

Secretary of State Hull anticipated a concerted action by all the American republics when he responded on June 18, 1940, four days before France formally capitulated. He dispatched notes to the governments of Germany and Italy advising them that the United States "would not recognize any transfer, and would not acquiesce in any attempt to transfer, any geographic region of the Western Hemisphere from one non-American power to another non-American power."[7] This was the historic no-transfer principle, closely related to the venerable Monroe Doctrine and to some extent growing out of it. Hitler's Germany and Mussolini's Italy were not overjoyed to be put on public notice that they were to be denied legitimate spoils of war illegitimately obtained.

A disquieting reply to Hull's note came from the Berlin Foreign Office on July 1, 1940. The Foreign Minister was unable to understand why Washington had addressed this warning to the Berlin government. Germany, quite in contrast with Britain and France, had no American possessions and had shown no disposition to acquire any. The German Reich would not regard as tenable or tolerable the implication in the Monroe Doctrine that certain European nations could hold territory in the Western Hemisphere and others could not. Nonintervention by Europe in the Americas could be rationally defended only if the American nations bound themselves not to interfere in the affairs of Europe.[8]

Hemispheric Neighborliness

The Monroe Doctrine was further strengthened against Nazi Germany by collective hemispheric action. On June 19, 1940, three days before the signing of the Franco-German armistice, Washington announced the summoning of the foreign ministers of the American republics to meet at Havana. Assembling in the last ten days of July, the delegates acted with unusual dispatch. Disregarding Nazi threats and responding to Secretary Hull's appeal for a "collective trusteeship," they unanimously approved the Act of Havana. By its terms those territories of European powers in danger of being seized by unfriendly hands might be taken over and administered jointly by the American republics. The final disposition of the areas in question could be worked out later, with the United States obviously having the strongest voice.

This Havana safeguard—anti-Nazi and anti-dictator—stands as a milestone in inter-American cooperation and in the sharing or multilateralization of the Monroe Doctrine.[9] Such a no-tresspass, no-hunting warning was naturally displeasing to both Hitler and Mussolini, against whom it was aimed. The Führer paid his disrespects to the Monroe Doctrine in his war-declaring speech of 1941, following the Japanese attack on Pearl Harbor.[10]

Even more important to Washington than Latin America was the ultimate fate of Canada, a belligerent fighting Hitler. In August 1940, less than a month after the Act of Havana, Roosevelt and the Canadian Prime Minister met at Ogdensburg, New York, near the St. Lawrence River. There they agreed on procedures for setting up a joint board of defense that would study strategic problems relating to the northern half of the Western Hemisphere.

In November 1940, the two governments agreed to modify the existing Rush-Bagot Agreement of 1817, relating to mutual disarmament on the Great Lakes. Under the new arrangements each side would permit the other to engage in the construction of ships and in other naval activity regarded as useful in the struggle against Nazi Germany. These were strange agreements indeed for a technical neutral to be making with an actual belligerent for the discomfiture of another unnamed belligerent. But the American people clearly

"Just So There'll Be No Misunderstanding" *S. J. Ray in the* Kansas City Star, *1940*

recognized that the defense of Canada was also the defense of the United States.

Offensive warfare against Germany was not the governing motivation in these Canadian-American negotiations, although Hitler evidently thought otherwise in his bellicose public indictment of December 11, 1941. He flatly accused Roosevelt of inventing "crises" from time to time to support his charge that America was "being threatened by [German] aggression."[11]

Hitler and Stalin: Twin Culprits

Aggressions and attendant "freezings" during these anxious weeks were not directed at Nazi Germany alone but also at Hitler's chief partner in aggression. Stalin had evidently hoped that Hitler's forces would destroy themselves in battering away at France's Maginot Line. But such dreams quickly vanished and the Soviets were left facing a fresh and battle-tested German war machine. The Russian dictator reacted in a manner that revealed panic. Between June 17 and 23, 1940, while France was capitulating, Soviet forces absorbed the neighboring Baltic republics of Estonia, Latvia, and Lithuania. These small states had once been a part of tsarist Russia but had enjoyed complete independence after World War I. A fearful Stalin was not content with putting these substantial pieces of real estate between him and the dangerous Germans. He also occupied the Romanian province of Bessarabia, which had once been Russian, and the Romanian province of Bukovina, which had not been.

Roosevelt's resolute response was predictable. Alarmed by this brutal extinction of three independent republics and by the unprovoked occupation of Romanian territory, he issued an executive order on July 15, 1940, freezing the financial assets of Estonia, Latvia, and Lithuania. In this action he further demonstrated that he disapproved not only of Hitler's aggressions but also of Stalin's.

On the face of the record, including Stalin's recent winter war on Finland, there was not a great deal to choose between the two bloodthirsty dictators. Roosevelt would resort to extraordinary means to fight lawless aggression anywhere in a world that was becoming increasingly contemptuous of what had long been cherished as international law. More than that, he had extended formal recognition to the fugitive Polish government in London after Stalin and Hitler, pursuant to their secret agreement, had divided that independent state between them in September 1939. Hitler belatedly responded in his 1941 declaration of war by accusing Roosevelt of having recognized this "so-called government in exile, a gang of Polish emigrants whose only political foundation was a few million gold coins taken with them from Warsaw."[12]

The Invasion That Never Was

France's unexpectedly rapid collapse left Hitler's frustrated armies on the coast of the English Channel without plans or preparations for invading the British Isles. Napoleon in 1803 had also found himself a maddening twenty miles from the white cliffs of Dover, with a turbulent moat between him and his sworn enemy. During the summer of 1940 Hitler's bombers ruthlessly blasted and burned large parts of London and other British cities. But the bulldog British, now led by Prime Minister Winston Churchill, stood firm and defiant among their smoldering ruins.

German strategists meanwhile pressed ahead with their plans for Operation Sea Lion, the code name for the massive invasion of England. The necessary barges and supplies were being assembled along the coast of France but, as in the case of Napoleon, all this effort was fruitless. A successful invasion of England required calm seas in the English Channel for the barges and a continuous flow of food, ammunition, and other supplies for the troops that would land. The attack had no real prospect of success unless the much smaller surface navy of Germany could control the sea in the teeth of the thundering British fleet.

The Germans also needed to control the air, especially if they expected to use their paratroops successfully. On September 15, 1940, German bomber raids on London cost more than 100 German aircraft. Two days later Hitler postponed Operation Sea Lion indefinitely—and, as events turned out, permanently.[13]

Obviously, Roosevelt's paper pronouncements and his freezing of foreign assets fell far short of substantial armed aid to the still worried British. What was left of their army had fled from France badly beaten, virtually all their heavy equipment abandoned. Faced with invaders by sea with barges and by air with parachutes, the embattled British were in desperate need of arms, even shotguns, to replace those left behind in France. At this point Roosevelt leaped into the breach with urgently needed aid by sanctioning various subterfuges. They were designed to justify departures from an international law that was by now largely dead—or at least widely disregarded.

Ever since Roosevelt had secured passage of the revised Neutrality Act of November 4, 1939, the British and the French had legally secured arms from the United States on a cash and carry basis in their own ships. But what Britain now urgently needed was an immense supply of aircraft and other weapons that could not be turned out overnight, even in the United States. Private manufacturers of airplanes could sell the same models that they were making for the government, but once title to these craft had passed to Washington, they could not be sold to the British without technically violating America's neutrality. To the delight of the British Ambassador in Washington, Roosevelt firmly resisted demands that the scanty supply of newly manufactured aircraft be kept in the United States for her own protection.[14]

Unneutral Aid to Britain

A godsend for the British came in the discovery and application of the musty law of May 12, 1917, still on the statute books since World War I.[15] By its terms Washington could make a deal with private manufacturers. The federal authorities would exchange old-model vehicles, airplanes, engines, and other materiel for newly fabricated equipment that could be used for the same purposes, only more efficiently. In short, Roosevelt would do what buyers of second-hand cars do: turn in old models for new. The outmoded equipment could then be sold to the Allies and shipped abroad on a cash and carry basis.[16]

This old-for-new swap began on a large scale in June 1940, when as a starter 50–100 attack planes and 80 bombers were made available. Under the same act of 1917 and a favorable ruling by the Acting Attorney General, Washington sold as unneeded "surplus" to private concerns a vast amount of equipment left over from 1917–1918. Of course, the supplies first had to be labeled surplus, with the understanding that they would be resold to the British. As a starter, this arrangement involved about 600,000 serviceable Lee-Enfield rifles, 800 French and British 75-millimeter field guns, as well as huge stocks of machine guns, mortars, and ammunition. All this equipment, though old, came as a godsend to the desperate British—and it was only a beginning. Thus the Washington government kept its nose clean, as far as the strict letter of the law was concerned, while extending arms across the sea to Europe's one remaining great democracy.

A scheme was also devised to provide the British with ten motor torpedo boats and ten submarine chasers that were then being constructed for the Navy Department in a private shipyard. The builder would obligate himself to deliver these craft to British purchasing agents and then build improved substitute models for the U.S. Navy. For legal justification another statute of 1917 was found, but it specifically forbade for watercraft what the other law permitted for aircraft. Amid outcries from isolationists of "shame and pretense," President Roosevelt terminated the proposed transfer. Yet in later months legal support was found for supplying the British with many destroyers and other smaller craft.

During June 1940 and subsequent months, the Washington legalists ruled that American planes could be flown directly to Canada. Formerly, they had been required to halt at the border, where they would be pulled or pushed across the line by tractors or teams of horses. A total of 105 "obsolete" tanks from an Illinois arsenal were sent to Canada for training purposes. Thousands of British pilots were permitted to train in sunny Florida, where flying conditions were far better than in Canada. Additionally, damaged British warships were allowed to undergo repairs in American ports. All this was closer to co-belligerency with Britain than it was to neutrality toward Nazi Germany.

Hitler, the premier violator of international law, repeatedly invoked international law against the United States in his bitter speech announcing Germany's declaration of war. Slapping at Roosevelt, he declared that in July 1940 the American President had tried to get ever deeper into the conflict by "enlisting American citizens in the British Air Force and by training British airmen in the United States." The Führer then went on to condemn the joint military program drawn up between the United States and Canada in August 1940.[17] It had obviously united America (a nominal neutral) with Canada (an active belligerent) against Nazi Germany (another belligerent). Yet Hitler was not coming into court with clean hands when he appealed for support from an international law that he had repeatedly trampled under foot.

CHAPTER 7

THE DESTROYERS-FOR-BASES DEAL

We need the fifty or sixty destroyers very much, and hope we shall obtain them. In no other way could the United States assist us so effectively in the next three or four months.

Churchill's cablegram to Ambassador Lothian
August 7, 1940

Churchill's Plea for Help

All previous acts of favoritism toward the Allies paled beside the destroyers deal, concluded by an exchange of notes between Washington and London, September 2, 1940. The United States agreed to transfer directly from the U.S. Navy to that of Great Britain fifty overage destroyers. In return, the Americans would receive ninety-nine-year leases for eight potential base sites scattered over some 4,000 miles of ocean from Newfoundland to and including British Guiana.

Winston Churchill had cabled President Roosevelt on this subject as early as May 15, 1940, the day after the Germans pierced French defenses near Sedan.[1] The Prime Minister knew that the United States had a fleet of about 120 four-funneled destroyers left over from World War I, all of them more than twenty years old. Although obsolescent, they were capable of being fitted with modern British sound-detection devices, radar, and late-model anti-aircraft guns. Once readied for combat these rusty old vessels would be invaluable in combating the ever-present U-boat menace, especially during that interval of several months when urgently needed British destroyers then under construction were being completed.

In this memorable telegram of May 15, 1940, Churchill included in his shopping list of requests "the loan of forty or fifty of your older destroyers. . . ." More startlingly, he asked that the United States "proclaim non-belligerence," which would involve helping Britain "with everything short of actually engaging armed forces."

Nonbelligerence was a term that was coming to be used to cloak ordinarily flagrant violations of a nation's neutral obligations—in short, a euphemism for belligerence. Roosevelt, in his response of May 16, 1940, ignored the invitation to join Britain in the fray and raised objections to the "possible loan of forty or fifty of our older destroyers." He pointed to delays in Congress, America's own defense needs, and the probable time lag in readying these old ships for action.[2]

Churchill renewed his request on June 11, 1940, as the French armies were disintegrating and the day after Italy declared war on France. This time he referred to thirty or forty overage destroyers. He was especially concerned about the 100 or so submarines that Italy was about to throw into the fray, and he knew that of all naval vessels the destroyer was most effective in combating underwater craft.

The redoubtable Prime Minister appealed again on July 31, 1940, after France had dropped out of the war and German bombers had begun their fearsome blitz of Britain. Now he asked for fifty or sixty old destroyers at once. He was aware that the Germans not only were stepping up their U-boat campaign and their aerial attacks but also were making elaborate plans to invade the British Isles. Such imminent dangers added urgency to his pleas.

Roosevelt was keenly aware of isolationist sentiment in his country, and he was extremely reluctant to respond affirmatively to Churchill's repeated appeals for help, especially formal belligerency. We should note that three and one-half anxious months passed between the Prime Minister's first overture and the consummation of the deal. Roosevelt was in the midst of a heated re-election campaign in which he had aroused angry cries of dictatorship by challenging the hoary no-third-term tradition. The President was enough of a politician to avoid stirring up the isolationists unnecessarily, and the very rumor that some kind of deal was in contemplation had generated bitter accusations.

The destroyer issue was undoubtedly loaded with dynamite. If Britain went under, as then seemed quite possible, these overage ships could prove invaluable in protecting American coasts and shipping lanes against the Nazi menace. Worse yet, the American vessels, if captured together with the British fleet, could be used in attacks on the United States or on American shipping. Among other concessions in any destroyer deal, Roosevelt wanted a safeguarding public pledge from Churchill. It should include assurances to the effect that if and when Britain was about to fall, she would not surrender her fleet to the Germans but would transfer it to Canada or other parts of the Empire, from which she could continue the war indefinitely. But Churchill was unwilling to link such a concession with a destroyer deal. British morale would suffer if word got out that the government, on the brink of defeat, was making plans to flee to Canada. Besides, as Churchill explained to Roosevelt with overtones of polite blackmail, the Nazis might successfully invade Britain. His successors might then have to yield the fleet to save all British cities from deliberate and systematic destruction.[3]

Swapping Ships for Sites

By August and early September 1940, the British plight had improved substantially, for the valiant fighter pilots of the R.A.F. had inflicted staggering losses on the attacking German aircraft. Despite the outcries of the isolationists in America, a Gallup poll (August 1940) showed that a clear majority of respondents giving opinions favored some kind of arrangement, 62 to 38 per cent, that would send fifty or so of the obsolescent vessels to embattled Britain while there was yet time. This proposed transfer surfaced even before Churchill had sweetened the deal with the eight base sites.[4] But under normal circumstances the disposal of any warships, obsolete though they might be, would provoke isolationist outcries, and the legislative process would take a nerve-racking amount of time. More than that, the isolationists were extremely vocal in Congress, and aside from the ordinary delays they might launch a filibuster against such a giveaway.

While the destroyer issue was being discussed behind closed doors the idea of a swap emerged—an exchange that would involve some six or eight bases off the eastern shores of the Americas. The prospect of acquiring such outposts, especially in the West Indies, had been a popular one in the United States for some years. An oft-repeated proposal was that Britain and France, the two major European debtors that had defaulted on their billion-dollar loans of World War I, might recompense the United States by turning over the British and the French West Indies. In March 1939 and again in October and December, isolationist Senator Lundeen of Minnesota had renewed this unsportsmanlike proposition. Now that the British and the French were busily fighting Hitler, he believed the time had come to demand prompt payment of their debts. If they failed to comply, then the Americans should seize these outposts.[5]

After considerable haggling, a complicated exchange was worked out in Washington. It involved the transfer of fifty destroyers on one side and eight sites for air and naval bases on the other, subject to ninety-nine-year leases. Precise locations were to be negotiated later. Technically, the yet undetermined sites in Newfoundland (Argentia) and Bermuda were outright gifts; the remaining six were part of the extraordinary deal.

Britain Involves the United States

Prime Minister Churchill believed that his own people would resent a one-sided deal with the tight-fisted Yankees—island jewels for rusted junk. The sites for bases were themselves intrinsically valuable, and in addition they could be highly useful to the Americans in defending their own coasts against Hitler. Ultimately they proved to be priceless in combating U-boats and in protecting Atlantic convoys during the dangerous months that loomed ahead.

In terms of 1940 dollars the 1,200-ton destroyers, if stripped of guns and other removables, were worth as scrap about $5,000 each, and on this basis the entire lot would fetch only $250,000. At least this was Roosevelt's rough estimate, and Churchill feared that the British public would react unfavorably to such a one-sided bargain. Actually, the replacement value of these ships was about $1 million each.

The problem was solved by an ingenious division of the bases into two parcels, one gift-wrapped. Six of the less useful sites were a direct part of the swap for fifty destroyers. In a separate package, at Churchill's insistence, the key outposts in Newfoundland and Bermuda were tendered as outright gifts for ninety-nine years, and hence immune from unfavorable comparisons. They were given, Churchill told the House of Commons, "in a spirit of confidence, sympathy and good will."[6] They were in fact an expression of gratitude for the unneutral help America had already given and, although this point was not put so bluntly, in the lively expectation of more favors to come. In the final exchange of notes there was added a written affirmation of Churchill's determination never to surrender or sink the British fleet but, if need be, send it overseas to continue the fight, presumably from Canada.

There can be little doubt that one of Churchill's reasons for engineering the exchange was to involve the United States inextricably in the Allied cause—and possibly co-belligerency. Speaking as a politician and "using the language of understatement" (that is, softened truth), the Prime Minister told the House of Commons on September 5, 1940:

"Only very ignorant persons would suggest that the transfer of American destroyers to the British flag constitutes the slightest violation of international law, or affects in the smallest degree the non-belligerency of the United States."

"I have no doubt that Herr Hitler will not like this transference of destroyers, and I have no doubt that he will pay the United States out, if he ever gets the chance. That is why I am very glad that the army, air, and naval frontiers of the United States have been advanced along a wide arc into the Atlantic Ocean, and that this will enable them to take danger by the throat while it is still hundreds of miles away from their homeland."[7]

Nine years later, in *Their Finest Hour,* Churchill could speak without "the language of understatement." He wrote bluntly that the transfer of the destroyers "was a decidedly unneutral act by the United States." It would have "justified" Hitler in declaring war. The deal brought the United States "definitely nearer to us and to the war" for it was one of "a long succession of increasingly unneutral acts" that edged the United States closer to the European conflict. As everyone could see, Churchill concluded, the transaction marked the elevation of America "from being neutral" to being "non-belligerent."[8]

Yet, as has often been noted, a nation cannot be only slightly belligerent, any more than a woman can be only slightly pregnant.

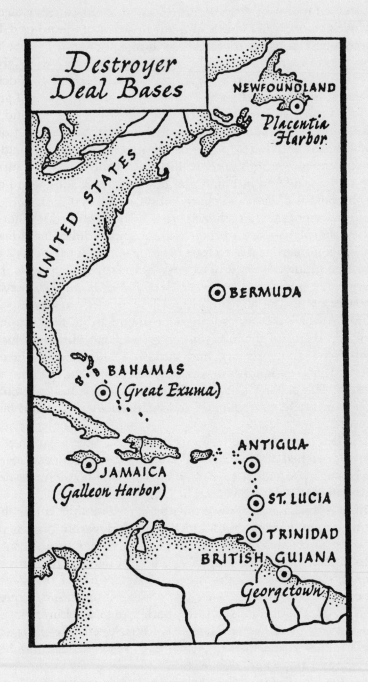

Destroyer
Deal Bases

NEWFOUNDLAND

Placentia Harbor

UNITED STATES

⊙ BERMUDA

BAHAMAS
⊙ (*Great Exuma*)

ANTIGUA
⊙

JAMAICA
(*Galleon Harbor*)

⊙ ST. LUCIA

⊙ TRINIDAD

BRITISH GUIANA
⊙
Georgetown

From the point of view of Hitler, the United States by this time had so far overstepped the bounds of neutrality as to be waging an undeclared war, but as yet on a severely limited scale.

America Flouts Neutrality

No one could argue today that the transfer of fifty warships from the Navy of the United States to that of Great Britain was a neutral act, that is, as the obligations of neutrality were conceived of in the era before Hitler rendered international law largely meaningless. Legislative opponents of the deal charged that it violated both domestic and international law. But the experts who were quoted on the subject were sharply divided in their opinions, much like the Supreme Court in its numerous five to four decisions.

In examining the views of experts, especially as expressed in the contemporary press and in the *American Journal of International Law,* one is struck with the realization that law-minded isolationists and internationalists alike were voting their prejudices.[9] One of the commonest arguments of the interventionists was that Hitler, by his aggressions and transgressions, had outlawed himself so far as any recourse to international law was concerned. We should note that neither the Hague Court nor the Supreme Court ever ruled on the destroyer deal, and consequently every citizen was his own court of last appeal.

The destroyers-bases deal on its face was a clear violation of the agreement reached at the Hague Conference of 1907, which made a brave but futile attempt to codify international law. Article 6 of Convention XIII was explicit: "The supply in any manner, directly or indirectly, by a neutral Power to a belligerent Power of war-ships, ammunition, or war materiel of any kind whatever, is forbidden."[10] In advance of the destroyer deal, the United States government by devious means had been supplying rifles, ammunition, and other war materiel to Great Britain.

Yet there was at hand a legalistic escape hatch from Convention XIII: Great Britain and Italy, both belligerents in 1940, had signed but never ratified it. Hence the other powers could claim a release from it, as specified in Article 28.[11] On the other hand, the Hague Conventions and Declaration were designed to codify, not negate, international law, and the transfer of ships from the navy of a nominal neutral to that of a belligerent had long been considered illegal. The Union government of President Lincoln had certainly taken this position in its difficulties with Great Britain over the *Alabama* and other Confederate warships during the Civil War.

Behind the scenes official Washington held the view that Hitler's repeated violations of international law justified retaliatory violations of that dead letter known as pre-Hitler neutrality. Roosevelt himself also found refuge in the ancient principle that self-defense and self-preservation are paramount to all law, including conventional international law. Even the Romans had a saying, "Inter arma leges silent" ("In the clash of arms the laws are silent").

Bypassing Congress

Domestic law had been another obstacle to the destroyer deal. A statute passed by Congress in 1917 had made it unlawful, while the United States was a neutral, to transfer to a belligerent nation any "vessel of war" that had been "built, armed, or equipped" for that nation.[12] Yet the fifty destroyers had obviously been constructed for the U.S. Navy. A law enacted in June 1940, some two months before the swap, had provided a further escape hatch when it declared that a warship could be transferred if the Chief of Naval Operations "shall first certify that such material is not essential to the defense of the United States."[13] Under pressure from President Roosevelt, the man who could hire and fire him, Admiral Stark, Chief of Naval Operations, formally certified that the fifty destroyers were not "essential" for the defense of the United States. Stark was convinced that the destroyers would be working in the interests of the United States, and he realized that the ships could be sunk but that the bases could not be.[14]

Everything hinges on how one interprets "essential." The very fact that many of the destroyers in question were already undergoing or had undergone reconditioning indicates that the Navy planned to use them for "essential" defensive purposes on the neutrality patrol, in part against a possible threat from Hitler's U-boats. But the solid advantages that would accrue from the yet unbuilt naval and air bases were also considerable, and after some prayerful consideration they could be regarded as more essential than the destroyers. This type of ship was already busy fighting Germans in European waters in a cause that concerned the security of the United States. The destroyers-bases deal was basically a trade-off, the results of which cannot be measured with precision but which conferred substantial advantages on the American people.

Roosevelt's Attorney General, Robert H. Jackson, provided a lengthy written defense of the domestic legalities of the transaction, including the proposed executive agreement that finally bypassed Congress in the form of exchanged notes. The Attorney General is the President's lawyer, who serves at his pleasure, and the presumption is that Jackson knew what side his legal bread was buttered on. His lengthy brief justified the destroyer deal on the ground that it would "strengthen rather than impair the total defense of the United States."[15] Privately Jackson believed that Hitler's aggressive violations of international law had released a neutral United States from the responsibility of abiding by the strict letter of international law.[16] Speaking to the Inter-American Bar Association in Havana some eight months later (March 27, 1941) Jackson declared that "international law provides an ample and practically unlimited basis for discriminatory action against states responsible for the violation of . . . treaties. . . . We need not now be indifferent as between the worse and the better cause, nor deal with the just and the unjust alike."[17]

Yet Jackson did not back Roosevelt on all counts. In his lengthy opinion he sanctioned the transfer of the destroyers by an executive agreement, but at the same time he held that the proposed addition of twenty anti-submarine "mosquito boats," then under construction for Britain, was illegal. The catch was that they had not been built for the U.S. Navy and hence presented a parallel to the Confederate *Alabama* of the Civil War. Oddly enough, these smaller craft were supposed to have gone with the fifty destroyers but were omitted by inadvertence from the final exchange of notes.

A Questionable Executive Agreement

The use of an executive agreement to transfer the destroyers had strong support in constitutional law. Public opinion polls at the time, by a comfortable margin, favored selling the destroyers, and Congress officially put the seal of its approval on the transaction by subsequently voting appropriations for establishing the yet unbuilt bases. Many of the voters, even isolationists, favored the sacrifice of the destroyers so as to provide further insurance that the war with Hitler would be kept on the other side of the Atlantic.

Roosevelt was well aware that the destroyers-for-bases scheme was unneutral by traditional standards, but he expressed his private view with great confidence nearly two weeks before the signings. In a letter to Senator David I. Walsh, the powerful chairman of the Senate Committee on Naval Affairs, he wrote that the proposed swap was "the finest thing for the nation that has been done in your lifetime and mine." He was "absolutely certain" that the transaction would not get the nation into war, and that America was not going to become involved in the conflict "unless Germany wishes to attack us." If and when Hitler wanted to fight the United States he would "do so on any number of trumped-up charges," as he ultimately did, December 11, 1941.[18] Roosevelt might have added that the Führer did not need any charges at all before launching an assault, as he had repeatedly demonstrated in attacking neighboring countries.

In short, the President reasoned, and correctly, that as long as Hitler had his hands full in Europe, the United States could with impunity openly aid the nations that the Nazis were fighting or occupying. This letter to Senator Walsh must be kept in mind when we later address the question of whether or not Roosevelt provoked Hitler into an all-out shooting war.

The Louisiana Purchase Parallel

On September 3, 1940, the day after the destroyers-bases deal was concluded, Roosevelt held an extraordinary press conference. In a briefing for "background" riddled with historical errors, he compared, "without attribution," the Louisiana Purchase of 1803 with the destroyers deal of 1940. Whether he knew better or not, his misuse of history was contrived to make the recent bargain with Great Britain look more acceptable to isolationist critics.

According to Roosevelt's version of the Louisiana Purchase, the two American negotiators in Paris did their work at a time when Napoleon (the Hitler of his age) was fighting Britain. The truth is that war had ended more than a year earlier with the short-lived Peace of Amiens. Roosevelt went on to say that President Jefferson's two negotiators brought back a "signed contract," that is, an agreement of the kind that had just recently been concluded on September 2 with Britain. The President then declared, as in the case of the destroyers deal, that there was considerable doubt as to the legality of the Louisiana Purchase (as was true). Consequently, Roosevelt alleged, "There never was a treaty, there was never a two-thirds vote in the Senate. . . ."[19]

The truth is that there were three treaties, all of which easily received the two-thirds vote of the Senate and the subsequent implementing appropriations by the Congress. Roosevelt was neither the first nor the last President to falsify the historical past to grease the wheels of the historical present.

On the same day as his Louisiana Purchase press conference, Roosevelt sent a special message to Congress, together with copies of the relevant agreements. He was aware that the destroyers deal was of value to the United States, offensively and defensively, and evidently with the isolationists in mind he soft-pedaled the offensive side. "This is not inconsistent in any sense with our status of peace," he asserted. "Still less is it a threat against any nation." The blunt truth is that the United States, a self-proclaimed neutral, had agreed to take the unprecedented step of removing from her naval arm fifty commissioned destroyers, overage though they might be. The ships would then be transferred to a belligerent nation, which had already lost or suffered severe damage to all but about sixty of its own destroyers. This deal was clearly a threat to the success of Hitler's naval war against Britain, and it was so recognized in Germany.

Roosevelt passed quickly over the offensive part of the deal, and then shifted his emphasis to its defensive aspects. "It is," he insisted, "an epochal and far-reaching act of preparation for continental defense in the face of grave danger." He went on to say, "Preparation for defense is an inalienable prerogative of a sovereign state. Under present circumstances this exercise of sovereign right is essential to the maintenance of our peace and safety. This is the most important action in the reinforcement of our national defense that has been taken since the Louisiana Purchase. Then as now, considerations of safety from overseas attack were fundamental."[20]

This analogy to the Louisiana Purchase in truth had much relevance. The transaction of 1803 was designed largely, if not primarily, to keep a militarily powerful France out of New Orleans and the Mississippi Valley. The destroyers deal was engineered to rescue Britain from collapsing and thus preventing the European dictators from working their will in the Americas. Roosevelt was at pains to point out to Congress that the leased base sites, if and when developed, would be used to defend the coasts not only of the United States but also those of Canada, Mexico, Central America, the Antilles, and much of northern South America, as well as the strategic Panama Canal. All this was in harmony with majority public opinion in the United States, as well as with the hemispheric declarations at Panama in October 1939 and at Havana in August 1940.

Praise and Blame for the Deal

As for American opinion, few informed citizens seriously challenged the value of the potential bases. With Hitler's air and naval power growing in destructiveness, the republic could hardly fail to perceive the desirability of having a "protective girdle of steel" well out into the Atlantic. The United States would not only find these sites useful for fending off an enemy, but, if left undefended, they might ultimately be seized and used by Hitler to mount offensive operations, including bomber attacks, against the United States.

Much of the criticism came during Roosevelt's third-term electoral campaign. The President, already accused of trying to become a dictator, showed commendable political courage by consummating the destroyer deal at a time when his Republican rival, Wendell Willkie, was showing formidable strength. Although Willkie personally favored aid to Britain, he publicly condemned Roosevelt for having bypassed Congress with "dictatorial action."

Most of the opposition to Roosevelt's destroyers deal came from a few hair-splitting legalists and from numerous isolationists who outwardly deplored negotiating in private instead of waiting for a slow-motion act of Congress. But, as Roosevelt wrote to King George after his triumphant re-election in November, "If I had done that, the subject would still be in the tender care of the Committees of the Congress."[21]

British opinion expressed itself in jubilation, although there was some minor grumbling over the hard bargain the Yankees had driven for their secondhand, overage, rusting "old iron." But with Hitler's aerial bombing still inflicting enormous damage, fifty destroyers in the hand seemed worth more than eight unbuilt bases in the bush. To sweeten the bargain for the British, there was the unwritten morale booster that the deal was a forerunner, as indeed it proved to be, of America's wading even deeper into the chill waters of co-belligerency.

Germany's military and naval experts were not misled by Roosevelt's heavy emphasis on defending American shores. Mussolini warned Hitler that America's active involvement in the war was an ugly "possibility" that had "to be faced any day now." German naval men anticipated that American war potential would soon be drawn closer than ever to Britain. Grand Admiral Raeder reckoned that the ultimate entry of the United States into the war must henceforth be regarded as a certainty. In vain he urged Hitler to take preemptive action against Britain's Gibraltar and Spain's Canary Islands. Raeder feared that the United States would "occupy the Spanish and Portuguese Islands in the Atlantic, possibly even the British West African possessions in an attempt to influence and if necessary take over the French West African colonies."[22]

Axis Reactions

The Nazi press in Germany naturally excoriated the destroyers-bases deal as illegal, unneutral, and warlike, although unlikely to affect the outcome of the war. The Italian Foreign Minister, Count Ciano, recorded in his diary, "In Berlin a great deal of excitement and indignation."[23] Hitler was provoked but could vent his wrath only by a concentrated bombing of England's population centers. As Roosevelt had predicted in his letter to Senator Walsh, the Führer would not fight at this time even on "trumped-up charges."

One is surprised to discover that Hitler did not single out the destroyers deal for more detailed condemnation in his lengthy war declaration after Pearl Harbor. Hitler noted, without particular emphasis, "In September 1940 he [Roosevelt] draws still nearer to the war. He turns over to the British fleet fifty destroyers of the American Navy in return for . . . several British bases in North and South America."[24]

Surprisingly, Berlin lodged no blistering official protest with Washington against the destroyer deal; that kind of reaction was generally left to the official Nazi press. But a diplomatic response later in the same month (September 27, 1940) was evidently related to the transaction. On that date Germany, Italy, and Japan, going beyond the anti-Comintern pact of 1936, drew closer together in a ten-year military and economic compact known as the Tripartite Alliance or the Rome-Berlin-Tokyo Axis. The Nazi Foreign Minister, Ribbentrop, advanced the argument that such an alliance would strengthen isolationist sentiment in the United States against Roosevelt's pro-Ally policy.[25] He probably was thinking that if America had to concern herself more actively with the Japanese threat in the Pacific, there would be less of a disposition to become involved with Great Britain in the European theater.

At all events, Ribbentrop evidently reasoned that the new pact with Japan would have a restraining effect on both Russia and America. He reassured the Italian Foreign Minister, Count Ciano, that the United States, "under threat of the Japanese fleet will not dare to move."[26] While the negotiation of the three-power pact was under way, Hitler informed his generals that America's armament program would not be effective until 1945, long after he expected the war to be ended. As events turned out, the unfriendly posture of both Germany and Japan forced Roosevelt to divide his navy between the Atlantic and the Pacific, thus weakening his hand in both areas.

Roosevelt meanwhile had not taken his eyes off the Japanese warlords, whose unpopularity in America had continued to mount, especially among China watchers. On July 31, 1940, he announced that the export of aviation gasoline would be limited to nations of the Western Hemisphere. He evidently desired to curb Japan's war-making powers against underdog China, and possibly to dissuade Tokyo from joining the Rome-Berlin Axis. On September 26, 1940, the day before the three-power coalition was revealed, Roosevelt announced that the exportation of scrap iron, a key item in Japan's war industry, would be prohibited, except to beleaguered Britain and the nations of the western hemisphere.[27] This overnight cutoff jarred Tokyo, but the big freeze on exports to Japan did not come until July 25, 1941. From that day forward the road to Pearl Harbor stretched sharply downhill.

Barnacled Bargains

Shortly after the destroyers-for-bases deal, the American naval authorities began to turn over the venerable fighting ships to the British at Halifax, the prime naval base in southeast Canada. The new crews promptly began necessary modifications because in the quick turnover such reconditioning as had already taken place was woefully inadequate. Naval engineers will testify that a destroyer of twenty-two years, especially one mass-produced and long laid up, is roughly comparable to an automobile of that age suffering from the rust and rot of disuse. The hull plating leaked; piping systems suffered from leaks and corrosion; boiler tubes gave out; electrical systems and gunfire control circuits proved defective.[28]

Many of the British replacement crews, about 125 men to a destroyer, were green recruits with no seagoing experience. Further, some of the ships were manned by displaced Norwegians, Poles, and Frenchmen who could not read the instructions posted in English for operating the machinery. Under the command of the British, a few of these overage four-stackers with faulty steering mechanisms collided disastrously with friendly vessels. Some of the ships barely made it across the Atlantic to Britain, where they took up repair space already needed for damaged but modern British destroyers. Overcoming such drawbacks, about forty of the fifty vessels managed to cross the ocean between September 1940, when the destroyers-bases deal was concluded, and the end of the year.[29]

Just as these floating antiques presented the British with problems, so the nonexistent bases proved to be a headache to the Americans. In a certain sense all that Roosevelt had done was to swap the destroyers for a license to hunt for sites. The precise location of such air and naval installations had to be worked out by Washington with the British government, as well as with the people inhabiting and governing the places in question.

The two most valuable sites finally granted after much haggling were at Argentia, in barren Newfoundland, and at Bermuda. The latter was a famed tourist resort, which the inhabitants did not want spoiled by an influx of rowdy Yankee servicemen. Argentia proved to be priceless as a base for air and naval patrols protecting the transatlantic convoys from Hitler's U-boats, while the American installations in Bermuda played a similar if somewhat less crucial role. The Argentia and Bermuda sites, we remember, were outright gifts.

The local regime in Trinidad turned out to be highly uncooperative; the governor wanted to reserve a fine bathing beach and locate the Yankee intruders in a swamp. Partly because of such difficulties, the fair island became a neglected naval base, and this was a lethal mistake—another classic case of too little and too late. In or near these waters the German U-boats in 1942 and 1943 took a terrifying toll of merchant shipping, particularly American, and only a relatively few anti-submarine ships flying the Stars and Stripes were near at hand to provide protection.

Fighting the Fuhrer by Proxy

Churchill seems to have oversold the immediate importance of the destroyers to Great Britain, moved as he was by a desire to boost his home-front morale and to involve the United States more deeply in the struggle against Hitler. His professed objective was to insure Britain's continued survival by thwarting Hitler's anticipated invasion of Britain and by combating the stepped-up U-boat warfare. As events turned out, the fifty rusting destroyers evidently played no significant role in Hitler's plans to postpone and then abandon the invasion of England. After all, Britain would still control the narrow English Channel with her powerful navy and locally superior air force.

The decrepit destroyers, many sidelined for repairs, could not begin their operational mission in significant numbers until the early weeks of 1941, some three or four months after Hitler had decided to postpone his projected invasion of Britain until after he had finished off Russia. The real contribution of these battered and bartered ships came in the Battle of the Atlantic as it mounted to its fateful climax in 1942–1943.

Despite their handicaps, these outmoded craft ultimately saw plenty of action. They sank or participated in the sinking of an impressive number of U-boats and in turn were sunk by them. Equipped by the British with the most modern radar and sonar units, they were especially useful in protecting convoys of Allied merchantmen across the North Atlantic to Great Britain. At one time during the furious Battle of the Atlantic in 1941 they made up between one-fourth and one-fifth of the escorting warships.[30] The outcome of the struggle in this theater, after frightful losses on both sides, turned eventually on a knife's edge. The deteriorating four-stackers certainly did something to provide the difference between victory and defeat for Hitler on the high seas—and hence on the land.

Early in 1942, shortly after the Pearl Harbor attack, the Germans launched their devastating U-boat raids on American coastwise shipping. One of the naval officers in Washington wrote to Admiral Stark, Chief of Naval Operations, wishing that the United States had those fifty destroyers back. He expressed the same thought regarding the transfer of ten other ships, which had received little or no publicity. These were Coast Guard cutters, 250 feet long and well designed for duty in escorting convoys. The Royal Navy had received them all by April 10, 1941, some seven months after the consummation of the destroyers-bases deal.

Admiral Stark's reply to this complaint was to the point. He wrote that as a result of the destroyer deal in September 1940 those ships had been working for the United States about a year longer than otherwise would have been possible.[31] He might have added that Roosevelt, in waging his back-door naval war with Hitler, had been fighting Nazi Germany for much more than a year. Indeed, Churchill may have been about as much interested in getting Roosevelt deeper into America's undeclared war with Hitler as in getting the obsolete warships into the conflict. But he could not say so publicly.

Roosevelt was determined to defend America by helping the British, even at the risk of open war with the Nazis. He astutely judged that the Führer would not then fight over his gross breach of neutrality. Making an outright gift of the destroyers was legally out of the question, but exchanging them for base sites made possible a plausible legal defense of the swap. At the same time Roosevelt would be safely carrying on his naval war with Hitler by proxy—all in what he conceived to be the interest of the nation and of mankind.

CHAPTER 8

LEND-LEASING A WAR

We must be the great arsenal of democracy. For us this is an emergency as serious as war itself. We must apply ourselves to our task with the same resolution, the same sense of urgency, the same spirit of patriotism and sacrifice as we would show were we at war.

Roosevelt's fireside chat,
December 29, 1940

F.D.R. as a Third-Termer

Lend-lease did not emerge as an issue during the presidential campaign of 1940. Roosevelt had good reason to be thankful, for he had enough of a task engineering the destroyers deal. Even the internationalist Republican candidate, Wendell Willkie, publicly condemned the "dictatorial" methods used to produce the historic exchange, although he personally favored aid to battered Britain. The British were pleased with both candidates, especially since Willkie was nominated by a Philadelphia convention that convened two days after France signed an armistice with Hitler, on June 22, 1940.

Roosevelt's much-criticized decision to challenge the hoary two-term tradition and run for an unprecedented third term could not have been an easy one. He indicated that at heart he preferred to retire to private life after eight grueling years of the New Deal, and on a purely personal basis this reaction was probably sincere. But his Republican and isolationist critics accused him of having developed a kingly complex that would not permit him and the "royal family" to bow out.

There probably was some truth in this charge, for power tends to corrupt. But Roosevelt explained with much plausibility that he had summoned a number of prominent men to serve with him in the government during the prolonged emergency, many of them at a sacrifice. He had no right to abandon them and the ship of state while breakers still loomed ahead. Depression-spawned unemployment still cursed the land, and there was no real assurance that Britain would survive the furious onslaught of Hitler's bombers, U-boats, and possible cross-Channel invasion by barges or other landing craft.

As a President who had been in power for more than seven years, Roosevelt undoubtedly believed that he had a better appreciation of the peril posed by Hitler to the democratic world, including America, than any possible successor, even the pro-British Willkie. Moreover, F.D.R. had a personal feud with the Führer. The elected head of a largely isolationist Republican party could not be counted on to take resolute steps to avert the impending disaster—a disaster not only to America but also to the free world. There can be little doubt that Roosevelt was regarding himself as something of an "indispensable man."

During the heated Willkie-Roosevelt presidential campaign, a foremost issue was the degree of America's prospective involvement in the Hitler-spawned war. The platform of the Chicago convention that nominated Roosevelt proclaimed: "We will not participate in foreign wars, and we will not send our army, naval or air forces to fight in foreign lands outside of the Americas, except in case of attack."[1] The "attack" qualifier was added at the urging of Roosevelt.*

As the campaign heated up, Willkie struck some heavy blows as he attacked the one-man rule that would lead the nation into war. He approved the destroyers-bases swap but disapproved of Roosevelt's bypassing Congress; he denounced this executive agreement as

* Charles A. Beard, an authority on American government, later accused Roosevelt of having broken his solemn "covenants" with the American people. Beard must have known that most citizens were skeptical of campaign promises and platforms. In July 1940 Gallup asked whether many voters paid much attention to "political platforms today." The response was 27 percent yes and 73 percent no. *Public Opinion Quarterly*, IV, 708.

"the most dictatorial and arbitrary act of any president in the history of the United States." Speaking in Chicago on October 22, 1940, he charged that American troops were "already almost on the transports." Raising his already husky voice, he declared in Baltimore on October 30 that "you may expect we will be at war by April, 1941, if he [Roosevelt] is elected."[2] This was an unnecessary prophecy, for Roosevelt's breaches of conventional neutrality had been so numerous and so serious that the nation was already in a limited, non-shooting, undeclared war with Hitler.

No Foreign Wars on Foreign Shores

Stung by Willkie's latest charges, Roosevelt addressed a large audience in Boston on the night of October 30, 1940. He appealed especially to the "mother vote" when he solemnly declared:

"And while I am talking to you mothers and fathers I give you one more assurance.

"I have said this before, but I shall say it again and again and again:

"Your boys are not going to be sent into any foreign wars.

"They are going into training to form a force so strong that, by its very existence, it will keep the threat of war far away from our shores.

"The purpose of our defense is defense."[3]

The first three sentences of this statement, which seem to form an iron-clad pledge, are among Roosevelt's most quoted words. The qualifying two sentences, which he immediately added, are usually omitted. Roosevelt was asked why he had not added the customary "except in case of attack." He had himself forced that phrase into the Democratic platform and had repeated it in campaign speeches. He replied in effect that such a qualification was repetitious and hence unnecessary. He also pointed out that if the United States were attacked, then the war would be an American war, not exclusively a foreign war.[4] But the suspicion remains that he omitted "except in case of attack" because he did not want to weaken the force of his ringing response to Willkie's heated charges.

In any event, Roosevelt's undeclared war on Hitler did not cost him the election. The President defeated Willkie by a comfortable margin, despite the destroyers deal and the formidable hurdle of the two-term tradition. During these months, as was true until Pearl Harbor, the polls showed that an overwhelming majority of the

American people wanted to stay out of war but a respectable majority of them wanted to aid Britain, even at the risk of war.[5]

Much of Roosevelt's opposition came from those elements that
were pro-German, pro-Italian, and anti-British. With good reason
the President could interpret his breaking of the third-term barrier
as a mandate of sorts to press on with his program of aid to Britain.
In a broad sense the victory was a stamp of approval on the destroyers-for-bases deal.

As for the "boys" fighting in "foreign wars," they were yet un-
ready to fight in any kind of war, foreign or domestic. On September
16, 1940, two weeks after the completion of the destroyer deal, Roosevelt's prodings bore fruit when he signed the Burke-Wadsworth
Selective Service Act. Incredibly belated, this legislation by a foot-
dragging Congress came three months after the shocking collapse of
France, and twelve months after Hitler had crushed Poland. The
new law provided for the nation's first "peacetime" draft.

Lots were drawn for the draftees on October 29, 1940, six days
before the presidential election. Rather than focus public attention
on drafting "boys" for a possible war, Roosevelt no doubt would
have preferred to postpone the drafting until after the election. But
the lion overcame the fox, and he courageously did his duty and
honored the occasion with a stirring radio address emphasizing "the
defense of our freedom."[6] Yet so badly prepared was the United
States for war that many of the draftees trained with broomsticks for
rifles and wooden sawhorses for machine guns.

Churchill's Palm Across the Sea

Hitler's bombing of Britain had meanwhile continued bloodily
though intermittently. The expected German invasion was thought
to be not far off, although Hitler had secretly issued orders for a
postponement in mid-September 1940.

In the midst of all these anxieties, Prime Minister Churchill
carefully prepared a 4,000-word letter to Roosevelt under the date of
December 7, 1940. He later described his appeal as "one of the most
important I ever wrote." Transmitted by wire to Washington, it was
delivered to Roosevelt, then vacationing in the Caribbean, on December 9.[7]

The essence of Churchill's persuasive plea was that the British
were in desperate shape and might go under unless the United
States came to the rescue with a huge outpouring of additional help.

Of special concern to Churchill was the imminent exhaustion of the dollars and gold with which to pay for the flood of war materiel now beginning to come from the United States. Millions of such dollars already had been used to build or expand American factories that were producing airplanes and other weapons for Britain. Ideally, these materials would have to be escorted by American warships—note the injection of the convoy issue—but the United States, argued Churchill, should have no fear of Hitler's making war on American ships. The Führer's maxim was "one at a time," and he would never move against the United States until the power of Britain was "gravely undermined." He had already shown that up to a point he was determined to avoid the Kaiser's mistake of forcing America into the conflict.[8]

Roosevelt's decision to respond to Churchill by proposing lend-lease help on an enormous scale may have been provoked by a speech that Hitler delivered on December 10, 1940 to the workers of a Berlin munitions plant. The Führer declared that the war in which Germany was then engaged involved a death struggle between the totalitarian and the democratic world. One of them must "break asunder."[9] These harsh words provided no comfort for American isolationists who insisted that a Hitlerian victory was of no real concern to the Americas.

Garden-Hose Neighborliness

After giving much thought to Britain's plight, Roosevelt unveiled the rough outlines of his lend-lease scheme at a press conference on December 17, 1940. In his opening statement he stressed a persuasive point, namely, that war orders from Great Britain were a "tremendous asset" to America's belated defense. They had created factories and other facilities for the production of arms, in which the United States was then dangerously deficient. Accordingly, from "the selfish point of view," the nation should continue to accelerate such an outpouring.

One possible solution of the problem, Roosevelt explained to the newsmen, would be to make an outright gift to Britain of the necessary defense weapons and materials. But he doubted "very much" if the proud British would accept this kind of charity, although he might have added that they would certainly have taken it in preference to nothing. Roosevelt then went on to say that he was seeking some way to "get rid of the silly, foolish old dollar sign." He retained unpleasant memories of the bitter controversies with Britain, France, Italy, and other ex-Allies after 1918 over the attempted collection of some $10 billion, mostly in arms and other munitions shipped to Europe.

By way of eliminating the "silly, foolish old dollar sign," Roosevelt continued with his famous garden-hose analogy. Suppose your neighbor's [Great Britain's] house "catches fire." You [the United States] lend him your garden hose. You don't ask for the $15 it cost. All you want is the "hose back" when the fire is out; if the hose is damaged, the neighbor will "replace it."[10]

This is roughly the idea that finally took form in the lend-lease program. Roosevelt's basic thought was that "you come out pretty well" if you have your war materials ultimately replaced after they have been used to good advantage. He did not say that one important reason for lending the hose was that the neighbor's burning house might set fire to one's own. Perhaps such a statement would have raised the ominous possibility that the lender himself could not put out his own fire if his neighbor had the hose. This objection had come up in connection with sending England fifty destroyers that might prove extremely useful in protecting American shores if the British collapsed, as seemed quite probable.

Responding to a question from one of the newsmen, Roosevelt replied that his lend-lease scheme would not require an amendment to the cash-and-carry provisions of the Neutrality Act of 1939. The war materials would be shipped in non–United States vessels. The President was also certain that his proposal would present no greater danger of embroilment in the war than already existed. "In other words," he declared, "we are furnishing everything we possibly can at the present moment. This will make easier a continuation of that program. That's all there is to it."

When asked if the proposed scheme "takes us any more into the war than we are," Roosevelt shot back, "No, not a bit."[11] His inner belief may not have been so emphatic, especially in the light of Churchill's advocacy of convoyed shipments in his recent lengthy letter. Or perhaps Roosevelt was gambling on Hitler's reluctance to provoke war with the United States as long as he could avoid it.

The Arsenal of Democracy

Roosevelt followed up the "garden-hose" news conference with a defiant fireside chat on December 29, 1940. This broadcast was more than a chat; it was actually a call to arms against the aggressors.[12]

At the outset the President announced that his purpose was to keep his own people and their descendants out of a last-ditch war to preserve the nation. "American civilization," he believed, had never been in such grave danger "as now." He noted that some three months ago, on September 27, 1940, Nazi Germany, Fascist Italy, and Imperial Japan had united in a treaty that threatened the United States if it should attempt to block their program for "world control." He quoted "the leader of the Nazis" as saying in a speech three weeks earlier that differences with the free world were irreconcilable and that "I can beat any other power in the world." F.D.R. tactfully refrained from mentioning Hitler by name.

If Britain went under, Roosevelt further declared, the Axis powers would control four of the seven continents and the intervening high seas. Every American would then be living at the point of a gun. The flying range of bombers was increasing dramatically; even then there were airplanes in existence that could fly (with bombs?) from the British Isles to New England and back without refueling. Nonintervention pacts with the dictators were meaningless, as events had abundantly proved. The Nazis "have proclaimed, time and again, that all other races are their inferiors and therefore subject to their orders." The wealth and resources of the American hemisphere, moreover, provided "the most tempting loot in all the round world." Events had obviously proved that "no nation can appease the Nazis. No man can tame a tiger into a kitten by stroking it." The lesson of history was that "a nation can have peace with the Nazis only at the price of total surrender."

As for the future, Roosevelt believed that "there is far less chance of the United States getting into war, if we do all we can now to support the nations defending themselves against attack by the Axis than if we acquiesce in their defeat, submit tamely to an Axis victory, and wait our turn to be the object of an attack in another war later on."

Roosevelt conceded that "there is a risk in any course we may take." But he believed that the program he proposed involved "the least risk now and the greatest hope for world peace in the future." Actually, the embattled peoples of Europe were not asking us "to do their fighting." They wanted only the tools to finish the job. There was no intention on the part of the Washington government to send armies to Europe: all such talk was "deliberate untruth." The national purpose was "to keep war away from our country and our people." Such a policy might seem unneutral but it, significantly, was no more "unneutral" than it was for Sweden, the Soviet Union, and other nations near Germany to send "steel and ore and oil and other war materials into Germany every day of the week." This was a telling point.

One part of the President's conclusion was especially moving, at least for the interventionists. "We must be the great arsenal of democracy," he asserted. "For us this is an emergency as serious as war itself. We must apply ourselves to our task with the same resolution, the same sense of urgency, the same spirit of patriotism and sacrifice as we would show were we at war." He might have added that the United States was already fighting an unofficial war against the Axis and would continue to do so. It finally became official nearly one year later.

Roosevelt's militant fireside chat evoked an overwhelming response. The President's secretary reported that the messages to the White House, including telegrams, were running 100 to 1 in their approval. The speech was judged to have generated the most favorable reaction that F.D.R. had ever received. It was evidence that the public opinion polls were not far from the mark when they were reporting that a majority of respondents favored all aid to Britain short of war.[13] As for the Germans, they chose the night of the speech to inflict a devastating night bombing on London.

Lend-Lease in the Lap of Congress

A few days later, in his annual message to Congress (January 6, 1941), Roosevelt gave a further boost to his lend-lease scheme by stressing the same sense of urgency that he had expressed so eloquently in his "arsenal of democracy" chat.[14] At the outset he solemnly declared that "at no previous time has American security been as seriously threatened from without as it is today." Recalling that Norway had fallen victim to Hitler through a combination of treachery and surprise, he went on to say that strategic parts of the hemisphere would ultimately be infiltrated by secret Nazi agents and their dupes. Many of these operatives were already at large in the United States and in Latin America. For its own preservation the republic would have to act as an arsenal to be used by those combatants who were fighting an "actual war with aggressor nations." Such weapons should be made available to them not as gifts or in the form of dollar loans but on a lend-lease basis that would require the ultimate return of what was loaned, or at least its equivalent.

HITLER'S AMERICAN AMBITIONS

COMMITTEE TO DEFEND AMERICA
Unify our spirit
Speed our defenses
Aid the allies

From the cover of a pamphlet issued by the Committee to Defend America. *Courtesy of the Hoover Institution, Stanford, California*

Roosevelt was evidently concerned about the egregious new breach of neutrality involved. But, he proclaimed, Americans would not be "intimidated by the threats of dictators." Such lend-lease aid was not an act of war, "even if a dictator should unilaterally proclaim it so to be." When the aggressors chose to attack they did not wait for an excuse, as Norway, Belgium, and the Netherlands had all discovered to their sorrow. As for the dictators, "Their only interest is in a new one-way international law, which lacks mutuality in its observance, and, therefore, becomes an instrument of oppression."

By thus supporting the victims of aggression, Roosevelt further declared that he looked forward to a world founded on his famous four freedoms: freedom of speech and expression; freedom to worship God; freedom from want; and freedom from fear.

The Democratic sponsors of the Lend-Lease Act, including Roosevelt, gave their bill the innocent appearing title of "An Act Further to Promote the Defense of the United States." This was the theme that Roosevelt had stressed when he unveiled the scheme in his "garden-hose" press conference of December 17, 1940. By building up America's arms factories while simultaneously pouring out arms for the British, the United States would be strengthening her own defensive muscle while keeping the war on the other side of the Atlantic. Yet some rabid interventionists promptly alleged that there was something immoral about arranging to fight Hitler to the last Britisher while America remained safe, smug, and prosperous on her side of the Atlantic.

By the autumn of 1941 the presence of U.S. naval escorts for lend-lease convoys to Britain had turned Roosevelt's non-shooting war with Hitler into a shooting war. Many I-told-you-so isolationists charged that Roosevelt had "planned it this way" all along. More than that, he had used all this talk about "promoting the defense of the United States" to pull wool over the eyes of a gullible public. Yet one need only point to the fallacy of arguing that because something turned out badly, it was deliberately planned that way from the outset. In December 1940, there was valid reason to believe that Roosevelt was thinking of the nations's defense, at least primarily, and that he meant what he was saying.

Aid to the Victims of Aggression

The lend-lease bill, though entitled "An Act Further to Promote the Defense of the United States," ironically helped to suck the nation into a shooting war. Introduced in Congress on January 10, 1941, it was cleverly numbered 1,776. This was a memorable date that added an aura of patriotism to the controversial measure. Skeptics to the contrary, Roosevelt did not "plan it this way." An obscure parliamentarian of the House of Representatives had come up with the happy inspiration.[15] Roosevelt might not have approved the number if he had been consulted, for although the date suggested patriotism it also reminded Americans that in 1776 they had formally cut loose from a "tyrannical" Great Britain—the same nation that was now proposing again to become an exploiter of the New World.

While the Lend-Lease Act was being exhaustively debated in Congress, Winston Churchill tried to speed it along by a radio broadcast (February 9, 1941). "Here," he said, "is the answer which I will give to President Roosevelt. . . . Give us the tools, and we will finish the job."[16] In this way the United States might hope to defeat Hitler with no risk at all or a minimum of risk. If America could only provide the tools, she could win a cheap victory over the aggressors without having to send over her own boys into "foreign wars."*

By the terms of the completed Lend-Lease Act, the President was authorized to manufacture or otherwise procure, to the extent that Congress voted the funds, "any defense article for the government of any country whose defense the President deems vital to the defense of the United States."[17] Note the unusual authority given to Roosevelt. A futile attempt was made in Congress to bar lend-lease aid to Communist Russia, for dictator Stalin was then a quasi-ally of dictator Hitler. But Roosevelt was left free to send enormous shipments of arms and other materiel to the Soviets, as he ultimately did.

Put bluntly, the Lend-Lease Act was a virtual declaration of war on the dictators, conspicuously Hitler. It was an unprecedented and all-embracing commitment by one ("neutral") nation to provide unlimited arms and other essentials of war to those countries that were resisting aggression, notably Great Britain. Yet this wholesale violation of international law was defended by interventionist international lawyers in the United States as an attempt "to restore respect for international law by assuming the responsibilities of a good citizen in the community of nations."[18]

Shepherding Lend-Lease Shipments

On the controversial question of convoying or escorting lend-lease supplies to Britain with American destroyers, Roosevelt was conspicuously evasive. As a knowledgeable naval man who had been Assis-

---

* A Gallup poll (January 23, 1941) found that of those with opinions 68 percent favored helping Britain at the risk of war, while only 32 percent were opposed. *Public Opinion Quarterly* V, 326.

tant Secretary of the Navy in the war of 1917–1918 against the German submarines, he certainly knew that lend-lease arms would inevitably be sunk when U-boats attacked British carriers. If these shipments were essential for the defense of the United States, as Roosevelt claimed, he would have to find ways and means to escort these non-American merchant ships with U.S. warships. Lend-lease would lead to escorting, escorting would lead to shooting, and shooting would lead to overt warfare in the North Atlantic. This is precisely what happened, and what many isolationist opponents of lend-lease repeatedly predicted.

Roosevelt was not as candid as he could have been in dealing with the explosive issue of convoying or, more precisely, of escorting convoys.* At his garden-hose press conference he had brushed aside the possibility of deeper entanglement in the war, and one reason for his evasiveness was the certain knowledge that the question of convoys and escorts would be freely ventilated by the opposition, in Congress and out. Defenders of Roosevelt have pointed out that no attorney has a moral obligation to raise damaging arguments that he knows full well will be voiced by his adversaries, as was certainly done in this case.

In Roosevelt's press conference of January 21, 1941, shortly after the lend-lease bill was formally introduced, one newsman referred to the current debate in Congress over lend-lease and the possibility of "convoying ships." He asked if such a course was likely in "the near future."

Roosevelt cautiously responded with "background" information, not to be attributed to anyone. The President reminded his hearers of his recent assurances that he had "never even considered" convoying "in any way at all." But he conceded that if one nation undertakes to convoy (escort) ships, either its own or those of other nations, through a danger zone, "there is apt to be some shooting—pretty sure that there will be shooting—and shooting comes awfully close to war, doesn't it?" But this was about the "last thing we have in our minds. If we did anything, it might almost *compel* shooting to start." (Isolationists later accused Roosevelt of having said "Convoying means shooting and shooting means war.")

At this same press conference, a perceptive reporter noted that two possibilities were being discussed in Congress. One was to have the U.S. Navy protect American merchant ships in British waters.

* In naval terms a warship "escorted" a "convoy" of merchant ships. Among laymen at this time and later, "convoy" was used as a verb in place of "escort," thereby introducing such confusion as "convoying convoys."

The other was to escort the convoys to Iceland "or thereabouts," where British escorts could take over. The President responded banteringly with, "That's a new one on me! How about the Falkland Islands [off southern Argentina]?" A questioner then asked, "Wouldn't you have that power now?" The President responded with, "Oh, I suppose so—yes. This is all, as I remarked the other day, cow-jumped over the moon, Old-Mother Hubbard stuff."[19] In short, the questioning was highly speculative and hence unworthy of serious consideration. Actually by July 19, 1941, American destroyers were directed to escort lend-lease cargo carriers to and from Iceland. On September 1, 1941, American warships were ordered to escort ships to and from the mid-Atlantic—the point at which the British navy took over.[20]

In a presidential press conference of March 18, 1941, seven days after the signing of the Lend-Lease Act, one newsman referred to "reports you were considering early convoying [escorting] of ships." Roosevelt replied that these rumors had been "going on four or five years," although in fact the war had been going on less than two years. As for the reports themselves, the President remarked, "I haven't paid any attention to them yet." This almost certainly was an understatement.[21]

The explosive convoy question popped up again at a regular press conference, April 22, 1941. One inquirer asked, "Mr. President, have matters yet got to the point where it looks as though convoys [escorts] would have to be seriously considered?" Roosevelt's rather flippant response was, "I never lived at Delphi"—a reference to the oracle through which ancient Greeks supposedly communicated with the gods through a resident priest.[22]

During these momentous months when the escort-convoy issue was before Congress and in the news media and polls, Roosevelt had certainly been giving more serious thought to convoys than he indicated. He was in fact aware that many of the fifty destroyers were earmarked for such duty by the British. Winston Churchill had even included a relevant paragraph, near the end of his lengthy appeal of December 8, 1940, on the "escorting" of U.S. merchant ships by American "battleships, cruisers, destroyers, and air flotillas."[23]

Experts on Parade

The two-month debate in Congress and in the press over lend-lease was prolonged, exhaustive, and exhausting. Public opinion had an ample opportunity to be informed (and misinformed) as to the nature of the legislation. In committee hearings held by both houses of Congress, the opinions and prejudices of isolationists and interventionists alike were fully aired.

Conspicuous among those who appeared before the Senate Committee on Foreign Relations was Dr. Charles A. Beard, a historian-political scientist with an awesome reputation as a scholar. With unscholarly extravagance, he declared that the title of the original draft of the bill should be changed from "An Act Further to Promote the Defense of the United States" to the following: "All provisions of law and the constitution to the contrary notwithstanding, an Act to place all the wealth and all the men and women of the United States at the free disposal of the President, to permit him to transfer or carry goods to any foreign government he may be pleased to designate, anywhere in the world, to authorize him to wage undeclared wars for anybody, anywhere in the world, until the affairs of the world are ordered to suit his policies, and for any other purpose he may have in mind now or at any time in the future, which may be remotely related to the contingencies contemplated in the title of the Act."[24]

Actually, Congress retained the power from the outset to vote or not to vote the necessary monetary appropriations, and in the amended version of the bill that body was specifically given the right to terminate lend-lease at its discretion.[25] Hence, "all the wealth and all the men and women of the United States" were not placed "at the free disposal of the President. . . ." Beard further testified, as many others were correctly predicting, that lend-lease would inevitably lead to convoying (escorting), convoying (escorting) would lead to shooting, and shooting would lead to war.[26] But the destroyer deal and the Lend-Lease Act themselves were widely regarded as belligerent provocations, and were certainly so belabored by Hitler in his vitriolic war speech of December 1941.

If Charles A. Beard was the foremost intellectual to testify for the noninterventionists, aviator-hero Charles A. Lindbergh was the foremost technical expert. Without convincing credentials as an expert on foreign affairs, he now found himself regarded as a leading authority on international relations, foreign policy, and military strategy as well. In 1936, 1937, and again in 1938, Lindbergh had been allowed to inspect German aircraft facilities, and even had been permitted to fly several of the most advanced models later used in World War II. He was tremendously impressed by what he saw and heard—overimpressed as events proved. But he was hardly to be blamed for regarding Nazi air strength as superior to that of France and Britain combined.[27] The "Lone Eagle's" friendly relationship with Marshal Goering and other leading Germans led to his being awarded a medal known as the Order of the German Eagle, an honor generally reserved for prominent foreigners who had materially aided Germany through trade, diplomacy, or propaganda. One must say in Lindbergh's defense that the medal was thrust upon him at an affair at which the American Ambassador was present, and he could not with good grace have thrown it back into the face of his hosts. The position that the eminent flyer took in regard to non-intervention happened to square with that of the Nazis, but they were extremely careful in their own extensive propaganda campaign in America not to associate themselves publicly with him lest they destroy his usefulness.*

Testifying before a Senate committee (February 6, 1941), Colonel Lindbergh was emphatic in his belief that the best solution was for Britain to settle for a negotiated Hitlerian peace, as France had done, only such terms were more dictated than negotiated. The famed pilot was confident that Germany could never be conquered, so formidable was German air power. A brilliant tactician but no global strategist, Lindbergh believed that the United States could ultimately make itself so strong with air power and other weapons as to be able to avert or beat off any ultimate attack by Hitler on the Americas, assuming that he had any such designs.[28]

Events proved Lindbergh completely wrong in his assessment of the invincibility of Hitler's air force, wherein lay the aviator's expertise. He could have been just as wrong in other areas where he had fewer claims to clairvoyance. Evidently by coincidence, Hitler had managed to blunt Lindbergh's oral testimony by a speech, on January 30, 1941, in which he threatened to torpedo every ship carrying lend-lease materials to England.[29]

Declaring War by Lend-Lease

While the Lend-Lease Act was still at the mercy of the Senate committee, a proposal was made by its friends that it be amended, as it finally was, by this clause: "Nothing in this Act shall be construed to

---

* Working unobtrusively through isolationist Congressmen, the German Embassy in Washington managed to have an immense amount of pro-German propaganda distributed under Congressional auspices. See *Documents on German Foreign Policy,* IX, pp. 624–625. A Gallup poll of May 8, 1941, found that of those with opinions 63 percent disagreed with Lindbergh and 24 percent agreed. *Public Opinion Quarterly* V, 496.

authorize or to permit the authorization of convoying [escorting] vessels by naval vessels of the United States."[30] Roosevelt readily assented, as well he might have. This addition would help to shorten debate and head off the really crippling restrictions that were being contemplated. Moreover, the amendment in no way prevented the President from convoying (escorting) at his discretion, except perhaps morally, and in this emergency old-fashioned morality did not seem to bother him unduly. In brief, the so-called restriction on the Chief Executive was meaningless, and its sponsors must have been aware of its uselessness. As Commander-in-Chief of the Army and Navy the President still had full power under the Constitution to give the Navy such orders as he saw fit.

Roosevelt made no attempt to put over lend-lease on the American people in the dark of night. It was no behind-the-scenes executive agreement, like the destroyers-for-bases deal. From the day the scheme was broached at the "garden-hose" press conference to the day it was signed—an interval of eighty-four days—it was debated in the press, in Congress, in public forums, and over "every cracker barrel in the land." Every conceivable argument was advanced for and against lend-lease, and the isolationists had ample opportunity to voice their objections to this "blank-check bill."

Senator Burton Wheeler of Montana was a slashing critic. Alluding to the plowing under of surplus crops during the most depressed New Deal days, he branded lend-lease as "the New Deal's triple A foreign policy—to plow under every fourth American boy." Stung to the quick, Roosevelt heatedly told a press conference two days later, "That really is the rottenest thing that has been said in public life in my generation."[31]

The final vote in the Senate, "highly satisfactory" to Roosevelt, was 60 yeas and 31 nays; in the House 317 yeas and 71 nays. Because lend-lease was an administration measure, most of the opposition naturally came from Republican members, many of whom were dyed-in-the-wool isolationists. Public opinion polls showed that impressive majorities of the people favored lend-lease aid to Britain even at the risk of war.*

The Lend-Lease Act was unquestionably an unprecedented breach of America's neutrality, but Secretary of War Stimson, a lawyer and a former Secretary of State, felt that "there was no obligation to be neutral in the face of aggression." He also re-

---

* A Gallup poll of March 8, 1941 (three days before the lend-lease bill was signed), found 56 percent favorable, 27 percent opposed, 8 percent qualified, and 9 percent without opinion. *Public Opinion Quarterly* V, 325.

garded lend-lease as a "declaration of economic war," as indeed it was.[32]

Roosevelt had already flouted neutral obligations so often that Hitler could logically have retaliated with warlike acts, if not a formal declaration of war. Although no beneficiary nation received specific mention in the law, Hitler was fully aware that lend-lease was aimed directly at him. If he had needed further evidence, there was Roosevelt's "Arsenal of Democracy" speech, delivered shortly before the lend-lease bill was introduced. It had pilloried Hitler, although not by name, as the aggressor to be thwarted. For full measure, the President had also held up as menaces the Fuhrer's two war-bent associates in the three-power Axis alliance.

A nation virtually declares war when it formally proclaims to the world that it is determined to provide arms without limit to those peoples resisting dictatorial (that is, Hitlerian) aggression. The Berlin government lodged no formal protest, perhaps recognizing the futility of such action, but the official Nazi press quickly raised an outcry. Hitler himself recognized the lend-lease challenge, although he did not formally accept it until December 11, 1941, coincidentally eight months to the day after Roosevelt signed the Lend-Lease Act.

The Fuhrer finally let himself go in his bitter declaration of war. After branding the destroyers deal as a hostile act, he turned to lend-lease to charge that Roosevelt, "with all his hatred of socialist Germany," decided to take over the British Empire "in the moment of its downfall." But since England was no longer able to pay cash for deliveries from America, the President "imposed" the Lend-Lease Act on the people of the United States. He thus received power to lend or lease to those nations who, in his judgment, might appear "vital to America's interest."[33]

An "Unsordid" Act?

Yet lend-lease did not prove to be as simple as lending a garden hose and then getting it back later, damaged or undamaged. Senator Robert Taft, Republican, remarked cynically that lend-lease was like used chewing gum: "You don't want it back." Obviously the United States did not expect the British or the Chinese to return battered and obsolescent tanks or airplanes. Legal provision was made for selling, transferring, lending, or leasing war supplies, including food, machinery, and services. They were to be repaid "in kind or property," and the first shipments went to the British.

An unhappy Hitler duly noted all this. In his war declaration he also pointed out that in April 1941 Roosevelt had promised to help Yugoslavia and Greece under the Lend-Lease Act. Further, the United States had subsequently frozen Yugoslav and Greek assets when these two countries fell to the Nazi invaders. The Führer also complained that after his attack on Stalin the Washington government had promised lend-lease aid to the hard-pressed Soviet Union. (The delivery was painfully slow in starting.)

Practically all of the formal allies of the United States in World War II were ultimately declared eligible for lend-lease aid, which finally totaled in excess of $50 billion. Much of this aid was not only a virtual gift but also a sacrifice of arms that the American armed forces could have used later. The British Commonwealth nations received some $31 billion in supplies and the Soviet Union $11 billion. Without lend-lease the Russians probably could not have beaten Hitler on their front, at least not as soon as they did. After the war had ended, settlements of accounts were achieved with the major beneficiaries, except the Soviet Union. The U.S.S.R. finally signed an agreement in 1972 that continued to generate disputation.

A delighted Churchill, speaking at the time in the House of Commons, referred to the lend-lease legislation as "the most unsordid act in the history of any nation."[34] This fulsome tribute could better have been used later to describe the Marshall Plan of 1947. If sympathy for Britain had been the prime motivation, the bill almost certainly would never have passed Congress. The American people wanted to strengthen Britain against Hitler, Roosevelt's undeclared foe, primarily in the interests of their own security. Hating Hitler more than they loved the British, many were willing to send a flood of arms so that, if need be, the war could be fought to the last Englishman. This aspect of the Lend-Lease Act was not completely unsordid.

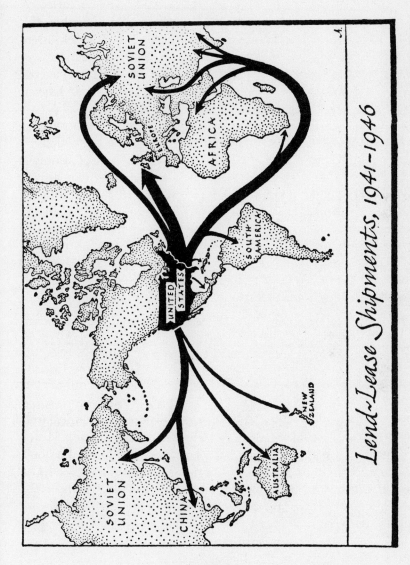

Lend-Lease Shipments, 1941–1946

From Thomas A. Bailey, A Diplomatic History of the American People, 9th ed., Prentice-Hall, copyright © 1974

CHAPTER 9

THE FIRING BEGINS

We believe firmly that when our production output is in full swing, the democracies of the world will be able to prove that dictatorships cannot win.

Roosevelt's address to the White House Correspondents' Association, March 15, 1941

Get Hitler First

Playwright Robert Sherwood, speechwriter for Roosevelt during the war, referred to the understanding reached with Britain at the time of lend-lease discussions as a "common law alliance." The analogy is apt. A common law marriage, often recognized as valid, is an informal union without formal commitments.

In January 1941, as the debate over lend-lease in Congress was beginning, representatives of the British Chiefs of Staff arrived in America for top-secret conversations with United States military and naval officers. To avert embarrassing speculation, they wore civilian clothes and passed themselves off as military advisers to the British Purchasing Commission in Washington. They had been invited to come during the previous December by Admiral Harold R. Stark, Chief of Naval Operations, with the full approval of President Roosevelt.[1]

These high-level, top-secret talks continued for two months, from January 29 to March 27, 1941. Both Roosevelt and Secretary of State Hull absented themselves from the meetings so that any agreements reached would be at the technical rather than the political or government level.

The main objective of the Anglo-American conferees was to prepare contingency plans for defeating Germany and her allies if and when the United States should be "compelled" (significantly, Roosevelt substituted this word for "decided") to resort to open warfare. The American officers did not see eye to eye with their British counterparts on certain important problems, notably the defense of Singapore and other British possessions in Asia. But on one issue of critical importance there was complete agreement, and it proved to be the basic strategy followed throughout the war. If Japan should enter the war against the United States and Great Britain, the joint strategy would be a holding operation in eastern Asia and a major offensive against Hitler's Fortress Europa.

After Pearl Harbor a vengeful cry rose from about six out of ten Americans, "Get Hirohito First."[2] But in part because a war plan already existed, Washington could weather this storm and hold fast to the unannounced slogan "Get Hitler First." Obviously, if Hitler collapsed, Japan would be less difficult to smash. But if time and energy were consumed in crushing the Japanese, Hitler might gain enough time to perfect secret weapons and render impossible the D day invasion of Europe. As events turned out, the early stages of the cross-Channel invasion of 1944 were touch and go. The Führer's foes do not like to think of what would have happened if he had been granted another six months or more in which to mass-produce long-range rockets and bombers, jet aircraft, long-submerged snorkel submarines, and other sophisticated weapons.

Secret Understandings with Britain

The secrets of the British-American staff conversations were well kept, fortunately for the concurrent passage of the Lend-Lease Act. If word had leaked out that the United States, a nominal neutral, was joining hands with belligerent Britain in formulating war plans against Hitler, Mussolini, and Hirohito, the resulting uproar among American isolationists might well have defeated the lend-lease legislation, at least in the form it finally took. The outraged reaction

would have been, "Why should a neutral United States be making
secret understandings to fight in a war beside a belligerent Britain—all in violation of neutral obligations as defined by international law?"

The blunt truth is that the United States was no longer a neutral; such doubts as had lingered before the destroyer deal of September 1940 and the Lend-Lease Act of March 1941 were largely
swept away. Besides, international law had been flouted so often by
both sides that realists could no longer speak of being bound by international law when a nation's own vital interests were at stake. Finally, although no hard and fast agreements were made during the
Anglo-American talks, there was considerable commitment in spirit.
As such, the conversations constituted one more giant step toward
an explosion in Roosevelt's undeclared war against Hitler.

From the standpoint of defending the United States, a refusal
to make such contingency plans with the British would have been
sheer folly. American relations with Hitler were fast deteriorating;
he already had a lengthening list of grievances against the United
States. If a shooting conflict came, the Americans would be well advised to have in hand a clear plan of action and enough strength to
put it into operation—all in concert with the British. Such precautions were made all the more urgent by Japan's joining the Hitler-
Mussolini Axis in September 1940.

For the war planners in Washington, the fateful example of
Belgium was worth pondering. In 1936 King Leopold, hoping to remain neutral, had declared that his little country would pursue a
policy "exclusively and entirely Belgian." He would make no alli-
ances with France or Britain that might provoke Hitler. He even
declined to enter into staff talks with the French and the British regarding his course of action should the Germans invade Belgium
(despite their solemn assurances to the contrary).[3]

Fortunately for Roosevelt, there were no serious leaks to the
press from the British-American staff conferences. In these and other
secret maneuvers, the President was well aware of the possibility of
immediate or ultimate impeachment.[4] The more rabid isolationists
were already voicing such a cry. Like Lincoln and all other presidents, Roosevelt had taken an oath not only to "uphold" but also to
"defend" the Constitution. He was to act in the light of his own
judgment, based on the fullest information available, much of it out
of reach of the public, including his critics.

Snuggling Closer to War

The secret Anglo-American staff conferences in Washington soon bore fruit. On February 1, 1941, Rear Admiral Ernest J. King's Patrol Force was designated the Atlantic Fleet, with King himself elevated to the rank of Admiral and Commander-in-Chief of the force. Following a visit of several senior U.S. naval officers to Britain in March 1941, Roosevelt allocated $50 million in lend-lease funds for the construction of U.S. naval operating bases on British soil, and work on them was begun three months later.[5]

At a press conference on April 4, 1941, the President revealed that the government had released $500 million in army and navy materiel for Britain and her Allies. Moreover, another $500 million of lend-lease funds had been earmarked for the construction of 212 cargo ships, 56 shipways, and facilities for the repair of damaged merchant ships.[6]

Anglo-American joint planning was also to continue at a high level. Scientific information was to be exchanged, including that relating to atomic energy and particularly radar, which had helped to save England during the recent Battle of Britain. There was likewise agreement that Britain would serve as a launching point for future strikes against Germany, and that the United States would protect the Western Hemisphere against Nazi infiltration or invasion. British and American negotiators alike agreed that maritime control of the Atlantic was absolutely essential.

Of special significance was the pooling of military intelligence, communications, codes, and tactical information. Close cooperation was achieved between intelligence operatives, following Roosevelt's orders and despite qualms in the State Department. These activities involved principally the Federal Bureau of Investigation, then under J. Edgar Hoover, and the hush-hush British intelligence agency, under a remarkable Canadian named William Stephenson—"A Man Called Intrepid." Both men were later decorated by the United States government for various exploits, including the thwarting of Nazi takeovers in Latin America.[7]

Undercover exploits were eclipsed by the steady flow of American military specialists to England to give instruction in the use of American weapons, and to learn combat operations at first hand from battle-toughened British. Plans were also being drawn up in Washington for the occupation by U.S. forces of various strategic areas, including Greenland, Iceland, the Azores, and Martinique. Only the first two sites were actually taken over, and they proved of immense value in protecting the British sea lanes to and from America. Additionally, damaged British warships were continuing to be repaired in American shipyards, while Royal Air Force pilots and crews were being trained under more favorable climatic and other conditions in the United States.

Most of these activities were contrary to the spirit or letter of international law that was still being invoked when war broke out. Taken all together, they were massive evidence of the existence and tightening of a de facto alliance between "neutral" America and belligerent Britain. Most of these flagrantly unneutral acts were publicly excoriated by Hitler when he finally declared war on the United States.[8]

Seizing Interned Ships

On March 30, 1941, three days after the initial lend-lease appropriation of $7 billion had passed Congress, the U.S. Coast Guard seized and took into "protective custody" certain Axis-controlled merchant ships lying in American harbors. The lot included twenty-seven Italian, two German, and thirty-five Danish vessels. (Denmark, as earlier noted, had been overrun by Hitler in April 1940.)

A key objective of these seizures was to make this valuable tonnage available to the British for lend-lease shipments, basically because the German U-boats were sinking a dismaying number of merchant ships. The German, Italian, and Danish (puppet) governments all protested to the State Department, and they had substantial grounds under pre-Hitler international law for their complaints. The German chargé d'affaires in Washington had already claimed that such seizures could be undertaken only by a belligerent nation, which the United States technically was not, and then only under conditions of "urgent public emergency."

Secretary of State Hull brushed aside these formal objections. His argument was that some of the crews, as was true, had deliberately sabotaged the machinery when seizure was imminent. Some twenty-five of the twenty-seven Italian ships had been crippled. Hull

THE YANKS ARE NOT COMING

Isolationist propaganda leaflet issued by a labor group, Maritime Federation of the Pacific. *Courtesy of the Hoover Institution, Stanford, California*

consequently argued that the crews, "in damaging their vessels to the detriment of navigation and the safety of our harbors, had committed felonies under United States law, in disregard of the hospitality we had extended to them."[9] Some of the Italian crewmen were jailed.

The German protest in this instance was a rare one; usually the
Nazi press had been encouraged to vent its spleen in undiplomatic
terms. Hitler underscored German objections when, in his lengthy
war-declaring bill of indictment, he complained wrathfully that all
German merchant ships in American ports had been unlawfully
requisitioned by the American authorities.[10] What is more, he was
right, at least according to the international law he had so grievously
flouted. If the United States had been a belligerent, the foreign vessels could have been seized lawfully, as had been done in World War
I.[11] But was the United States at this point a nonbelligerent?

Balkan Battles

Roosevelt was meanwhile extending his long-range resistance to
Hitler as far as the Balkans. The Fuhrer, by applying both political
and military pressure, had forced unhappy Bulgaria into his iron
embrace early in March 1941. The United States responded by
freezing Bulgarian assets in the United States.

Hitler followed up this success by attempting to force the government of Yugoslavia to yield to the threat of his armed might.
While all this was occurring, a top-secret agent from the United
States, war hero Colonel William J. ("Wild Bill") Donovan, was
operating in the Balkans, particularly Yugoslavia and Greece. He
urged these luckless peoples to resist Hitler's takeovers and conveyed
assurances of lend-lease aid from the President if they did resist. But
the Yugoslav government, intimidated by superior force, bent the
knee to Hitler, and on March 24, 1941, Roosevelt froze some $50
million of Yugoslav assets in the United States.

Quite unexpectedly, the more nationalistic elements in Yugoslavia arose and overthrew the weak-kneed government, March 27,
1941. They realized that they would be overwhelmed by Hitler's
armies, as indeed they were in three weeks. When the Germans invaded on April 6, 1941, Roosevelt cabled a pledge of "all material
aid possible" to Yugoslavia although he conceded in a subsequent
press conference that there was little hope of getting much war materiel there in time "to be of use."[12]

The doughty Greeks were the next victims of a German blitzkrieg despite some 60,000 British soldiers diverted from North Africa
to help them. The President learned of the heroic resistance of the
Greeks on April 6, 1941, and took steps to send lend-lease aid to
them. Neither the large amount of encouragement nor the promises

of inadequate aid had prevailed; the Greeks were speedily over-whelmed and the British were driven out in another mini-Dunkirk. On April 28 Roosevelt froze some $40–50 million of Greek assets in the United States.

Superficially, Roosevelt and his agents had merely made empty gestures when they encouraged the Yugoslavs and the Greeks to re-sist. But the final reckoning for Hitler was yet to come. By diverting his divisions into the Balkans, he slowed down his timetable for in-vading the Soviet Union by about six weeks. As events turned out his armies were stopped at the very gates of Moscow in December 1941, when paralyzing cold and Russian resistance forced back the shivering invaders. If Hitler, as planned, had started some two months earlier, he probably would have penetrated so deeply into Soviet Russia as to win a sweeping victory rather than suffer igno-minious defeat and eventual self-destruction. The world owes much to the Yugoslav and Greek patriots who sacrificed their lives more usefully than they could possibly have known.

The Red Sea Reopened

Another by-product of Hitler's overwhelming Balkan triumphs, temporary though they proved to be, related to North Africa. On April 10, 1941, Roosevelt issued a proclamation removing the Red Sea from the list of forbidden combat zones under the Neutrality Act of 1939. He evidently did so because he wanted to rush lend-lease material by way of Egypt to the British forces fighting in North Africa. In fact, Roosevelt cabled Churchill the day after issuing his proclamation that he proposed to send "all types of goods in un-armed American flagships" for the British armies near Egypt.[13] Churchill later made grateful reference in his memoirs to this help-ing hand.

Hitler resented all this interference by the United States. In his bitter war-declaring speech he noted that Roosevelt had first sent Colonel Donovan, "a completely unworthy creature," to Bulgaria and Yugoslavia to plot an uprising against Germany and Italy. The American President, "who stands against every aggression," had backed the "aggression" of the revolutionists who had removed "the lawful government" of Yugoslavia. In addition, Roosevelt had promised lend-lease help to Yugoslavia and Greece in April 1940. He also formally recognized the governments in exile of Yugoslavia and Greece, and contrary to "international law" froze Greek and

Yugoslav assets in the United States.[14] The Führer further complained that Roosevelt had opened up the Red Sea to American ships so that they could bring supplies to the "British armies in the Near East" through the back door of the Suez Canal. Hitler thus continued to pile up his list of charges against his meddlesome adversary in Washington.

In his press conferences Roosevelt was evasive as to why he had declassified the Red Sea as a combat zone. Churchill states that all the ships of the Italian navy had been cleared from this area, which in one sense was no longer involved in the fighting.[15] Consequently, American ships could properly transport supplies to the British army in North Africa. Under the cash-and-carry Neutrality Act they could bring no munitions but they could carry materiel useful to the British. At the White House press conference of April 22, 1941, a questioner asked whether it would be a "defense secret" to disclose that "any American ships" were "delivering supplies through the Red Sea?" Roosevelt replied simply and frankly, "Yes, it would."[16]

Berlin responded to Roosevelt's provocative proclamation by insisting that the Red Sea was still a danger zone, and the Germans made clear that American shipping would be subject to attack. Roosevelt was asked, in his press conference of May 16, 1941, if he recognized the action of the Nazi government "in extending combat zones to the Red Sea area?" Roosevelt answered with a lengthy disquisition on "freedom of the seas." As pointed examples, he referred to American successes in upholding that principle by fighting the North African pirates in the Mediterranean in the early 1800s and the French in the West Indies in the undeclared war of 1798–1800. A reporter asked whether there were "any modern counterparts of the Barbary pirates?" Roosevelt quipped, "Well, I told you to use your haid [sic]." An outburst of laughter followed. The clear implication was that the United States had fought two undeclared shooting wars against marauders and might do so again.[17]

At the same press conference of May 16, 1941, one newsman asked, "Under the Neutrality Act, sir, no supplies ultimately destined for a belligerent could be delivered to a neutral country, could they?" Roosevelt replied that he did not know because the question brought up some disputed questions of international law, such as "continuous voyage." He added that the House of Representatives had been "on all four sides of that subject." A reporter asked, "one is a good side, isn't it?" Roosevelt replied with one word, "Yes." The ensuing merriment revealed that the newsmen had got the point:

transporting "neutral" American supplies to the British army in North Africa was the "good side."[18]

The Greenland Grab

We remember that Hitler had engulfed Denmark in April 1940, simultaneously with his surprise assault on Norway. The enormous and frigid island of Greenland, now a motherless Danish colony, was left in the hands of a few Danish colonists and their administrators. Fears began to mount in Britain, Canada, and the United States that the Nazis might seize a lodgment there. Apprehension deepened after Berlin had proclaimed, on March 25, 1941, an extension of the German war zone to include Icelandic waters and the eastern coast of Greenland.[19] German aircraft were reported to be flying at times over Greenland, as if to locate strategic sites for aircraft bases, which could be used for searching out British naval convoys. Such activity was all the more worrisome because of the defenseless position of the few inhabitants, who had asked for United States protection as early as May 3, 1940.[20]

Most important of all was the strategic location of Greenland on the flank of the lend-lease route from Newfoundland, to Iceland, to Britain. German submarines were already sinking thrice Britain's capacity to build new ships, and the destructiveness of the U-boats would be markedly increased if they could secure an effective lodgment in Greenland. Weather reports radioed from here to Germany would also be of great help to German aircraft about to take off on their missions.

In deep secrecy Roosevelt wrote Churchill on April 11, 1941, that he was about to extend the "security zone and patrol areas" in the North Atlantic far enough east to include strategic Greenland. He would then employ American aircraft and naval vessels operating from the United States, Greenland, Nova Scotia, Newfoundland, Bermuda, and the West Indies to seek out the ships and planes of the "aggressor" nations. These patrols would "immediately make public [by radio]," for the benefit of the British defenders, the presence of the enemy.*

On April 18, 1941, Admiral King, pursuant to orders from the White House, extended the neutrality zone (safety belt) as far east as longitude twenty-six degrees west, which would embrace Green-

---

*Roosevelt was so deeply concerned about American isolationists that he wanted this decision to appear "unilateral" and not after "diplomatic conversations." Loewenheim, *et al., Roosevelt and Churchill,* p. 137.

land.[21] As for the United States, the huge island would be of great value in establishing weather stations for reconnaissance by sea and air, and in the transatlantic delivery of short-range aircraft. The weather stations ultimately turned out to be invaluable in mounting the later bombing raids on Germany.

Roosevelt and his advisers conceived of Greenland as a part of the Western Hemisphere, and hence covered by the blankets of the Monroe Doctrine of 1823, by the Declaration of Panama of 1939, and by the Declaration of Havana of 1940. Thus Monroe's ancient dogma, plus the multinational security arrangements engineered by the United States, could be invoked to take over Greenland preemptively until Denmark was freed.

The Nazi-dominated puppet government in Copenhagen was represented in Washington by the marooned minister, Henrik Kauffmann. The American officials had little difficulty in persuading him to sign the necessary agreement on April 9, 1941. By its terms Denmark would permit the United States to occupy Greenland for defensive purposes and without detriment to Denmark's sovereignty until the emergency was over. Kauffmann undoubtedly felt that such a course was in the best interests of his Nazi-controlled country.

But the Danish minister in Washington had done more than exceed instructions. He was totally without authority to enter into such an agreement. The Nazi directed regime in Denmark promptly disavowed Kauffmann's action and recalled him. Secretary Hull, in a defiant reply, declined to recognize the recall and continued to regard the discredited envoy as the regularly accredited minister.[22]

This action was without precedent in American diplomatic experience, and plainly ran counter to conventional international procedures as of 1914. But by this time two world wars had either eroded or outmoded many time-honored practices. The United States was dealing with an unprincipled and bloodthirsty opponent, and in the interests of hemispheric safety, not to mention the Monroe Doctrine, was fully prepared to fight the Nazi devil with fire.

Hitler was outraged by the defiance of Minister Kauffmann and the barefaced collusion between him and the Washington government. In his blistering war declaration of December 11, 1941, he assailed the hypocrisy of Roosevelt in thrusting his clumsy hands into European affairs while invoking the Monroe Doctrine to keep Europe out of American affairs. He did not in this context specifically mention Greenland, or the Declaration of Panama, or the Declaration of Havana, but he must have had them in mind. Later on this same occasion he named June 4, 1941, as the date on which the first American troop transports arrived in Greenland to provide personnel "to build airdromes."[23]

The *Niblack* Fires First

The strategic island of Iceland, some 450 miles westward from Scotland and about 530 miles from the Nazi bases in Norway, had assumed increased significance as the war rose in fury. As far back as 1918 the outpost had become a sovereign state in union with Denmark, but in April 1940, after Hitler overran the mother country, Iceland became completely orphaned. The next month, at the invitation of the local government, British army units landed for protective purposes.

A new era opened for Iceland on March 25, 1941, when Hitler proclaimed an extension of his so-called blockade area or "operational zone." Henceforth it would extend much farther west to include all of Iceland and embrace the waters of the Atlantic up to the three-mile limit of Greenland. Within this vast area all neutral merchant ships, as well as belligerent ships, could be sunk on sight. Obviously, intruding warships, including those of the United States, would be endangered.

Admiral Stark, U.S. Chief of Naval Operations, had earlier alerted Roosevelt to the immense strategic value of Iceland to the United States for bases and convoys, especially if the undeclared war between Hitler and the United States should escalate into an all-out shooting war. The President, with the obvious intention of forestalling a Nazi occupation, ordered a preliminary reconnaissance of Iceland.[24]

This mission was assigned to the U.S. destroyer *Niblack,* commanded by Lieutenant Commander Edward F. Durgin. Also on board was the division commander, Commander Dennis L. Ryan. On the morning of April 11, 1941, some 500 miles southwest of Iceland the warship slowed down to take on board from three lifeboats about sixty survivors of a Dutch freighter that had been torpedoed by a U-boat several hours earlier. The sunken ship had evidently been a straggler in a convoy.

As the last survivors were being rescued, the sound man (sonar operator) reported a hostile contact, which he identified as a submarine approaching off the starboard beam at a distance of about 1,400

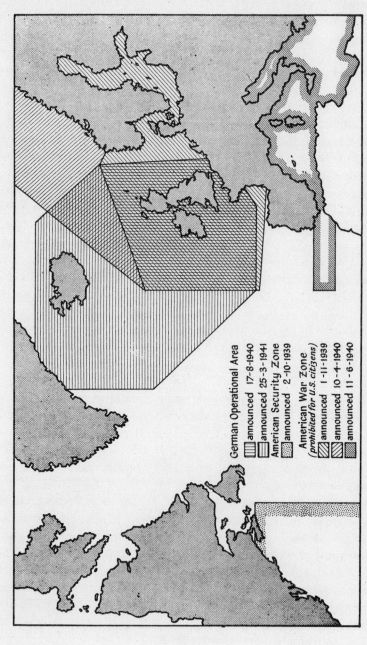

Political zones in the area of hostilities

From Der Seekrieg by Vice Admiral Friedrich Ruge. Copyright © 1957, U.S. Naval Institute, Annapolis, Maryland

German Operational Area
announced 17-8-1940
announced 25-3-1941

American Security Zone
announced 2-10-1939

American War Zone
(prohibited for U.S. citizens)
announced 1-11-1939
announced 10-4-1940
announced 11-6-1940

yards. Whatever the suspected object was, it seemed to be moving toward the *Niblack* as if to attack. But the periscope was never seen. To Commander Ryan the prudent course was to strike first rather than try to evade the U-boat's torpedoes.

The supposed submarine could have fired a torpedo using sound (not periscope) bearings, an admittedly less accurate method. The division commander, sensing danger, realized that depth charges would probably discourage attack, and he acted accordingly. His decision to order Durgin to take the offensive may have been prompted in part by a suppressed desire to strike back at the supposed U-boat, for German submarines had already made life miserable for the U.S. destroyer escorts.

Five minutes after the first sonar contact, the *Niblack,* on an intercepting course, launched three depth charges at ten-second intervals. Evidently nothing was hit, for there were no subsequent oil slicks or other signs of wreckage in the water. The destroyer then zigzagged away from the scene at a speedy twenty-eight knots. Nearing Iceland the next morning, the lookout spotted what appeared to be a periscope some 300 yeads distant but the American warship swerved and easily passed out of range.

The Incident That Never Was

When the *Niblack's* mission in Iceland was completed in eleven days, the destroyer returned to Newport, Rhode Island, on April 28, 1941. There the commander told Admiral Bristol about the alleged sonar contact seventeen days earlier. The admiral, properly skeptical, did not believe that the alleged assailant had been a U-boat. He noted that "false contacts" were common at sea; that they could be caused by schools of fish, by submerged objects (there was much submarine-created wreckage in these waters), and by turbulent wakes. He could well have mentioned inexperienced and jittery operators of relatively primitive sonar equipment. The commander of the *Niblack* himself came to believe, after more experience with anti-submarine warfare, that he had made a false contact, possibly a whale. He might even have mentioned prolonged patrols and strained nerves, with a consequent proneness to overreact.

On the German side, there is overwhelming evidence of a non-incident. The torpedoed Dutch freighter, from which the sixty men had been rescued, had been attacked by the *U-52*, which reported no depth-bomb attacks to Berlin. The submarine had not lingered in the area of the torpedoing, as was true of *U-92* and the *U-94*, which likewise reported no brush with the *Niblack*. The lookout of *U-101* had seen a ship in the area in question, but had not suffered an attack. Such records were kept with Germanic thoroughness by the U-boats on patrol. After word of the *Niblack* affair finally reached the American press, the German navy undertook a careful investigation of the alleged attack but came up with nothing. We should note that not even Hitler mentioned the supposed incident in his war speech, although he did refer by name to the destroyers *Greer* and *Kearny*.

Not until June 9, 1941, did reference to the incident occur in the American press. Columnists in the *Washington Post* used it to support their charge that the President was employing the navy in such a way in the Atlantic as to provoke an incident that would enable him to justify more active participation in the Battle of the Atlantic. Roosevelt was furious. As he wrote to Secretary of the Interior Ickes, the story "ought not have been printed whether it was true or not."[25] F.D.R. evidently welcomed a clash so as to justify stronger anti-submarine measures, but his guideline was that the first shot should come from the Nazis so that he could claim self-defense.[26] In this case all the firing had come from a United States destroyer.

The *Niblack* incident has been incorrectly labeled the first shot in Roosevelt's undeclared war with Hitler. Actually, there were three shots, and if they had been directed at a U-boat, the Germans, including Hitler, remained unaware of their peril. But one indisputable conclusion emerges in retrospect. Actual clashes with U-boats were inevitable as long as U.S. destroyers, armed with depth bombs, continued to patrol these North Atlantic waters and thus to place themselves in the path of approaching trouble.

CHAPTER 10

INCREASED FRICTION AND THE *ROBIN MOOR*

Notice is served on us, in effect, that the German Reich proposes so to intimidate the United States that we would be dissuaded from carrying out our chosen policy of helping Britain to survive.

Roosevelt's message to Congress on the *Robin Moor,*
June 20, 1941

Stalin and Japan Clasp Hands

The diplomatic gamesmanship involving Germany presented Roosevelt with a disagreeable jolt on April 13, 1941, while Yugoslavia and Greece were collapsing under the lightning blows of Hitler's armed forces. On that historic day Moscow announced the signing of the Soviet-Japanese Neutrality Pact. It was supposed to last five years, and it would be automatically renewed unless either party terminated the agreement before the expiration date. By the pact's provisions neither Russia nor Japan would ever aggress against the other.* From Stalin's standpoint the pact was a stunning coup, for it

---

* With a regard for the proprieties not common among dictators, Stalin gave notice of the termination of the treaty on April 5, 1945, in anticipation of his declaration of war on Japan, August 8, 1945.

strengthened his back-door Siberian defenses as he faced the threat of an assault by the untrustworthy Nazis in Europe. Henceforth Hitler could not count on Japan's stabbing Russia from the rear in the event of his invasion of the Soviet Union, which in fact he was already planning.

To Roosevelt the signing of the Moscow-Tokyo pact came as highly unwelcome news. It meant that the Japanese, freed of worry about being assailed by their traditional Russian foe in the rear, could concentrate on their lagging conquest of the Chinese, whom the President was supporting as best he could. But more immediately alarming was the undisputed fact that the Japanese were now freer to strike Hong Kong, Singapore, and other valuable British holdings in the Far East. If possible, the British would have to divert some of their spread-thin naval strength from their desperate struggle against Hitler to defend their highly vulnerable Asiatic outposts.

As a result of the Russo-Japanese Neutrality Pact, the Americans were immediately put under greater pressure to keep more of their naval strength at Pearl Harbor. Roosevelt was prompted to write to a cabinet member during these anxious months that he did not have "enough Navy to go round," that is, for the Battle of the Atlantic against Germany and for adequate watchdog operations in the Pacific.[1]

The jarring Russo-Japanese Neutrality Pact bore fruit in yet another quarter. Roosevelt was already on record as proclaiming that the United States would defend the Western Hemisphere against intrusions by hostile sea forces in the Atlantic. No one should have been greatly surprised when Admiral King, Commander-in-Chief of the U.S. Atlantic Fleet, took bold action. On April 18, 1941, as we have seen, he announced to his ship captains that the Western Hemisphere now extended from approximately 26° westward, including all of Greenland and the Azores.[2] This vast expanse overlapped the German combat zone of March 25, 1941, and virtually guaranteed some kind of clash with the Nazis sooner or later.

To enable Admiral King to patrol this awesome new area more effectively, the President took another fateful step. Early in April 1941 he authorized Admiral Stark to transfer from the Pacific to the Atlantic three battleships, an aircraft carrier, four cruisers, and supporting destroyers. The signing of the Soviet-Japanese Neutrality Pact presumably caused Tokyo to regard the withdrawal of so much naval strength as a sign of weakness. Accordingly, during the weekend of April 19–21, Roosevelt rescinded the proposed transfer and fell back on intensified patrols rather than naval escorts of convoys.

The next month, May 1941, the President rescinded this rescission. As a compromise with his advisers, he reduced the transfer to three battleships, an aircraft carrier, and supporting vessels. This withdrawn force represented about a quarter of the remaining Pacific fleet that subsequently suffered severe damage at Pearl Harbor.[3]

Extending American Patrols

By a presidential order of April 24, 1941, Roosevelt countermanded a previous directive and ordered the Navy to conduct only patrol operations in the North Atlantic. American warships were merely to report by radio (to British patrols) the movements of German ships west of Iceland, and there was to be no shooting except when shot at.[4]

At his press conference of April 25, 1941—one of the longest on record—Roosevelt, as a former naval person, responded to newspaper rumors by giving the reporters a lecture on the proper use of nautical terminology.[5] The words "convoy," "patrol," and "escort" were being used interchangeably, and Roosevelt wanted everyone to know that there was as much difference among them as between horses and cows. A convoy, he explained at length, was a group of merchant ships sailing together and usually being escorted by destroyers. A person should never say that a warship convoys a convoy; a destroyer escorts a convoy. American fighting ships in the Atlantic were only patrolling or scouting, not convoying, just as scouts in covered-wagon days scouted several miles ahead of the wagon train to discover if hostile Indians were lurking there.

Yes, conceded Roosevelt, American warships were then engaged in "patrol" duty but not "convoy" duty. They were merely roving the waters of the North Atlantic routes and alerting the British lend-lease convoys by radio to the presence of enemy submarines or surface raiders.* Roosevelt revealed that he had already extended (April 18, 1941) the patrol area far beyond the 300-mile minimum limit of the Pan-American Security Zone to 26° west. (It was to be extended even farther some two months later, in July 1941, all the

---

* At about this time the U.S. carrier *Wasp* was assigned to the neutrality patrol. Not surprisingly, her search aircraft carried "no armaments of any kind," her scout planes being equipped only with "smoke bombs." These could have been used to alert British warships. Captain F. L. Palmer to Paul B. Ryan, October 28, 1977.

way to Icelandic waters.)⁶ If necessary, Roosevelt asserted, he would expand the U.S. patrols over "the seven seas" in defense of the "American hemisphere." He was protecting not only British shipping but also North and South America "under the Monroe Doctrine."⁷

At this same conference Roosevelt discounted reports that 40 percent of the lend-lease material was being sunk by German U-boats. He was asked bluntly if the government had "any idea" of "escorting convoys." "No, no," he replied as he threw cold water on the sensationalists, and that "will be awfully bad news to some of you."⁸

The President may well have been telling the truth. Some of his closest advisers were pushing for the escorting of convoys, and he had spurned their advice recently in rescinding an order to escort. But as the Battle of the Atlantic grew more desperate, F.D.R. was forced to reconsider this hands-off decision and provide armed escorts, which in turn were bound to tangle with the U-boats.

Attention focused anew on the Battle of the Atlantic when the German monster battleship *Bismarck* sortied into the North Atlantic southeast of Greenland on May 26, 1941. She presumably had left to wreak havoc with convoys and possibly to intimidate potential American escorts. The warship was ranked with her sister, the *Tirpitz,* as the most powerful battleship in the world. After destroying the British battle cruiser *Hood* with one salvo, she was run down and destroyed by pursuing British ships and aircraft over a period of three days. The *Bismarck* almost got away but was located from the air by an American-built Catalina (PBY). The plane was operated under the British Coastal Command with an American naval officer assigned as pilot-instructor to the Royal Air Force.⁹ As the arsenal of democracy, the United States had a good day, although at the time Hitler could not have been aware of these details.

During the nerve-racking two days when the *Bismarck* was lost to view, Roosevelt anxiously consulted his advisers. He feared that the battleship might show up in the Caribbean, where the United States had some submarines. Suppose he ordered an attack and the *Bismarck* was sunk? "Do you think the people would demand to have me impeached?" He was told by his hawkish advisers that he would risk impeachment only if the Navy "fired and missed."¹⁰ What had appeared to be proper tonic in the spring might not seem like adequate medicine in the fall.

Vichy France and the *Zam Zam*

During these critical weeks Roosevelt was becoming increasingly worried about ominous developments in France. On May 15, 1941, the government of Marshall Pétain, which had been installed as Hitler's quasi-puppet in Vichy France, announced its intention of moving closer toward collaboration with Nazi Germany. In quick response, Roosevelt issued a public appeal on that very same day. It amounted to going over the head of the Vichy government to the French people—something strictly forbidden by diplomatic protocol. But protocol had gone the way of international law.[11]

In his unorthodox plea, Roosevelt emphasized his concern over the obvious threat to the Western Hemisphere. He especially feared that the Vichy government would deliver to Hitler, as an accomplice, France's overseas colonies, especially those on the coast of West Africa facing the Americas. Yet such officious presidential intervention was an obvious attempt to thwart Hitler's supposed expansionist designs on the American continents. To underscore Washington's deep concern, Roosevelt ordered the U.S. Coast Guard to place armed men as "protective custody" on all ten French ships currently berthed in U.S. ports, including the enormous and ill-starred liner *Normandie.*

More bad news for the United States came on May 20, 1941. On that day, Berlin announced that an Egyptian passenger steamer, the *Zam Zam,* with about 140 American passengers on board, had been shelled and sunk by the *Atlantis,* a German surface raider, in the South Atlantic. The sinking occurred west of the African Cape of Good Hope, far from Egypt.[12]

A number of American citizens were injured, but providentially no American was killed. They were all safely transferred to the German supply ship *Dresden.* The tragedy took place in an area that was not designated as a war zone by the belligerents or by the quasi-belligerent United States. Many Americans were angered by the brutal destruction of a so-called neutral merchant ship on which they felt they had every legal right to travel. Actually, Egypt's neutrality was badly compromised because her military facilities and naval bases had been placed at the disposal of the British. Several pitched battles had been or were to be fought on Egyptian soil, including crucial El Alamein.

In partial reply to Nazi ruthlessness, Roosevelt signed a bill (June 6, 1941) that was designed to take over all foreign merchant ships, about eighty in number, immobilized by the war in United States ports. This legislation came in belated response to a special message by Roosevelt (April 10, 1941) requesting authority to act vigorously.[13] Significantly, both houses of Congress rejected amendments stipulating that none of the vessels so seized, whether neutral or belligerent, be turned over to the British. Hitler was thus warned that Roosevelt retained a free hand, as he obviously wanted, to use these ships to transport lend-lease materials under convoy to the enemies of Nazi Germany.

Torpedoing the *Robin Moor*

While Roosevelt was debating with himself and his advisers whether to escalate from patrolling to escorting on the North Atlantic run, ominous news came from the South Atlantic. On May 21, 1941, for the first time in the war, a German submarine, in this case the *U-69*, had deliberately torpedoed and sunk a merchant ship, the *Robin Moor*, legitimately flying the American flag. The sinking took place at a point at sea 700 miles between the bulge of Brazil and the west coast of Africa. Although the ship was not sailing in a danger zone announced by one of the belligerents, she met her fate near the outer edge of the pan-American security zone proclaimed in October 1939.

The *Robin Moor*, a 5,000–ton freighter built in 1919, was operated by the Robin Line of New York.[14] The vessel was outbound from New York for Cape Town and other ports of South Africa. We should note that Cape Town was a major shipping center of the Union of South Africa, a part of the British Commonwealth, and as such a belligerent in the war against Hitler.

The torpedoed ship was carrying a general cargo, including steel rails and trucks, as well as an insignificant number of small-caliber target rifles and a trifling amount of ammunition. All these items and others were now listed as contraband by both camps of belligerents, although this fact alone did not justify the kind of sinking that occurred. The vessel was flying the American flag and prominently displaying other painted markings that proclaimed her nationality. Such ships had hitherto been spared torpedoing outside the belligerent danger zones recognized under the Neutrality Act of

1939, and consequently the owners of the *Robin Moor* had reason to expect immunity.

On May 21, 1941, the *Robin Moor* encountered a submarine, the *U-69,* commanded by Kapitänleutnant Jost Metzler, who was then on the lookout for enemy shipping, particularly that headed around the hump of Africa for British Commonwealth ports. The submarine signaled the ship to stop, to cease using the radio transmitter, and to send over a boat with the ship's papers to the surfaced U-boat. Metzler was unwilling to come close to the *Robin Moor* or to board her with his own men, partly because he suspected that his quarry might be a British entrapment ship (Q-ship) armed with screened guns. In fact, the deck cargo seemed to him suspiciously high.[15]

After the ship's papers revealed that there was much contraband on board, as defined by the Germans, Metzler decided to torpedo the vessel. The eight passengers, male and female, and thirty-eight crew members were granted a scant twenty minutes (later extended to thirty) in which to scramble into the four lifeboats. A torpedo was then launched, and when it failed to inflict sufficient damage, Metzler completed the sinking with gunfire.

The *U-69* flew no flag, and the commander did not announce his nationality. But he spoke English with a thick Germanic accent, and his victims quickly and correctly assumed that only a German U-boat would be prowling as a commerce raider in these vulnerable waters. According to the master of the *Robin Moor,* Metzler promised that he would broadcast by radio the position of the survivors in the hope that nearby ships would rush to the rescue. Evidently such an appeal was never sent, or at least it was not reported as received. Perhaps Metzler had second thoughts about also apprising nearby British warships of his own presence. His memoirs omit any mention of sending out the position of the sunken ship and her survivors, although he does report that he told the master what course to steer. He also relates that he gave the castaways "provisions," which actually were a meager supply of bread, water, and brandy.

Metzler may even have reasoned that no one on board this mystery ship would ever reach shore. In this case the *Robin Moor* would be written off as just another casualty in the age-old list of mysterious disappearances, not uncommon before the radio was introduced—and still continuing. His conduct in abandoning the survivors to the stormy Atlantic may also explain why he evidently did not risk getting off a radioed S.O.S. Perhaps they would all be swallowed up by the sea, and their disappearance would remain a mystery.

The Legalities of the Sinking

This attack on an unresisting American merchant ship is surprising because it was plainly contrary to Hitler's wishes and specific orders. In spite of pressure from Admiral Raeder to unshackle the U-boats, the Führer was continuing to lean over backward to avoid creating an "incident" that would justify either active American interference or an outright declaration of war. He was then intent on completing preparations for his mighty assault on Russia, delayed as he was by the costly and time-consuming diversion into Yugoslavia and Greece.

The U-boat skipper published in his book a further justification for acting as he did. First of all, there was one thing highly suspicious about the *Robin Moor,* a possible entrapment ship. When he asked for her identity he could not find a listing in his copy of *Lloyd's Register.* The explanation is that her name had recently been changed from the *Exmoor* to the *Robin Moor* when the new owners took over. Further evidence of dangers came from the unkempt appearance of the crew and what Metzler regarded as a simulated panic on board. Moreover, he probably felt that international law was on his side, once he had issued the conventional warning and had ascertained that the ship was carrying contraband.

But Metzler ignored one key condition, whether consciously or not. In 1936 Germany had voluntarily accepted the London Protocol, which minced no words when it declared that no warship, submarine, or surface craft could sink or disable an unresisting merchant ship without observing certain time-honored formalities and "without having first placed passengers, crew, and ship's papers in a place of safety. For this purpose the ship's boats are not regarded as a place of safety unless the safety of the passengers and crew is assured, in the existing sea and weather conditions, by the proximity of land, or the presence of another vessel which is in a position to take them on board."[16]

Metzler had plainly violated international law as of 1936, at least in the eyes of the United States and Great Britain. His most serious offense was in leaving the crew and passengers, male and female, in open boats, some 700 miles from land, exposed to stormy winds and waves, lack of water, and shortages of food, as well as other hazards. Probably no American or British jurist would have regarded Metzler's treatment of human life as consonant with the "place of safety" enjoined by the London Protocol of 1936. True, no one perished, and in a narrow sense the outcome proved that the passengers had been accorded reasonably safe treatment. Yet their survival was largely a matter of pure luck.

Unrepentant Germany

One lifeboat from the *Robin Moor,* occupied by ten crew members and one passenger, sailed toward Brazil and almost miraculously found itself in the coastal shipping lanes in eighteen days. On June 9, 1941, the survivors were picked up by a Brazilian ship, which radioed the news of the *Robin Moor*'s sinking to the world on June 10, 1941. As hope gradually faded for the thirty-five people in the other three lifeboats, word was finally flashed from Cape Town and published in the press on June 17 that all of the remaining castaways had been rescued alive. A British ship bound for Cape Town had picked them up on June 2.

A surprising aspect of the *Robin Moor* incident was that the American public did not respond with a volcanic outburst of indignation. Feelings did not run especially high, and Roosevelt, to his credit, soft-pedaled the incident by immediately calling for a "suspension of judgment."[17] Word had not yet arrived about the second batch of survivors.

By this time reports of sunken steamers, from the *Athenia* on, were monotonously common, although they were not American ships. The rescue of the second lot of the *Robin Moor*'s passengers and crew followed an anxious period of waiting, and it came as an anticlimax, accompanied by a grateful "Thank God" from the American people. The Germans could be billed for damages, and if they refused to pay, Washington could secure recompense by seizing German assets under American jurisdiction.

A defiant Berlin government figuratively poured gasoline on the burning dispute. A spokesman for the Wilhelmstrasse airily told a newspaper correspondent that "Germany won't be buffaloed. . . . Whenever any ship with contraband sails for England we'll shoot at it." Noting that the *Robin Moor* had carried steel rails, which were regarded by the British and Germans as contraband, he added, "We really can't understand what all the fuss is about."[18] Americans could now reasonably assume that henceforth such torpedoings

without regard for human life, whether of ships of belligerent or
nominally neutral nations, bore the approval of the Berlin
government.

Despite the relatively mild reaction in America, the *Robin Moor*
was one of the most significant "crisis ships" to make the headlines

BLACKOUT: The dark menace of Nazi Germany. *Holland in the* Nashville
Banner, *c. 1940*

in the many months between Hitler's attack on Poland in September 1939 and the Japanese assault on Pearl Harbor in December 1941. This luckless steamer was the first American vessel of any kind to be sunk, or even attacked, by a German warship. Up to this point virtually all of the acts of provocation or aggression in German-American relations had come from the American side. The time span involved ranges from the earliest days of unneutrality up to and through the unorthodox destroyers deal and the sweeping Lend-Lease Act. German apologists in the United States repeatedly replied that in view of the implicit declaration of war in the Lend-Lease Act, Americans should not be surprised to find the forbearing Germans at last striking back with a retaliatory act of their own.

Roosevelt Breathes Defiance

As was often the case during these suspenseful months, the interventionists among Roosevelt's advisers urged the President to respond to the sinking of the *Robin Moor* with strong countermeasures. Harry Hopkins, the President's closest adviser, pressed F.D.R. to provide naval escorts for all United States vessels sailing outside the danger zones.[19] Secretary of War Stimson, a war hawk, favored an even stronger stance, as did Secretary Ickes.[20] Under such pressure the President wavered and then backed off. By way of reprisal he had seriously considered seizing a German merchant ship, the *Windhuk,* interned in a Brazilian port, but he soon dropped the scheme.[21] He also declined to seek authority from Congress to arm American merchant ships. Such a move might endanger the critical aid-to-Britain program, which the isolationists were still decrying.[22] Antiwar spokesmen like Senator Wheeler of Montana were proclaiming that the Germans were morally, if not legally, justified in sinking a ship carrying contraband of war to their enemy. At this time, concluded Hopkins, Roosevelt was not going to lead the country into war; he would have to be pushed in.[23] Evidently, he would rather follow public opinion than lead it.

On May 27, 1941, six days after the *Robin Moor* was sunk, Roosevelt delivered a long-deferred fireside message in which he proclaimed an "unlimited national emergency."[24] We must not assume that this stroke was in response to the *Robin Moor* incident, because the President did not get full word of the sinking until about three weeks later. The plight of the British alone was depressing enough to warrant strong language.

At the outset, Roosevelt observed that the war had developed, "as the Nazis always intended it should develop, into a world war for world domination." This time he attacked Hitler by name, for the gloves were now off. The President then went on to list the steps that he had taken to fortify resistance to Nazi domination, including the destroyers-for-bases deal and lend-lease. His basic purpose was to keep the dictatorial menace away from the Western Hemisphere. If Hitler won, he would move into both Latin America and Canada, and thus put an intolerable squeeze on the United States. The American way of life would vanish, for, "The Nazi world does not recognize any God except Hitler. . . ." The Hitlerites were threatening to move into Spain, Portugal, North Africa, and the Cape Verde Islands, which were only seven air hours from Brazil for bombers and troop-carrying planes.

The Nazis could not conquer North America, Roosevelt continued, without control of the sea, and he was doing all he could to thwart such control. He had extended American naval patrols far out into the North Atlantic and had greatly strengthened the Atlantic Fleet. The patrolling U.S. ships and planes were warning British convoys of German raiders and consequently were helping to shepherd needed supplies to England. And "all additional measures necessary to deliver the goods will be taken."

In concluding his two-fisted address, Roosevelt announced that he had that night issued a proclamation stating that "an unlimited national emergency exists and requires the strengthening of our defense to the extreme limit of our national power and authority." He had earlier proclaimed, we recall, a "limited" national emergency (September 8, 1939), five days after Britain and France entered the war.[25] Both proclamations granted F.D.R. a sweeping but temporary expansion of presidential powers.

This latest stirring message from the White House evoked an overwhelmingly favorable storm of telegrams.* Yet to the dismay of the interventionists, the President did not follow through with positive action in any direction. He explained at a press conference the next day that to implement his proclamation he would have to issue executive orders, and "none have been issued."[26]

---

* A *Fortune* poll asked (June 1941) if America was not already in the war for all practical purposes. The responses were 79.5 percent affirmative, 10.9 percent negative, and 9.6 percent without opinion. *Public Opinion Quarterly,* V, 477.

Roosevelt Refuses to Cower

On June 14, 1941, seventeen days after the proclamation of an unlimited national emergency, Roosevelt acted in what was assumed
to be retaliation for the *Robin Moor* sinking. He ordered the freezing
of Axis-held funds not previously frozen, including those of Nazi-
conquered Albania, Austria, Czechoslovakia, Danzig, and Poland.[27]

Two days later, on June 16, 1941, the President directed all
German consulates in the United States closed and their staffs withdrawn by July 10. The official reason given was "activities" outside
"legitimate duties"—that is, propaganda and espionage. Yet this
drastic step was widely interpreted in America as retaliation for the
Robin Moor affair. For their part, Germany and Italy struck back by
expelling all United States consular officials for engaging in improper acts, and by ordering the consulates closed.[28]

On June 20, 1941, Roosevelt reacted to these reactions in a
blistering message to Congress on the *Robin Moor* outrage. This time
he did not appear in person but sent up his message to Capitol Hill,
from which it would be certain to get international publicity in the
press and on the radio. In his recent fireside chat, he had already discussed freedom of the seas, and he may not have wanted to appear
unduly repetitious and suffer from "overexposure."[29]

After recounting the basic facts of "the ruthless sinking of the
Robin Moor," contrary to neutral rights under international law, the
President branded this act of inhumanity as the work of "an international outlaw." "Full reparation" for such an "outrageous and in-
defensible sinking" would be expected of the German government.
Yet the foul deed could not be considered apart from Hitler's long-
pursued policy of "frightfulness and intimidation," especially
against "the innocent and the helpless" of other countries.

Roosevelt further stated that the United States, unlike other
Nazi victims, would "neither be intimidated" nor "acquiesce" in
Germany's plans for "world domination." No faith could be placed
in Nazi declarations "to the contrary," especially in view of what
had happened in Austria and at Munich in 1938. The *Robin Moor*
sinking appeared to be "a first step" in Germany's plan to "seize
control of the high seas." Henceforth no American ship or cargo
could "consider itself immune from [German] acts of piracy."

Roosevelt rose to dramatic heights in his concluding paragraph.
The Nazis, he declared, had served notice "upon us" that the United

States was about to be intimidated into abandoning her "chosen policy of helping Britain to survive." The *Robin Moor* incident was really a Hitlerian warning to the Americans not to resist "the Nazi movement of world conquest." Roosevelt's final resolute words were, "We are not yielding and we do not propose to yield."

Hitler Ignores the *Robin Moor*

Roosevelt's tough-fisted message to Congress constituted his informal protest to the Berlin government. On the day of its release (June 20, 1941), Secretary of State Hull sent a copy to the German Embassy in Washington with the request that it be passed on to Berlin. Chargé Thomson replied four days later by saying, "I do not find myself in a position" to comply with Secretary Hull's request.[30] Significantly, this was two days after Hitler had launched his furious and fateful assault on the Soviet Union.

The State Department dutifully undertook to gather data on the bill for damages to be presented to Germany for the destruction of the *Robin Moor*. On September 19, 1941, Secretary Hull wrote to Chargé Thomson to say that the United States would accept $2,-867,092 as compensation. This bill was forwarded to Berlin, but the envoy was sharply rebuked for having even accepted it and for having cabled it to Germany. Smarting from this reprimand, Thomson replied to Hull that the latter's two recent communications (the stinging Roosevelt message and the large bill) "are not such as to lead to an appropriate reply by my government."[31]

On its face, the defiant reaction of Berlin to the *Robin Moor* incident is somewhat puzzling, for the U-boat commander had plainly violated Hitler's admonition not to create an incident with the United States. If so minded, the Führer could have mollified the Americans with an apology explaining that the errant Metzler had misunderstood his orders or had been confused by the suspicious appearance of the ship and her unconfirmed name.

Special circumstances evidently prompted Hitler to ignore the incident. For one thing, the American public was not so seriously aroused as Berlin had reason to expect. More important, during the days just before and after the uproar over the *Robin Moor* the Führer was deeply involved in planning and launching his colossal invasion of the Soviet Union with Operation Barbarossa. At the same time, he was fearful that the British might take advantage of his involvement to attack Norway and cut off his priceless naval and air bases

Hitler (foreground) and Mussolini (center right) in Italy, 1937
Courtesy of the Hoover Institution Archives

Mussolini (center) and Hitler (left) in Germany, 1937
Courtesy of the Hoover Institution Archives

Above: Churchill and Roosevelt on the Prince of Wales, *Argentia. Note at extreme left are two civilians: Harry Hopkins and W. Averell Harriman. Immediately behind Roosevelt and Churchill are Admiral King, General Marshall, General Sir John Dill, Admiral Stark, and Admiral Sir Dudley Pound. Courtesy of the U.S. Naval Historical Center*

Left: Roosevelt and Churchill, seated at left of muzzle of big gun (far left), singing at services on the Prince of Wales, *Argentia Courtesy of the U.S. Naval Historical Center*

Part of the 150 mothballed, four-stack destroyers
Courtesy of the U.S. Naval Historical Center

*The destroyer USS Greer on convoy duty in the rough North Atlantic, June
1943, nearly two years after the brush with the U-652. Note torpedo mounts
on each side.*
Courtesy of the U.S. Naval Historical Center

The destroyer USS Kearny *in the Atlantic*
Courtesy of Captain Frank K. B. Wheeler, USN (Ret.)

Facing page:
The Kearny *after torpedoing at Reykjavik, Iceland, October 19, 1941*
Courtesy of the U.S. Naval Historical Center

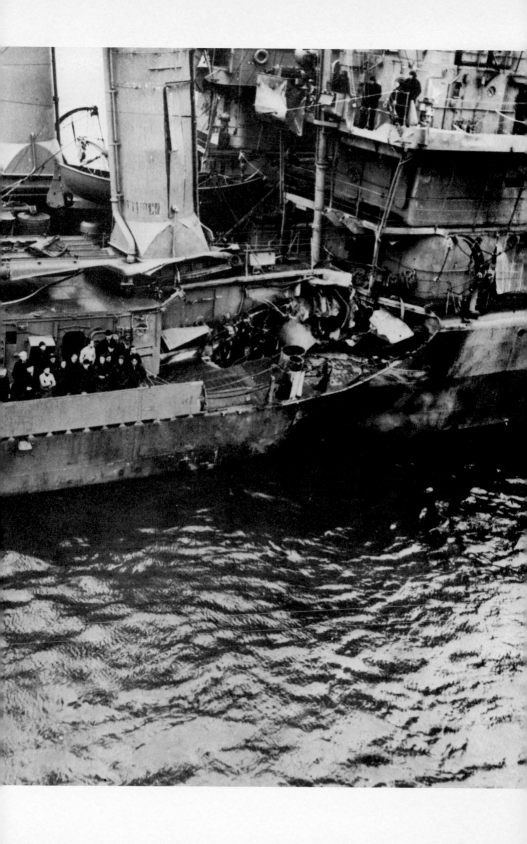

The destroyer USS Reuben James *at Philadelphia in 1932*
Courtesy of the U.S. Naval Historical Center

Camp Snafu, Reykjavik, Iceland, completed and occupied by a naval-air patrol squadron
Courtesy of the U.S. Naval Historical Center

in that conquered country. He needed all his strength, including aircraft, for the far-flung Eastern Front.

Hitler conferred with his top naval advisers on June 21, 1941, the day before the invasion of Russia. In reference to the *Robin Moor* case, he expressed the wish that "incidents with U.S.A. warships and merchant ships outside the closed area" be avoided "under all circumstances." Later the same day he voiced the desire to "avoid any possibility of incidents with the U.S.A." until Operation Barbarossa "becomes clearer, i.e., for a few weeks."[32]

As the weeks passed and success in Russia grew increasingly difficult, Hitler became even more determined to avoid a showdown with the United States. On July 25, 1941, more than a month after the invasion of Russia started, he declared in a conference with the Commander-in-Chief of the German Navy that his views had "undergone no changes whatever." He would like to avoid having the United States declare war while the Russian campaign was "still in progress, also out of consideration for the Army, which is involved in heavy combat." But he would "never call a submarine commander to account if he torpedoes an American ship by mistake." When the Russian campaign ended victoriously, he reserved "the right to take severe action against the U.S.A. as well."[33]

Nearly two months later, September 17, 1941, a Führer conference reported no change in policy, for by this time Hitler fully realized that his far-flung irruption into Russia was approaching a crisis. The morale of the U-boat personnel was flagging because of the prohibition on offensive action against American warships, and the submarine officers were to be reassured that the reason for this temporary restraint was the all-engulfing invasion of the U.S.S.R.[34]

Isolationist critics of Roosevelt have accused him of seeking an "incident" during these months that would justify a declaration of war on Nazi Germany. If so, why did he not seize upon the case of the *Robin Moor* and dispatch an ultimatum to Berlin, as Wilson had done in 1916 over a French passenger ship, the *Sussex?* One reasonable explanation is that Roosevelt did not want a full-fledged war with Nazi Germany, only the opportunity to aid the British and other foes of the dictators, primarily through lend-lease. Perhaps he remembered all too well what had happened when President Wilson had gone out on the end of a limb; certainly he must have realized that majority opinion favored aid to Britain at the risk of war.*

---

* If Britain seemed certain to be defeated, public opinion favored using U.S. warships to escort ships carrying supplies to Britain. Gallup (April 22, 1941) found 71 percent approving, 21 percent opposing, and 8 percent undecided. *Public Opinion Quarterly* V, 486.

The Near Attack on the *Texas*

On the same day that Congress received Roosevelt's ringing message on the *Robin Moor,* June 20, 1941, a near-explosive incident occurred in the North Atlantic. A German submarine, the *U-203,* sighted an American battleship, the *Texas,* zigzagging and escorted by three destroyers. The encounter took place about ten miles inside the so-called German blockade zone around the British Isles—an area in which the Nazis claimed the unrestricted right to sink all intruders, civilian or military.

The U-boat commander was undecided whether to attack what was clearly an American battleship or one recently transferred by the United States to Britain. The vessel was steaming in an area in which he was free to attack all warships, on the well-founded assumption that they belonged to the enemy. Yet U.S. fighting ships were still forbidden quarry. What the *Texas* was doing so far east in the German blockade zone mystified the commander of the *U-203,* for such warships previously had been barred from this battle area.

Admiral Dönitz states in his memoirs that the U-boat commander suspected that this American battleship was one recently transferred by the United States to the British, much like the fifty destroyers. He consequently decided to stretch his orders and strike, but he was unable to maneuver himself into a position to fire his torpedoes. After he had vainly pursued his intended victim for about 140 miles, the *Texas* finally steamed out of sight, completely unaware of her peril.[35]

The aging *Texas,* vintage 1912, carried a complement of about 1,200 officers and men—and no lifeboats, only life rafts. If the torpedoes of the *U-203* had struck home, the loss of life would doubtless have been heavy. In retrospect, the sweeping movement of the *Texas* and her escort into the German combat zone was an act of sheer recklessness, probably traceable to Roosevelt's known desire to assert American dominance in the central and western Atlantic. But if the battleship had been sunk by the *U-203,* Hitler probably would have blamed the British for torpedoing the *Texas* with one of their own submarines in the hope of dragging the United States into the deep waters of full belligerency.

In German naval discussions at the highest level, the *Texas* was bracketed with the *Robin Moor* as presenting the kind of incident that

Hitler wanted to avoid on the eve of the invasion of Russia. Under instructions from the Führer himself, the German naval authorities immediately issued orders to the U-boats to refrain from attacking American warships, even within the blockade zone, because such offensive operations did not "coincide with the Fuehrer's political intentions."[36] In short, pick no fight with the Americans until the imminent invasion of Russia had succeeded.

Their hands tied by the new naval orders of June 21, 1941, U-boat commanders could not attack enemy destroyers, only cruisers, battleships, and aircraft carriers. Yet destroyers were the most common and effective defenders of the transatlantic convoys, and the German submarine commanders greatly resented this Hitler-imposed handicap. The reason was obvious. With the fifty American destroyers now incorporated in the British Royal Navy, the U-boat commander could not determine whether his potential victim was British or American. This galling self-restriction is in itself further evidence of Hitler's determination not to provoke the United States while he was in the partial embrace of the Russian bear. Later a modifying order was issued to permit the U-boats to defend themselves against attacks by destroyers while a battle involving convoys and submarines was in actual progress. But once pursuit had broken off, there was to be no counterattack.[37]

Hitler in a Death Trap

Hitler's partial shackling of the U-boats became more comprehensible two days following the fruitless attempt to torpedo the *Texas*. On June 22, after prodigious preparations, Hitler launched his all-out invasion of the Soviet Union. As was his habit, he did not bother to declare war, as was traditional under international law, nor did he denounce his Nonaggression Pact with Stalin. Negotiated in 1939 for ten years, it had nearly seven years to run.

There is an English proverb, "When thieves fall out, honest men come by their own." When these two bloody-handed dictators began to tangle with each other, the democratic world rejoiced. The intense heat was now off the British—at least temporarily. Hitler, believing that he would have to attack Stalin ultimately, evidently wished to dispose of his untrustworthy accomplice before he turned and settled accounts with the British. Besides, the conquest of Russia was the key part of his blueprint for conquest unveiled in *Mein Kampf* nearly two decades earlier.

Interested observers could now perceive why Hitler, during the months before the June assault, had made strong efforts not to provoke the United States by fighting back against the Americans in the North Atlantic. Hitler still did not have an adequate comprehension of the productive capacity of the American industrial giant. But he did remember that in 1917 the United States had been prodded into war by the U-boats, and that the Yankees had helped turn the momentum against Germany in 1918. He did not want history to repeat itself at his expense.

During the tense months before the fateful assault on Russia, Roosevelt and dozens of other outside sources had known that Hitler was preparing a devastating attack. United States officials and others warned the Kremlin well in advance.[38] But Stalin evidently did not believe that his partner in crime would be so mad as to try to stab him in the back so soon and so hard, especially before the Nazis had finished off Britain. Certainly, Stalin did not want to provoke such an attack by taking provocative precautions. Nor did he wish to be duped by anti-Hitler propaganda fed to him by so-called friends in the West.

Roosevelt's instinctive feeling that Hitler did not want to arouse the United States explains why the President could safely take disagreeably strong measures against the Führer. Under other circumstances, Roosevelt's flagrant violations of neutrality might well have provoked vigorous, not to say violent, responses from Germany. After the Russian campaign had begun, the President could clearly perceive that he had his Nazi adversary over a Bolshevik barrel.

CHAPTER 11

QUASI-ALLIES OF STALIN

*I tell the American people solemnly that the United States will never survive as a
happy and fertile oasis of liberty surrounded by a cruel desert of dictatorship.*

Roosevelt's speech at Hyde Park
July 4, 1941

Hitler Assaults the Soviets

From the standpoint of the United States there were three great
turning points during the uneasy two years when the nation was
nominally neutral. The first was the collapse of France in the spring
of 1940; the second was Hitler's overpowering assault on the Soviet
Union in the spring of 1941; and the third was the Japanese "sneak
attack" on American outposts, conspicuously Pearl Harbor, on December 7, 1941. All three of these great turning points were in the
nature of surprises. The attack on France was fully expected, but not
the fatal flanking movement and the complete collapse. The
Führer's assault on Russia was widely anticipated in the Western
world, but it evidently caught Stalin off guard.

On June 22, 1941, the day of Hitler's initial onslaught on Russia, disturbing rumors were circulating in the United States that the
two dictators had buried their differences and were about to unite in
a military alliance that would certainly spell the doom of Britain,

and possibly of the United States as well. We now know that Stalin and Hitler had undertaken high-level negotiations some months earlier but that Stalin had insisted on greater influence in southeastern Europe than Hitler was willing to grant, especially in Bulgaria and at the Dardanelles.[1]

The truth is that Stalin suspected Hitler of readying for an eventual attack, for the German army was massing along the western frontier of the Soviet Union, while Marshal Goering's aircraft were violating Russian airspace by numerous and deep penetrations. The Soviet dictator evidently felt that if he took aggressive defensive measures, the Führer would find in them provocation for an attack. Why he should have reasoned this way, if he in fact did, is indeed surprising because Stalin should have known that Hitler did not need valid excuses for an attack. Nor for that matter did Stalin.

Military experts in Britain and America were almost unanimous in their agreement that Hitler's mechanized might would knock Russia out of the war in a few weeks. This judgment was one reason why Roosevelt cautiously approached the problem of dispatching substantial help. What he did provide might be thrown away by arriving too late, or worse yet, be used by Hitler against the British and possibly the Americans. But the embattled Churchill was in such a perilous position that he was willing to take a chance. Reminding people that from the beginning he had been an unrelenting foe of "the foul baboonery of Bolshevism," he remarked, "If Hitler invaded hell, I would make at least a favourable mention of the Devil in the House of Commons."

Many American interventionists advocated all possible aid to Russia, even at the expense of some lend-lease shipments to Great Britain. To them a golden opportunity had come to save England by encouraging Hitler to waste his strength in the vastnesses of the Soviet Union. They were naturally joined by the few vocal Communists in the United States; overnight these leftists had shifted from praising Hitler, the ally of Russia, to condemning him as the foe of Russia.

But many American isolationists raised vehement objections to supporting the double-dealing dictator, Joseph Stalin. He had made no secret of his intentions, if possible, to communize the world. The Catholic church, moreover, had always been and continued to be an unforgiving foe of atheistic Communism. "I have no more confidence in Stalin," declared Archbishop Curley of Baltimore, "than I have in Hitler." If Russia triumphed, the Communist menace to the free world would emerge as a substitute for Hitlerism.

The British lion snuggles up to the Russian bear after Hitler invades Russia. So does the American eagle. *Fitzpatrick in the* St. Louis Post-Dispatch

The isolationists had yet other arrows in their quiver. Why risk war with the Führer by thus openly and unneutrally aiding another of his enemies? But the strongest argument went back to the summer of 1939, when the free world was hoping that the two dictators would bleed each other white on the vast steppes of Russia. Now that blessed day had at length arrived, and the free world could breathe easier while standing approvingly on the sidelines with folded arms. Leading citizens, including ex-President Hoover and Senator Harry S. Truman, voiced such views. But the unknown factor, a frightening one, was the strong possibility that Hitler would crush Stalin and bestride all of Europe. Many Americans saw that there was much wisdom in facing up to one menace at a time—and preferably the more menacing one first.

Roosevelt Promises Aid

In the face of such conflicting counsel Roosevelt moved cautiously but quickly. On June 24, 1941, two days after the Nazis struck, the Treasury released some $39 million in Soviet securities that had previously been frozen in the United States. At his press conference that day the President indicated that he would permit some aid to go to the embattled Soviets, although he did not know what they wanted or needed.[2] On June 25 the announcement came that Roosevelt would not invoke the Neutrality Act of 1939 to proclaim that a state of war existed between Germany and Russia, although the Hitlerian attack was by far the most massive the world had ever witnessed. This concession was of considerable value to the Soviets because it enabled them at once to undertake to import a limited quantity of necessities through the Siberian port of Vladivostok, tauntingly past a Japan immobilized by the Soviet-Japanese Neutrality Pact of April 13, 1941.

As for extending massive lend-lease aid to Russia, Roosevelt certainly did not act with indecent haste. He sent his top adviser, Harry L. Hopkins, to Moscow some five weeks following the German invasion. After conferring with Stalin and making personal observations, the American envoy could report favorably to Roosevelt on the prospects that the fall-back Russian defenses would hold. German advances were definitely slowing before late summer. On October 30, more than four months after the initial invasion, Roosevelt offered the U.S.S.R. $1 million worth of lend-lease material, a small beginning toward the ultimate $11 billion.

The great bulk of the American lend-lease aid to Russia came after Pearl Harbor was blasted in December 1941. Probably for this reason Hitler did not give such assistance prominent billing when he denounced Roosevelt in his declaration of war. Referring to the occupation of Iceland by American troops on July 7, 1941, he did note, "At the same time [Roosevelt] promised American help to the Soviet Union." Actually, the rather vague assurance of help at the press conference of June 24 had come two days after Hitler invaded Russia.

Occupying Isolated Iceland

Roosevelt's occupation of the strategic island of Iceland with a brigade of nearly 4,000 U.S. Marines, on July 7, 1941, dealt a major blow in the undeclared naval war against Hitler. The President dispatched Marines instead of army personnel because under the Selective Service Act draftees could not legally be sent out of the Western Hemisphere. Another barrier was the President's pledge in the Democratic platform and in his campaign speeches that American "boys" were not going to be sent into foreign wars, "except in case of attack." The Marines regarded themselves as professional fighting men, not "boys," and they were volunteers, not draftees.

Iceland was then, as now, an independent republic, with Norwegian and Danish antecedents. In 1918 Denmark had recognized Iceland as a separate state with unlimited sovereignty but still nominally under the Danish king. By the fortunes of war the island was strategically located near the route of the transatlantic convoys that were carrying lend-lease shipments from Newfoundland to Great Britain and later to Russia. The British had early recognized the disaster that would befall them if the Nazis occupied the island with paratroops and used it as a base for aircraft and U-boats to launch attacks on the watery lifeline linking North America with Great Britain and Russia.

The British had bought some insurance in mid-May 1940 when they landed an infantry brigade in Iceland to avert a possible German takeover. In June–July 1940 reinforcements of Canadian and British soldiers were added. But Winston Churchill had urgent use for these troops elsewhere, and he was eager to have the Americans replace the British force as soon as possible. The new troops would have to be supplied from the United States, which in turn could be more easily persuaded to escort its own convoys and beat off German U-boats. One of Churchill's most cherished objectives was to involve the United States ever more deeply in the war.

Significant preliminaries preceded the American occupation of Iceland. On April 18, 1941, Admiral King had announced, certainly with the sanction of Roosevelt, that "the Western Hemisphere [and the Monroe Doctrine] extends from approximately 26° W to include all of Greenland. . . ." King warned his command that entrance into this zone by German ships or planes was to be viewed as "unfriendly."[3] Incidentally, this vast new expanse of the ocean partially overlapped the German combat zone, which was extended on March 25, 1941, the previous month, all the way westward to the coastal waters of eastern Greenland.

On June 16, 1941, six days before Hitler smashed into Russia, Admiral Stark carried out a Roosevelt directive by ordering Admiral King, Commander in Chief of the Atlantic Fleet, to occupy Iceland with an American force of Marines. The assumption had been that the Icelanders would be willing to extend an invitation, but they developed a bad case of cold feet, largely because they feared Hitlerian retaliation. Not until July 1 were terms agreed upon, and these included a withdrawal of American troops promptly on the coming of peace; a recognition of the complete independence and sovereignty of the Icelanders; and a pledge not to interfere in the internal affairs of the island.[4]

On July 7, 1941, the first U.S. Marines landed. Eight days later Admiral King announced that the Western Hemisphere (and the Monroe Doctrine) now included Iceland, even though the island was about three times closer to the mainland of Europe than to the North American continent.[5]

Convoys to Iceland

On the day the Marines landed, Roosevelt apprised Congress (July 7, 1941) of his decision in a memorable message to that body.[6] At the outset he declared that a German occupation of the strategic island would pose an intolerable threat to the "independent nations of the New World." The establishment of hostile naval and air bases there would pose a menace to Greenland, to the shipping of the North Atlantic, and to the "steady flow" of munitions to Great Britain, in itself "a broad policy clearly approved by Congress." Therefore, as Commander-in-Chief, he had "issued orders to the Navy that all necessary steps be taken to insure the safety of communications in the approaches between Iceland and the United States, as well as on the seas between the United States and all other strategic outposts."

By this time Roosevelt evidently had in view using the Navy to escort convoys of freighters to Iceland, as advisers like Secretary of War Stimson and Secretary of the Navy Knox were urging. He would thus safeguard not only American ships but also British vessels and any others that chose to accept such protection. The President presumably had decided that it would be politically disastrous to state his intentions in such blunt terms, but in the light of what was to come, this is plainly what he was trying to say. In explaining the deployment of Marines he stressed elemental self-defense and the blank check that Congress had reluctantly given him to escort convoys when it passed the Lend-Lease Act.

Roosevelt's fears of some kind of public explosion never materialized. A Gallup poll found that 61 percent of the respondents approved the occupation of Iceland and only 17 percent were definitely opposed. A question arose in a subsequent press conference as to whether or not Iceland was in the Western Hemisphere. Roosevelt refused to be pinned down when he concluded that the real test was whether an area in question was "terribly important" for the defense of the Americas.[7]

New orders were issued by U.S. Navy headquarters in mid-July, obviously with the approval of Roosevelt, whose interest in ship operations was unflagging. American warships, now empowered to engage in the defense of Iceland, were "to escort convoys of United States and Iceland flag shipping, including shipping of any nationality which may join such United States or Iceland flag convoys, between United States ports and bases, and Iceland."[8] The U.S. Navy, joining thirty Canadian and Free French destroyers and corvettes, thus began escort operations from Canadian waters to Iceland. The British continued to take care of the transatlantic routes, including the protecting of convoys from Iceland to England.

In theory, the U.S. Navy was escorting only American and Icelandic ships to Iceland, but the official orders included "shipping of any nationality" that chose to sail along in the convoy. And many so chose. This was precisely the sort of development that foes of lend-lease, in Congress and out, had feared.

Hitler Controls His Anger

The American occupation of Iceland in July 1941 was essentially a blow aimed at Hitler. The same may be said of the accompanying orders to provide escort protection for all ships that chose to take advantage of such guardianship. As Roosevelt stepped up his military and naval operations against the Nazis, he was clearly counting on Hitler's entrapment in Russia to curb any impulse the Führer may have had to strike back in force.

The German documents reveal that Roosevelt's estimate of Hitler's intentions was completely correct, even though the official reaction in Berlin to the American occupation of Iceland was prompt and violent. Admiral Raeder hurried to Hitler's headquarters, where the Führer was directing the Russian campaign. He asked for a decision as to "whether from the political viewpoint the occupation of Iceland by the U.S.A. is to be considered as an entry into the war, or as an act of provocation which should be ignored." Hitler then explained in detail that he was "most anxious to postpone the United States entry into the war for another one or two months." The entire air force would be needed for the Russian campaign, and the Führer did not want to divert even a part of it. A victorious campaign on that front, declared Hitler, would probably have a "tremendous [cooling] effect on . . . the attitude of the U.S.A." As a consequence, he wanted ship incidents involving the Americans to be avoided "as far as possible. . . ."[9]

Two weeks later, in connection with a Führer conference of July 25, 1941, Admiral Raeder prepared a lengthy report embodying existing military and naval policy. He recorded that Hitler still wished to avoid war with the United States while "the Eastern Campaign" was in progress. After the expected victory, Hitler reserved the right to settle accounts with Roosevelt.[10]

In declaring war with the United States on December 11, 1941, Hitler made more than a passing reference to the Iceland occupation. He proclaimed that the island, located well within the German war zone, was occupied by American forces under orders from Roosevelt. The President aimed "to force Germany to make war and to make German U-boat warfare as ineffective as it was in 1915–1916."[11]

There can be little doubt that F.D.R. at this point was determined to reduce greatly the effectiveness of the U-boat attacks on lend-lease shipments, but he probably still wished to achieve his ends without provoking the Germans into a full-scale shooting war. Hitler had already shown great forbearance; his initial successes in Russia had been awesome. Yet wintry weather would arrive about late October (as it did), and Hitler seemed blissfully unaware that he might yet suffer Napoleon's fate (as he did) in succumbing to General Frost, General Distance, and General Mud.

The Japanese Menace

We recall that the three-power alliance of September 27, 1940, bound together Germany, Italy, and Japan in the Tripartite Pact.

By its terms the three signatories agreed to fight any power not then a belligerent (except Russia) that should aggress against one of their number. In short, if the United States attacked Japan, then Germany and Italy would join in fighting the Americans. Or if any one of the signatories entered upon a defensive state of war with the United States, the others would come to the rescue.

Obviously, the three dictator powers had military operations primarily in mind, but the spirit of the treaty certainly embraced aggressive economic warfare or accumulations of incidents on the high seas. America's Lend-Lease Act was in effect an economic declaration of war on Germany, but the Japanese did not feel obligated to fight the United States in response to treaty obligations. Nor did Hitler judge that the Tripartite Alliance bound him to tackle the United States when Roosevelt embarked on retaliatory economic warfare against Japan, as he finally did.

Roosevelt clearly had majority opinion behind him in support of the destroyers-for-bases deal, lend-lease, and ultimately the escorting of convoys. But in taking strong measures against Japan, Roosevelt lagged well behind American public opinion, which from the start of the China incident of 1937 had been overwhelmingly favorable to the underdog Chinese. He declined to proclaim the existence of the Sino-Japanese war, although it lasted from 1937 to 1945 and proved to be one of the bloodiest and most destructive in history.

Roosevelt had his reasons for inaction. For one thing, if he had proclaimed a state of war under the Neutrality Act of 1937, he would have had to cut off war materiel for both China and Japan. Not much materiel was going to the Chinese over the rugged, winding Burma Road, but that little was desperately needed and would be cut off if America's flood of oil, gasoline, and scrap iron were denied Japan. Further, if Roosevelt should shut off this critical oil supply, the oil-thirsty Japanese militarists might be forced to attack the Dutch East Indies, which did have large reserves. The Japanese might at the same time overrun the American Philippines and other outposts in the Pacific (as they did at the time of Pearl Harbor). Finally, Roosevelt could risk ignoring pro-Chinese public opinion because, while widespread, it lacked burning intensity.

Roosevelt gradually tightened the screws and waged economic warfare on Japan, Hitler's valued partner located on the Pacific flank of Russia in the Far East. Following a surprise move by the Japanese warlords into Vichy France's stepchild Indochina (Vietnam), the President resorted to severe retaliatory measures when he issued an order freezing all Japanese assets in the United States, July 25, 1941. This drastic move—for the Japanese an economic Pearl Harbor—was combined with new embargo restrictions and cooperative action by the British and the Dutch. As the oil gauge dropped and the time bomb ticked, the Japanese militarists felt that they had either to accept American terms to clear out of China or to break out of the blockade. They emphatically registered their choice at Pearl Harbor on December 7, 1941.

The President's act of economic aggression against Japan roughly resembled the more positive acts of aggression, such as lend-lease, that the United States had pursued against Hitler. In his vehement speech of December 11, 1941, justifying a declaration of war, the Führer listed dozens of German grievances against the Roosevelt government, and then added, "I do not need to mention what this man has done for years in the same way against Japan."[12]

The Roosevelt-Churchill Conference

One of the most surprising features of Hitler's war indictment of the United States in 1941 was the absence of any specific denunciation of the Roosevelt-Churchill Atlantic Conference—the parley that begot the Atlantic Charter, August 9–12, 1941. The meeting was a spectacular example of an act which, if not actually belligerent, was the antithesis of neutrality. The conference further cemented the informal Anglo-American alliance and served as a precursor to numerous other summit conferences in this troubled decade.

For nearly two years Roosevelt and Churchill had kept up a lengthy and increasingly intimate correspondence. The President finally concluded that a better understanding of their common objectives could be reached by a face-to-face meeting. Hitler's increasing preoccupation with the invasion of Russia provided a convenient lull, and Churchill jumped at the opportunity to visit with his overseas correspondent.

A trip across the submarine-infested North Atlantic was risky business, and the Germans would have liked nothing better than to torpedo or bomb the ship bearing their archfoe. Churchill sailed in the *Prince of Wales,* one of Britain's newest and biggest battleships, with an escort of destroyers to protect the zigzagging vessel. En route the presence of several German submarines was reported by radio, but nothing came of these scares.

The rendezvous was scheduled for Placentia Bay, Newfoundland, bordering Argentia, the northernmost base that Churchill had presented to the United States as a gift in the destroyers deal of September 1940. Roosevelt quietly departed from Washington by train. At New London, Connecticut, he boarded the presidential yacht *Potomac,* and after two days at sea transferred to the cruiser *Augusta,* where he joined General Marshall and Admirals Stark and King. The various conferences took place in both the *Prince of Wales* and the *Augusta,* mostly on board the latter because of Roosevelt's crippled condition.

The sessions lasted four days and involved not only the two leaders but also the highest naval and military authorities of both nations, including the Chiefs of Staff and the commanders of the air forces and fleets. Also present were members of the War Plans Divisions, as well as representatives of the London Foreign Office and the U.S. Department of State. The expectation was that better cooperation could be achieved if these officers and officials became better acquainted with their opposite numbers.

At the military level there were extensive discussions of precisely what each side would do in the event that the United States became openly involved in the war against Hitler and his two Axis partners, particularly Japan. These conversations were an extension of the military staff discussions in London, beginning in August 1940 and continuing in the United States from January to March 1941, preceding the Lend-Lease Act. We have already noted that from these earlier interchanges had emerged the decision to "get Hitler first" (Plan Dog) rather than Hirohito, should Japan enter the war, as seemed increasingly probable. This topic, as earlier observed, was a strange one for a nominal neutral to be discussing with an actual belligerent.

Much of the discussion among the military men at the Atlantic Conference focused on what strategy both nations should pursue if Japan should join her two Axis partners in the fight. The basic concept of Plan Dog was reaffirmed, but there was still considerable disagreement as to how it should be implemented. The British, with their memories of the slaughter in France and Belgium of World War I, were clearly reluctant to throw a new mass of cannon fodder across the English Channel onto the European continent. They were much more friendly to the idea of securing enough bombers from the United States to blast Germany out of the war. But the American officers were strongly of the opinion that a cheap victory could not be won by air alone and that a large D-day army would have to assault Hitler's fortifications across the Channel. They were right. After several years of postponement on the part of the British, the D-day invasion of Normandy was finally launched on June 6, 1944, nearly three years later. But no final decision was reached on this subject at the Atlantic Conference.

The Fruits of Argentia

War-bent Japan—now Hitler's Axis partner—presented the conferees off Newfoundland with their most urgent problem. The recent Japanese takeover in Indochina posed an increasing threat to the heavily fortified British base at Singapore, which, in the British view, was the keystone to the defense of Australia and New Zealand. Churchill insisted on a stern note to the Japanese that would bluntly threaten war unless Tokyo ended its aggressions. Roosevelt finally agreed, but this demand was softened somewhat, at the urging of Secretary of State Hull, before it was presented to Ambassador Nomura.[13]

The Anglo-American military and diplomatic talks were conducted in secrecy, and little news was given out except in the official press release that contained the unsigned Atlantic Charter.[14] The preliminary part of this statement reported that the conferees had discussed the problem of supplying munitions under the Lend-Lease Act for American armed forces (in Iceland?) and for "those countries actively engaged in resisting aggression. . . ." (This observation delicately covered the completion of plans for escorting British convoys as far east as Iceland.) Also discussed were the problems resulting from "the dangers to world civilization arising from the policies of military domination by conquest upon which the Hitlerian government of Germany" and its associates had embarked. This direct thrust at Hitler was not veiled in diplomatic language.

The remainder of the Roosevelt-Churchill press release listed the eight points of the so-called Atlantic Charter. This formulation, though never signed and sealed, nevertheless carried immense weight. It proclaimed that Britain and America sought no "territorial aggrandizement" and desired no "territorial changes that do not accord with the freely expressed wishes of the people concerned." This was warmed-over Wilsonian self-determination, and it gave new hope, as was intended, to the Czechs, Poles, and others who had fallen under the heel of Hitler. The same ethnic groups were appealed to by Point Three, which upheld the right of people to choose their own form of government and to have their former rights and regimes restored to them.

Point Four held out hope to victor and vanquished alike of equal access to the "trade and raw materials of the world. . . ." Point Five expressed a desire to improve "labor standards, economic advancement, and social security."

Point Six was an astonishing statement for a so-called neutral nation to be promulgating with a leading belligerent in the anti-Nazi camp. After "the final destruction of the Nazi tyranny," both governments hoped that universal peace would be established in which people could live "in freedom from fear and want."

The final two points advocated freedom of the seas, the abandonment of "the use of force" (such as the three Axis powers were employing), and universal peace. These lofty goals were to be established by "a wider and permanent system of general security" (the United Nations?) and would involve the "disarmament" of those nations that "threaten, or may threaten, aggression outside of their frontiers" (by implication Germany, Italy, and Japan).

Criticisms of the Conference

The mimeographed press release, of which the Atlantic Charter was a part, seemed to assure the public that no joint commitments had been made. Yet Roosevelt had promised Churchill that Washington would send a sharp warning to Japan, and also step up the defense of British convoys. On the whole the American people approved the high-sounding principles publicly proclaimed, even though they were reminiscent of President Wilson's ill-fated but largely forgotten Fourteen Points. The British people were keenly disappointed, for they had hoped for some kind of pronouncement indicating that at long last the United States was going to come into the war on their side with both fists.

Naturally, Nazi Germany was highly displeased with the conference, and particularly with a charter that was so obviously aimed at Hitler and his fellow dictators in the Axis triumvirate. They did not appreciate being branded tyrants and aggressors, especially by the "neutral" and meddlesome United States. The revival of hated Wilsonian principles was a red flag to the Nazi bull.

American isolationists, a noisy minority, could hardly believe that so many top officials would take so much time to travel so far to

produce so little. Despite official denials, they were certain that secret commitments and understandings had been reached, as indeed
they had, but not for all-out war. Isolationist Congressmen in particular were aroused, for they saw in the conference one more gingerly
step into the chill water of co-belligerency with Britain, as indeed it
was. The *Chicago Tribune* wanted to know what business it was for the
head of a neutral Washington government to discuss problems of
co-belligerency with a nation already at war. This journal, like the
American public, did not fully recognize the brutal fact that the
United States for some time had been waging an undeclared war on
Hitler. Nor did the ordinary citizen sense that the Führer had shown
remarkable forbearance. Having made the lethal mistake of starting
a two-front war by attacking Russia, he had no stomach for making
it a three-front war.

Churchillian Strategy

Prime Minister Churchill cabled the Prime Minister of Australia on
August 15, 1941, that the United States was taking over for escort
purposes the "America-Iceland stretch of the Atlantic."[15] One can
easily fall into the error that this decision was reached at the Chur-
chill-Roosevelt conference. Actually, Admiral Ernest J. King had issued such orders on July 19, 1941, in connection with the American
takeover of Iceland.[16] Churchill estimated the relief thus given to
Britain to be over "fifty destroyers and corvettes" that could soon be
transferred for service in British home waters and in the South
Atlantic.

    Especially noteworthy is Churchill's subsequent assessment in
his memoirs of the Atlantic Charter as an act of quasi-belligerency,
if not actual belligerency. He found "astonishing" the fact that the
United States, "still technically neutral," could join with a "belligerent power" to issue such a declaration. He had himself contributed
the phrase "the final destruction of the Nazi tyranny," and he believed that it "amounted to a challenge which in ordinary times
would have implied warlike action."[17] Most Americans at this time
probably regarded their nation as on the sidelines, but Churchill
knew better.

    In his memoirs Churchill relates that on Sunday, August 10,
the Americans and British, officials and ordinary seamen, gathered
on the quarterdeck of the *Prince of Wales* for religious services. The
sailors, as if to symbolize the unity of the two peoples, shared the

same songbooks and joined together in the prayers and hymns. Churchill had chosen the music himself: "For Those in Peril on the Sea," "Onward Christian Soldiers," and "O God Our Help in Ages Past." "Every word," the Prime Minister later wrote, "seemed to stir the heart. It was a great hour to live. Nearly half those who sang were soon to die."[18]

The sequel was short and tragic. In the vain hope of restraining Japan, Churchill unwisely sent the powerful but inadequate *Prince of Wales* and *Repulse* to Singapore, where proper air cover was unavailable. On December 10, 1941, three days after Pearl Harbor, both warships were sunk by Japanese aircraft with the loss of about 1,000 men.[19] Ironically this event was directly related to the tough stance against Japan that was agreed on in the Atlantic Conference.

In returning from Newfoundland to England, Churchill recorded that he sailed by way of Iceland, with an escort of two American destroyers. Serving in one of them was Ensign Franklin D. Roosevelt, Jr. Churchill further noted that en route from Iceland to England, his battleship met a homebound convoy of seventy-three ships, all in good order after a "fortunate passage" across the Atlantic. Evidently, substantial lend-lease shipments were then getting to England without overwhelming interference from the U-boats.

Secrets of the Conference

The suspicion that there were well-kept secrets at the Atlantic Conference is borne out by British documents released some thirty years later.[20] The confidential oral reports that the returning Prime Minister gave to the British War Cabinet, August 19, 1941, would have been seized upon with horror by American isolationists.

Churchill stated that on September 1, 1941, the United States would have "a convoy system in full operation" all the way to Iceland. This arrangement would pose a painful dilemma for Hitler: if he attacked the convoys, he would be counterattacked by U.S. warships. If he did not attack, he was insuring victory for the British lifeline in the Battle of the Atlantic. Meanwhile the Americans were confronted with the immensely difficult problem of turning out production to supply their own armed forces, as well as those of the British and Russian armies.

From the top-secret Secretary's File came additional observations by Churchill for the War Cabinet. Roosevelt was supposedly under pressure from his family, including two sons in uniform, who were insistent that American help to Britain in money and supplies "was not enough." Churchill had the impression, but only an impression, that Roosevelt was "determined" that the United States "should come in." Yet the President was restrained by a refractory Congress, which only recently had passed additional appropriations for lend-lease by a "very narrow majority." If the President should put before that body "the issue of peace or war," the members would debate it "for three months."

Roosevelt had stated that he would "wage war" but that he would "not declare it." (Actually, only Congress can declare war.) But he would become "more and more provocative," and if the Nazis "did not like it, they could attack American forces."

The President's orders to the American destroyers escorting convoys were "to attack any U-boat which showed itself, even if it were 200 or 300 miles away from the convoy." Admiral Stark was determined to "carry out this order literally," and he would approve the action of any commander who sank a U-boat. All necessary steps would be taken to force an "incident," thus compelling Hitler either to fight the United States or to permit the convoys to go through unharmed. Churchill then suggested that in a few weeks the British might well taunt Hitler "with this difficult choice."

Churchill next reported that he had twisted Roosevelt's arm a bit in connection with Russia. He had suggested that if Stalin were compelled to sue for peace, and hope died in Britain that the United States was "coming into the war," then Churchill could not answer for the consequences. Roosevelt had responded that he "would look for an 'incident' which would justify him in opening hostilities." In truth, the United States for many months had been "in the war"—but only on an undeclared basis.

Churchill's hush-hush recollections for the benefit of the War Cabinet were based largely on impressions. Possibly, to boost British morale, he made Roosevelt appear to be more eagerly interventionist than he actually was. Moreover, the cheerful and ingratiating President was notorious for telling visitors what they wanted to hear; he hated to hurt peoples' feelings by bluntly saying no.

Twenty-three days after the Atlantic Conference ended, there came the first so-called attack—actually a counterattack by a German submarine on the U.S. destroyer *Greer*, which was approaching Iceland. With undue haste Roosevelt seized upon this incident as justification for fighting defensively, not to "get into the war" but to protect lend-lease convoys.[21] Yet no official orders seem to have been issued, certainly not to the *Greer*, to attack U-boats that were "200 to

300 miles away from the convoy." Until Hitler declared war on the United States, December 11, 1941, the only other American warships damaged or destroyed by German submarines—the destroyer *Kearny,* the armed tanker *Salinas,* and the destroyer *Reuben James*— were all actively engaged in regular convoy or escort operations.

To the bitter end Roosevelt realized that he could not count on a declaration of war from Congress against Nazi Germany. On the very last day of the Atlantic Conference, the House of Representatives had voted, by the agonizingly close margin of one vote, to extend the Selective Service Act for eighteen months. For months Roosevelt had fought defensively, if informally, to insure the delivery of war supplies to the enemies of Hitler, chiefly Great Britain but secondarily Russia. And there is no conclusive evidence that he really intended to go further as long as the Nazi invasion of Russia hung in the balance. It might so hang for several years, as it finally did. Meanwhile, Roosevelt presumably would exercise restraint and resist pressure from his hawkish cabinet advisers and other interventionists for all-out war.

On August 9, 1941, two days before Churchill and Roosevelt met off Argentia, the German chargé d'affaires in Washington sent a telegraphed dispatch to Berlin. He reported that America's two-ocean navy would not be ready for five years, that the fleet was divided between the Pacific and the Atlantic, and that it would have to be so divided as long as Russia was in danger of collapse and Japan remained a menace. Roosevelt, "even under British pressure," would continue a "median course" of "postponing decisions and prolonging the war"—in short, undeclared quasi-belligerency.[22]

As events turned out, the Japanese spoiled Roosevelt's strategy by attacking Pearl Harbor. The irony is that the German chargé in Washington, who was not present at Argentia, evidently fashioned a more accurate assessment of the President's intentions than did the wishfully thinking Churchill. No proof has yet appeared that F.D.R. really wanted or intended to come to grips with Hitler on the continent of Europe with "American boys." The voluminous secret correspondence between Roosevelt and Churchill reveals the presidential state of mind before the Pearl Harbor debacle. Roosevelt repeatedly ignored, brushed aside, or flatly rejected the Prime Minister's numerous hints, suggestions, and invitations to join Britain in the Hitlerian blood bath.[23]

CHAPTER 12

THE DISPUTED
GREER AFFAIR

In the waters which we deem necessary for our defense, American naval vessels and American planes will no longer wait until submarines lurking under the water . . . strike their deadly blow—first.

Roosevelt's fireside chat,
September 11, 1941

The *Greer* on Patrol

The nine-hour duel between the U.S. destroyer *Greer* and the German submarine *U-652* was the first instance in this war of a battle involving warships of both Germany and the United States. It was a milestone on the downhill slope from an undeclared conflict to Roosevelt's shooting war with Hitler.[1]

Early in the morning of September 4, 1941, the German *U-652*, commanded by Oberleutnant Fraatz, was cruising some 165 miles southwest of Reykjavik, Iceland, well within the danger zone proclaimed by Hitler in March 1941, and overlapping Roosevelt's expanded security zone. The submarine was lurking near the rich hunting grounds in which British-American convoys bound for England might be encountered ("Torpedo Junction"). Suddenly, a British patrol bomber sighted the submarine and sped to the spot where the U-boat could be attacked with aerial depth bombs. But by this time the intended victim had dived and only her general location was known.

The *U-652* now lay deep in the water some miles ahead of the U.S. destroyer *Greer*, an old four-stacker left over from World War I, now steaming about 175 miles to the southwest of her destination, Iceland. The skipper was Lieutenant Commander Laurence H. Frost, who had been in command only one month. Also on board was Frost's immediate superior, Commander George W. Johnson, commanding Destroyer Division 61. The *Greer*, having sailed from Argentia in Newfoundland, was not on regular patrol duty but was carrying mail, much-needed freight, and eleven military passengers, representing both Navy and Army.

At 8:40 A.M. the watch on the *Greer's* bridge sighted the British bomber, which promptly sent a message by flashing blinker signal. The aircraft reported that a U-boat had been observed about ten miles ahead and slightly to port of the American destroyer. Commander Johnson immediately directed Frost to ring up full speed and steer a zigzag course for the submarine.

Johnson's intention was not to attack but, in conformity with his orders as he interpreted them, merely to shadow the submerged U-boat and broadcast by radio her position to his naval superior in Washington. Nearby British warships and reconnaissance planes could easily pick up his messages. The *Greer's* officers were keenly conscious of their lack of authority to attack, for the official orders, as given to other Atlantic Fleet destroyers, were only to "trail and report." Such orders did not cover the action of a lone U.S. destroyer that chanced to encounter a submerged U-boat. Nor did Frost and Johnson foresee that they would be called upon to team up with British aircraft and a British destroyer to hunt down a German submarine. The *Greer* was not engaged in escorting United States shipping and in these circumstances would be taking the offensive. On the other hand, Commander Johnson deemed it improper to ignore a hostile U-boat prowling in waters through which vulnerable American ships were then passing, whether freighters or warships. To take up the search for a German submarine seemed consonant with both Roosevelt's policy and standing fleet orders, even though the *Greer*, now engaged in a special mission, was not escorting a convoy.

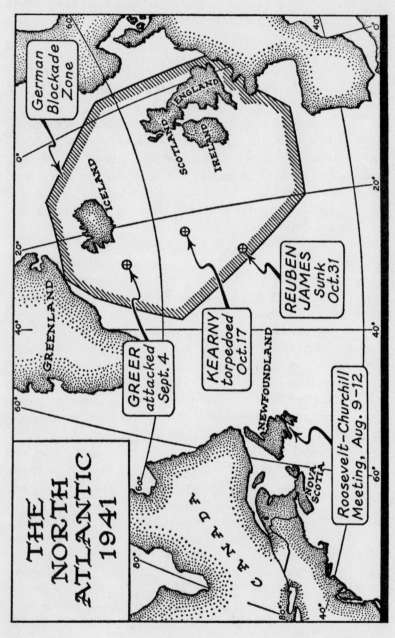

THE NORTH ATLANTIC 1941

German Blockade Zone

GREENLAND

ICELAND

ENGLAND

SCOTLAND

IRELAND

GREER attacked Sept. 4

KEARNY torpedoed Oct. 17

REUBEN JAMES Sunk Oct. 31

CANADA

NEWFOUNDLAND

NOVA SCOTIA

Roosevelt–Churchill Meeting, Aug. 9–12

From Thomas A. Bailey, The American Spirit, 4th ed., Volume II, copyright © 1978, D. C. Heath and Co.

The Hunter Becomes the Hunted

At 9:15 A.M. (Greenwich time), thirty-five minutes after sighting the British bomber, the *Greer* reduced speed to ten knots, thus enabling her sonar equipment to be more effective. Shortly thereafter a contact was reported at 2,000 yards dead ahead. The destroyer kept "locked on" to her quarry and continuously presented a narrow bows-on target, holding this position for the next three hours and twenty-eight minutes. Meanwhile, the *U-652* was moving below the surface at about four knots, while the *Greer*'s blinker was reporting the location of the submarine to the nearby British bomber. The airplane finally signaled to ask if the destroyer was going to attack; Commander Johnson replied in the negative.

At 10:32 A.M. the roving British bomber, several thousand yards ahead of the American destroyer, dropped four random depth charges. All of them missed the submarine by a considerable margin. The aircraft, now low on fuel, returned to base. Meanwhile the commander of the German U-boat believed that the bombs had been dropped by the pursuing *Greer*. The trailing had been going on for over an hour, with the destroyer and the submarine both maintaining sonar contact with each other. The U-boat commander had no way of determining for certain whether his pursuer was an American or a British destroyer, although he had glimpsed the four-stacker through his periscope and had recognized her as one of the type now transferred to the British navy in the destroyers-for-bases deal. From all the evidence that he had his boat was under a prolonged attack by a single destroyer or by a hunter-killer team of aircraft and destroyers. Either way, from his point of view, he was being attacked and hence felt fully justified in fighting back. A completely submerged submarine crew could not tell for certain whether the bombs were being dropped by a destroyer or an airplane or both.

Oberleutnant Fraatz had no choice but to remain submerged, although from time to time he ventured to take a cautious periscope observation. If he surfaced, he might face a salvo of gunfire from a British or an American destroyer or an attack by a British bomber or both. His best course was to run as silently as possible and hope to give his pursuer the slip, even though the *Greer* continued to trail him relentlessly. The men in the submarine realized that the destroyer was seeking to maintain contact until the U-boat's electric storage batteries ran down, thus forcing the *U-652* to the surface. Then the submarine would be at the mercy of the destroyer, British or American, and possibly of accompanying aircraft, British or American. Fraatz had no alternative but to stay deep and shut down all machinery, except his electric propulsion motors, and occasionally rise to periscope depth to make a quick observation. He could then fire his torpedoes with fair accuracy and full justification, for in his eyes the destroyer had attacked first and was begging for trouble.

At 11:30 A.M., the *Greer,* using the international distress frequency, transmitted by radio the U-boat's position. Thirty minutes later another British airplane appeared and the destroyer promptly flashed to it the location of the U-boat. The newcomer then commenced a visual search for the submarine.

Sometime after noon, when the *U-652* had been under enemy observation or attack for nearly four hours, Fraatz decided to strike back. Still submerged, he swung toward a course parallel with that of the trailing *Greer.* The sonar operator on the destroyer then called out a warning that the U-boat was turning toward the *Greer.* With the range down to 150 yards, the American warship swung to the starboard to keep the U-boat more nearly head on. This maneuver evidently forced Fraatz to fire sooner than he had planned, and his torpedo missed. Ten minutes later his second torpedo passed harmlessly through the foaming wake of the *Greer.*

The pursuing *Greer* itself was now under attack. Lieutenant Commander Frost, responding to orders from Commander Johnson, ordered a pattern of eight depth charges dropped at 12:56 P.M. The explosions did not come close enough to do serious harm, and the officers and men on the *Greer* could see no signs of wreckage. The U-boat suffered some rather minor damage, as we now know from Fraatz's war diary.

More than an hour later, at 2:15 P.M., a British destroyer arrived on the scene and by signal inquired if the Americans wished to join in a coordinated search. Commander Johnson replied in the negative. Still mindful of his "trail and report" orders, he did not want to become more deeply involved with the British than he was already. The intruding destroyer dropped a going-away depth charge in the general neighborhood of the U-boat and then steamed away.

Before leaving the area, Commander Johnson decided to make one more sweep. His persistence was rewarded, for at 3:12 P.M. the *Greer*'s sonar picked up what was believed to be a submarine contact 900 yards ahead, evidently the same U-boat that had been trailed and depth bombed over a period of some six hours. Again the *Greer* attacked, this time with eleven depth charges, but they evidently did not come nearly as close as those of the first encounter. Actually the contact was a false one, for the log of the *U-652* reveals that at this very time the depth charges exploded "distantly." At 6:40 P.M., the *Greer* broke off the hunt, some ten exhausting hours after the initial encounter.

American Overreactions

Back in Washington, Admiral Stark had received by radio from Commander Johnson the initial reports of the early contact with the *U-652*. Thus, allowing for the time differential of five hours between the *Greer* and Washington, a report radioed from the destroyer at 10 A.M. would probably have been received, decoded, and ready for Admiral Stark at 8 A.M., Washington time. The Admiral notified the President, who was aware that the *Greer* had been attacked when he referred to the subject at his next press conference, which began at 10:55 A.M. that same morning.

Soon after learning of the clash, Roosevelt ordered a message sent by radio to Rear Admiral R. C. Giffen in Iceland, instructing him to have the U-boat "eliminated." But the Admiral, doubtful of the reality of the "attack," feared the possible consequences of two-fisted action by the U.S. Navy. So he did nothing, to the great disgust of Admiral King, Commander-in-Chief of the Atlantic Fleet.[2] Actually, the "elimination" order from Washington was pointless, for the search for the U-boat had already failed.

Despite what Roosevelt promptly announced about an unprovoked attack, on the basis of incomplete reports, the *Greer* affair had turned into a slam-bang naval duel in which the hunter was sometimes the hunted, much like a man with a rifle stalking and being stalked by a man-eating tiger in the jungle. To the crew of the U-boat the *Greer* was initially in the position of locating the target for the British "hit man." In this sense the U.S. destroyer was the attacker as much as the British bombers or the British destroyer. As far as the Germans could tell, they were being attacked by either the British or the Americans or both—in any event by an enemy. Certainly any U-boat commander, like any normal skipper under any flag, would have felt justified in fighting in self-defense, as Hitler wished. In fact, Fraatz believed that his assailant might be one of the fifty American destroyers "sailing for England."

The *Greer* presented a classic "incident" in which each side could sincerely claim that it had been attacked first, the U-boat with more reason than the American destroyer. Lieutenant Commander Frost himself was aware at the time that the U-boat commander may have thought "the battle was joined" after the British bomber had dropped the depth charges. Yet, oddly enough, Commander Johnson, who evidently believed the *Greer* to be in no danger, was surprised and "very angry" when the U-boat discharged her torpedoes.[3]

The *Greer* attack highlighted the changing role of the United States from innocent bystander to Britain's not-so-silent partner. Indeed, in a broad sense the *Greer* episode constituted a counterattack against Hitler's assault on the legal, moral, and ethical foundations of Western civilization.

Roosevelt Gets His "Incident"

For weeks the isolationists had been openly charging that President Roosevelt was either hoping for an "incident" or scheming to stage one that would justify his asking for a formal declaration of war. A patriotically aroused Congress would surely honor his request, and the nation would at last be officially in the conflict to help the British and save democracy from the tyranny of the dictators. Evidently the "deliberate attack" on the *Greer* now released Roosevelt from his campaign promises and pledges to keep out of war "except in case of attack."

F.D.R.'s reactions did much to support the theory of a contrived incident, such as the President needed to justify an undeclared shooting war against Hitler's U-boats. On September 4, 1941, the Navy Department gave the press the story that a submarine of unknown nationality had attacked the *Greer* that morning. Torpedoes had been fired at the American destroyer, and she had counterattacked with depth charges, with results that were unknown. The American destroyer, the Navy Department further stated, was then a part of the Atlantic patrol established during the spring by Admiral King and was carrying mail to Iceland.[4]

The next day, September 5, 1941, radio dispatches from Iceland added details.[5] The *Greer* had arrived in port undamaged, a German submarine had attacked her, and the destroyer had been supported in repelling the attack by British airplanes participating in the Atlantic patrol. The press additionally reported that the President had issued orders to "eliminate" the submarine, and that he regarded the torpedo attack as deliberate. He had also hinted that the attacker may have been a U-boat.

Five minutes before noon that same morning (September 5, 1941), the President opened his regular news conference.[6] Confirming the press reports, he said that there was "nothing to add, except that there was more than one attack, and that it occurred in daylight, and that it had occurred definitely on *the American side of the ocean.*" (It will be recalled that Roosevelt had extended the American security zone to include Iceland on July 15, 1941, at the time he sent in the U.S. Marines. Oddly enough, the expanded zone overlapped the already delineated German combat zone.)

As for the dangerous implications of the *Greer* incident, Roosevelt was reminded of an "allegory." Once upon a time, he said, there were two children out in the country on their way to school when some unknown assailant fired several shots at them from the bushes. The father argued that since no one had been hit "there wasn't anything to do about it," such as searching the bushes or taking other energetic action. By implication Roosevelt indicated that the father was wrong and strong measures were required following the so-called attack on the *Greer.*

A newsman then asked about the problem of identification of the *Greer* by the U-boat. Roosevelt replied that she had "an identification number on her, plus the flag. And the fact remains that there was more than one attack." (We now know that when Fraatz took hurried periscope observations, he did not see much identification, except for the four funnels. The *Greer* was headed at him, bows on, and he could hardly have observed clearly the numerals on the bow or the national colors streaming from the mast.)

Continuing, Roosevelt next dismissed the charge that the *Greer* had been operating in the German combat zone. He observed that the United States had never been formally notified of that zone's existence, and besides "everyone knows that a blockade is never recognized unless it is effective." The President in fact was citing outdated international law, for in World War I and World War II the traditional close-in, effective blockade had been discarded in favor of the long-range, unorthodox blockades established by both Great Britain and Germany. If international usage is international law, these new practices were becoming the new international law.

The President was then asked, in reference to his allegory, if a search was being made of the (watery) bushes for the assailant who had fired the shots. He replied that he was not acting in the role of the unconcerned father of the children, but as the schoolmaster who had a broad responsibility for his pupils. The unconcerned father was here cast in the role of isolationist, and Roosevelt, an interventionist, was the worried schoolteacher. When asked what the pedagogue would do when he found the guilty marauder, the President replied, "Eliminate him." By implication American destroyers were then seeking to "eliminate" the menacing U-boats. Roosevelt then refused to provide any more details, although he apparently had some, because he assured his listeners that the attack had come in clear daylight with little chance of mistaken identity.

Who Attacked Whom?

Apologists for Roosevelt claim that at first he had not received a full report of the incident, including details about the *Greer*'s guidance of the attacking British bombers, and hence he had not deliberately misled the public.[7] Yet six days later, in his blistering fireside chat, September 11,1941, he still spoke of the attack as entirely unprovoked. One can hardly believe that the Navy Department would have risked withholding the critically important details for so long from the Commander-in-Chief. We should note that Commander Johnson, after arriving in Iceland, was promptly flown to Washington to make a firsthand report.

Yet the Navy Department insisted that the initial attack had been made by the U-boat. This assertion was true only if one does not regard as offensive action the prolonged "tailing" of the German submarine by the *Greer,* as well as the pursuer's signaled guidance of the bomb-dropping British aircraft and all British destroyers within radio range. In the criminal courts of the United States the accessory may be judged as guilty as the actual attacker.

As a former Assistant Secretary of the Navy, Roosevelt was a faithful watchdog of fleet operations, and most likely he pressed the Navy Department for full details. In his press conference on the *Greer* affair, he repeatedly stated that he could not give out certain facts. He did not make clear whether he was unwilling to divulge classified information or whether he did not then know all the details. It could be that he did not want to know them and thus take the sting out of the "incident." Or he could have known all the essential facts but did not wish to reveal the full extent of the Navy's cooperation with the British in searching for the U-boat. He apparently had not foreseen a case in which an American destroyer would team up with

British destroyers and aircraft to hunt down a German submarine. Obviously, the American public, especially the noninterventionists, was not yet ready for a showdown. The Navy was in a shooting war, but the nation was not.*

Nazi Cries of Outrage

On September 6, 1941, two days after the *Greer* incident, Berlin issued to the press a formal communiqué, obviously based on an official radioed report from the *U-652*. It stated that a German submarine was attacked with depth bombs and "continuously pursued in the German blockade zone. . . ." The U-boat commander was unable to establish the nationality of the hostile destroyer and, probably because of his extreme caution, he mistakenly thought that the destroyer had pursued him "until midnight."

The Nazi communiqué sharply challenged the allegation of the U.S. Navy Department that the attack was "initiated by the German submarine." This excuse, Berlin charged, was given to cloak a "complete violation of neutrality" with the appearance "of legality." Roosevelt not only had ordered American warships to report the location of German submarines "in violation of neutrality," but he was also now ordering direct attacks. He was thus attempting to provoke incidents, "with all the means at his disposal," in order to incite the American people into war against Germany.[8]

This communiqué was evidently the only official cognizance taken of the incident by the German government. There was no protest to the State Department, as one might have expected. But the Nazi press unleashed a volley of invective against Roosevelt, the "calloused liar" and the "betrayer of his people." One charge was that his policy was to "shoot first and ask questions afterward."[9]

In Japan, the ally of Hitler in the Tripartite Pact, the reaction of the press to the *Greer* incident was less bellicose.[10] Several of the most important Tokyo newspapers believed that the United States was still cautious and would not "plunge itself into the war." The Americans were fully aware, so the Japanese believed, that they were not yet prepared to enter this conflict and that they would have to build up a sufficient supply of munitions if they expected to be-

*A Gallup poll released September 2 (two days before the *Greer* incident) asked whether or not the U.S. Navy should "convoy" war materials to Britain. The result was 52 percent yes, 39 percent no, and 9 percent without opinion. *Public Opinion Quarterly* V, 680.

come involved openly in a protracted war. As a matter of fact, Roosevelt was keenly aware that America's war production was lagging; that he could not spare lend-lease aid for both Britain and Russia in the volume needed; that a United States force for the massive invasion of Europe did not exist; and that (as he privately confessed) he did not have enough navy for both the Atlantic and the Pacific.[11]

In lieu of an official protest, Foreign Minister Ribbentrop sent the published Nazi communiqué to Chargé Thomson in Washington, in a telegram of September 6, 1941, marked "Most Urgent." He was instructed "immediately" to "get in touch with the leading isolationist members of Congress." He should, "in a suitably confidential manner," expose "Roosevelt's war-mongering policy" and thus "deal it a decisive blow to the advantage of the isolationists." Thomson could perhaps persuade "one or more of the most influential isolationist members of Congress" to refer to the Berlin communiqué and make motions to recall the *Greer,* to interrogate her crew, and to reveal the identity of those officers who had given the destroyer orders to shoot.

Ribbentrop went on to say that there was a "a unique chance here to deal a decisive blow to the Messrs. Roosevelt, Knox and Stimson" and thus expose them as men who, contrary to the will of the people, were seeking to provoke war with Germany. There was a special interest "at the highest level [Hitler]" in the *Greer* case.[12]

Three days later, on September 9, 1941, Thomson reported to the Foreign Ministry in a dispatch marked "Most Urgent" and "Top Secret."[13] Through "suitable contacts" he had reached friendly senators (Wheeler, Taft?), congressmen, journalists, and "suitable organizations" (the America First Committee?). His contacts had gone "to work so circumspectly that one will not be able to see the German influence." Their success would depend on Roosevelt's upcoming fireside chat, two days later. Thomson also predicted that Roosevelt's scheduled speech would probably use the *Greer* incident to whip up war passions in the hope that the people would increase war production to the point where America would truly become "the arsenal of democracy." The President would announce measures for increasing the shipment and protection of military supplies to England, while blaming Germany for having initiated aggressive warfare. In the light of subsequent events, Thomson's prognosis was not a bad one.

The record strongly suggests that Roosevelt was eagerly looking for a "*Greer* incident" that would justify America's shooting defensively at U-boats. Hitler, on the other hand, was trying his best to avoid such a provocation—at least until he could see the light at the end of the long and cold Russian tunnel.

Roosevelt Declares War on Piracy

On September 11, 1941, Roosevelt responded to the *Greer* incident, which had occurred a full week earlier, by delivering his "rattlesnake" fireside chat. It was really a bombshell speech to the nation, delivered sitting down.[14]

The President by now had been accorded ample time to get the essential facts straight, as was his solemn responsibility. But his address, based substantially on a misrepresentation of the explosive *Greer* incident, was in effect a presidential declaration of war on Hitler's submarines. In tone and content it bears a strong resemblance to the Führer's anti-Roosevelt declaration of war of December 11, 1941. Like Hitler, Roosevelt listed a number of incidents that the United States had found provocative, and like Hitler, he urged strong countermeasures. Avoiding diplomatic niceties, F.D.R. condemned the Führer by name about ten times and the Nazis more than a dozen times.

At the outset Roosevelt outlined the *Greer* episode from the vantage point of the White House. The destroyer had been on a "legitimate mission" in waters declared by "Congressional action" (lend-lease?) to be essential "for the defense of our own land." In broad daylight and with the American flag flying, a German U-boat had fired first, "without warning, and with deliberate design to sink her." This "deliberate attempt" by the Germans to destroy "a clearly identified American warship" was "piracy—piracy legally and morally."

The President then began to list other outrageous acts of the Nazis against the United States. He mentioned first the *Robin Moor,* sunk cold-bloodedly in flagrant violation of international law. Yet, as he said, the Germans had not come forward with an apology, an allegation of mistake, or an offer to make reparation.

He next mentioned the narrow escape of an American battleship, evidently the *Texas,* although he did not mention the vessel by name or acknowledge that she had been cruising the Atlantic in the German combat zone, where she had no business to be. Roosevelt charged that a German submarine, its periscope visible, had followed the American battleship for a long time while seeking to "maneuver" itself into "a position of attack." The pursuer must have been a German submarine, Roosevelt concluded correctly, because

no British or American submarines were "within hundreds of miles
of this spot at the time. . . ."

Continuing with his fireside indictment against Hitler, Roosevelt observed that five days earlier a U.S. Navy patrol ship had
picked up three survivors from the freighter *Sessa*. He declared that
she was an American-owned vessel, even though she was flying the
"flag of our sister Republic of Panama." As Roosevelt told the story,
the ill-starred vessel had been torpedoed without warning on August
17, 1941, and then shelled. The sinking of this ship, then carrying
provisions and construction supplies to Iceland, had occurred near
Greenland. The remaining members of the crew were presumed lost.
Roosevelt concluded that there could be no reasonable doubt as to
the identity of the attacker, especially in view of "the established
presence of German submarines in this vicinity. . . ."

Additional facts that we now know about the *Sessa* are relevant.
She formerly had been a Danish vessel and was acquired by the U.S.
Maritime Commission under the authority of Public Law 101,
which permitted the requisitioning of idle foreign flagships in
American waters. She was, Roosevelt conceded, sailing under Panamanian registry, which meant (although he did not say so) that
technically she was not a United States ship at all and as such was
not entitled to the protection of the American flag. The Panamanian colors in this case were a subterfuge to provide greater protection against German submarines. By referring to the "sister
Republic of Panama," Roosevelt evidently hoped to emphasize the
concept that the twenty-one republics of the Americas were as one,
especially following the Declaration of Panama establishing the Pan
American Safety Zone in October 1939, and the colony-protecting
Act of Havana in July 1940.

The luckless *Sessa* was carrying foodstuffs, lumber, and other
general cargo to Iceland, presumably in part for the U.S. Marines
who had been landed there in July 1941. She was torpedoed and
sunk while the visibility was poor and her lights were darkened. In
all, twenty-four members of her crew were unreported and presumed lost.[15]

Sunken Ships

Continuing his fireside chat of September 11, 1941, Roosevelt cited
the case of an unquestioned attack on a U.S. merchant ship, the *Steel
Seafarer*. She was sunk in the Red Sea on September 5, 1941, by a
German bomber, some 220 miles south of Suez, while en route to an

Egyptian port. She was under American registry and legitimately flying the American flag.[16]

Additional facts were ultimately made public. Not only was the *Steel Seafarer* flying the Stars and Stripes, but she also had a large U.S. flag painted on each side. She was carrying, among other cargo, a deck load of large cases, which may have been aircraft for the British armies in Egypt, that is contraband of war. She was sunk by bombs dropped from an airplane, although the ship's side lights were burning and the visibility was good. No lives were lost.

We remember that the narrow Red Sea had been declared off limits to American merchant ships early in the war, but that the ban had been lifted in April 1941 to permit military supplies to go to the British armies in Egypt.[17] If the *Steel Seafarer* had been halted by a German U-boat or surface raider, she could have been sunk lawfully after passengers and crew had been permitted to take to the lifeboats, for the vessel was relatively close to land. But the bomber could not visit and search, and the Germans could not observe international law when they attacked from the air. Their alternatives were either to sink the ship with bombs or permit it to pass unscathed, carrying war materiel to their sworn enemy. In Hitler's heyday precautions took precedence over proprieties.

If informed, Roosevelt could have inflated his list of jeopardized or sunken ships by adding the freighter *Montana,* sunk by a German torpedo on September 11, 1941, the very day of the fireside chat. She was en route to Iceland with a cargo of lumber, possibly to build more barracks for the recently landed U.S. Marines. Yet the *Montana* would not have added much strength to Roosevelt's bitter charges because, like the *Sessa,* she was under Panamanian registry, though American owned. The entire crew was saved.[18]

Shoot-on-Sight Orders

Roosevelt further observed in this same *Greer* speech that one should not exaggerate an "isolated incident," but that the recent attacks were a part of Hitler's general plan to take over the Atlantic Ocean and menace the United States. The Führer already had agents busily engaged in subverting Uruguay, Argentina, and Bolivia. Recently, secret airfields had been discovered in Colombia, "within easy range of the Panama Canal." The broad Atlantic Ocean, if no longer defended by the British Navy, would menace rather than protect the United States. The *Greer* incident was but a part of a recognizable jelling pattern.

No violence by Hitler, Roosevelt asserted, would intimidate the Americans into abandoning their right to sail the high seas. The Nazi U-boats and raiders were "the rattlesnakes of the Atlantic." America sought "no shooting war with Hitler," but "when you see a rattlesnake poised to strike, you do not wait until he has struck before you crush him." The very presence of these vipers "in any waters which America deems vital to its defense constitutes an attack."

At this point Roosevelt summoned American history to his support. In 1798–1800, the second President, John Adams, had ordered American warships to attack "European [French] ships of war" that were ravaging American commerce. (F.D.R. refrained from saying that Congress had formally authorized Adams to act.) Similarly, Thomas Jefferson, the third President, had ordered American warships to attack the "corsairs of the nations of North Africa." (This undeclared war of 1801–1805 by the United States against these piratical nations had followed a formal declaration of hostilities by the Pasha of Tripoli.)

Citing these strained analogies, Roosevelt concluded that his "obligation as President is historic; it is clear. It is inescapable." If America struck back at the Nazis, such a response would be "solely defense" in defense of "freedom of the seas." Henceforth German or Italian warships would enter waters deemed "vital to American defense" only "at their peril." Orders had been issued to shoot in such circumstances, but there would be "no shooting unless Germany continues to seek it." We should note that there was to be only *defensive* shooting and *only* in waters "vital to American defense"—that is, on what Roosevelt had earlier called "the American side of the ocean." In this way, F.D.R. would honor his pledge not to send American boys into "foreign wars," except "in case of attack." And he did not use the fearsome phrase, "shoot on sight."

The President concluded his memorable *Greer* speech by asserting that he had not reached this decision "hurriedly or lightly" but as a result of "months and months of constant thought and anxiety and prayer. In the protection of your nation and mine it cannot be avoided." These carefully chosen words had the ring of finality. They obviously were intended to whip up a fighting spirit, and in this endeavor Roosevelt certainly succeeded.*

---

*A Gallup poll of October 2, 1941, found that 62 percent favored "shoot on sight" and that only 28 percent opposed. As was usual in these polls, more Democrats than Republicans supported the administration's policy. *Public Opinion Quarterly* VI, 163–164.

We should further note that Roosevelt repeatedly invoked the sacred American doctrine of "freedom of the seas" not only in the *Greer* speech but at other times as well. He would use this principle to support the armed escorting of American freighters laden with contraband for British ports, where they could be used against an enemy, in this case Hitler's Germany. This interpretation was, of course, a perversion of America's ancient concept of a free sea. Roosevelt, as the belligerent nations pointed out, had parted company with freedom of the seas for so-called neutrals by repeatedly forsaking the obligations of a neutral. Most notably, he had created a safety zone around the Americas south of Canada and had finally pushed its new boundary eastward, to embrace all of Iceland, in July 1941.[21]

Roosevelt's deliberate misrepresentation of the *Greer* incident proved to be one of the most savagely criticized deceptions of his controversial career. But it provided a needed pretext for his belligerent shoot-on-sight address to the American people—and the whole world, including Hitler and Mussolini. His defiance naturally brought great cheer to the battered British, who had just entered upon the third year of this dreary and shattering war. They would joyously welcome as even a partial ally their reluctant but giant daughter in the west.

Roosevelt's officially proclaimed shooting war (but not a declared one) ultimately led to two more armed clashes between U.S. destroyers and Hitler's U-boats. But these were spread over the dozen weeks from the rattlesnake speech of September to the Pearl Harbor attack of December 7, 1941, and they occurred under such circumstances as to make clear that Hitler then had no stomach for accepting Roosevelt's challenge. We must not forget that the Führer did not declare war on the United States until December 11, 1941, four days after the Japanese forced his hand at Pearl Harbor.

Roosevelt's War Powers

We now know that from the early days of the war Hitler had issued orders not to provoke incidents with the United States. He clung to this course despite repeated pleadings by his admirals, especially after he had plunged into the disastrous Russian campaign. By September and October he was fully aware that he had a bear by the tail, and he had all the more reason not to arouse the United States.

Roosevelt did not need American spies to fathom German intentions; he could deduce what they were from Hitler's extraordinary forbearance. Even before the invasion of Russia, the Führer had officially ignored America's flagrantly pro-British acts of unneutrality, notably the destroyers-bases deal and the Lend-Lease Act. In this crisis atmosphere F.D.R. could enjoy the luxury of talking tough and acting tougher, without fear of immediate retaliation of a serious nature. Actually, on September 17, 1941 (six days after F.D.R's shoot-on-sight speech) Hitler issued instructions "to avoid any incident . . . before about the middle of October."[22]

Firmly ensconced in the driver's seat, Roosevelt would have been less than human if he had not welcomed the *Greer* incident with open arms. He naturally grasped this opportunity eagerly and hastily, without having carefully scrutinized and weighed all relevant facts. He obviously read too much into the *Greer* affair in his shoot-on-sight speech. The destroyer-submarine attacks and counterattacks in themselves were not proof that Hitler had serious intentions of enslaving the New World.

Isolationists angrily charged that Roosevelt had usurped the authority of Congress and was edging the nation into war. Herbert Hoover, who had occupied the White House during four troubled years, emphatically voiced this view in a Chicago speech.[23] His well-known distaste for Roosevelt may have partially colored his opinion.

Bound by his oath to the Constitution, the President cannot *declare* war, but there is no clause that forbids him to *proclaim* it, as Roosevelt did. The President can wage war but not declare it. Roosevelt had said that the Nazis were making war on the United States, as was true in a broad sense, and that he had issued orders to shoot back. But there would be no shooting unless the Germans and the Italians appeared on the scene as so-called aggressors.

We recall that Lincoln fought the Confederacy during the Civil War without a congressional declaration of war; that Harry Truman engaged in the Korean war without one; and that Lyndon Johnson waged the Vietnam war without one, although he had the near unanimous support of Congress in the Gulf of Tonkin resolution. And he had promised the voters in the presidential campaign of 1964 that "Asiatic boys," not "American boys," would have to do the fighting. The suspicious Gulf of Tonkin episode was Johnson's *Greer* incident and, ironically, it also was badly misrepresented. As Senator Fulbright observed, "FDR's deviousness in a good cause made it much easier for LBJ to practice the same kind of deviousness in a bad cause."[24] The troublesome question then arises, "Who shall determine the goodness or badness of a cause: the Congress, the President, public opinion, or posterity, including historians?"

Aroused isolationists charged that Roosevelt had deliberately bypassed Congress. This was no doubt true because the noninterventionist minority in that body would have fought the declaration of a shooting war to the bitter end. If necessary, they doubtless would have resorted to the filibuster—the last-ditch resort of the minority in the Senate. Keenly aware of such dangers, Roosevelt had engineered the destroyers deal as an executive agreement, despite the inevitable storm of protest from the neutrality-minded citizenry.

In Roosevelt's partial defense we must note that he had consulted Democratic leaders in Congress, and had even read to them his startling fireside chat. They evidently indicated their tacit approval.[25] This same Congress had voted lend-lease with the unwritten understanding that the supplies would reach England and not be destroyed en route.

The Question of National Interest

A major defense presented by the interventionists was that Roosevelt's shoot-on-sight doctrine was not sprung on an unsuspecting, unwilling, and disapproving people. A nation that had by strong majority opinion supported lend-lease should not have been greatly surprised by the inevitable U-boat attacks on American escorts. The public opinion polls during this period and later showed that the masses strongly favored aid to Great Britain at the risk of war, but how could such aid get there if not sent under a protective naval shield? The American people suffered from a split personality. By an overshelming majority they wanted to stay out of the war, and yet they desired by strong popular majorities to help the British survive, even though such a course might mean a shooting involvement in the war. The American people were vulnerable to the human failing of wanting to eat their cake and have it, too.

Apologists for Roosevelt argued that his aggressive course was in the national interest and hence took precedence over all platform promises and campaign pledges to stay out of war. Yet historian Charles A. Beard, in his book *President Roosevelt and the Coming of the War 1941,* called such assurances sacred "covenants" with the American people. This was a gross exaggeration. Beard, as an astute student of American government, well knew that platforms are made to get in on, not stand on. Traditionally Jove laughs at the "promises" of lovers and politicians. There is also a principle in international law, especially with reference to treaties, known as *rebus sic stantibus,* or literally "things remaining as they were." More commonly one hears the phrase "circumstances alter cases."

Dr. Samuel E. Morison, in an unrestrained rejoinder to Beard's attack on Roosevelt and his solemn "covenants," wrote that "all promises have implied predicates."[26] In this instance one of the unmentioned predicates was that the chief executive would keep out of war *provided that* the crisis situation did not deteriorate to the point where, in the view of the President and his counselors, abstention would result in the possible enchainment of the American people by Nazi tyranny.

Roosevelt could see the whole picture because he had access to piles of classified information that was not available to the ordinary American. His judgment was confirmed by the leading military men, who were better able to assess the military and naval dangers than was the workaday citizen. He was being prodded toward a wraps-off war by Secretary of War Stimson, Secretary of the Navy Knox, Secretary of the Treasury Morgenthau, and Secretary of the Interior Ickes—whom the isolationist *Chicago Tribune* called "the belligerent old men in his Cabinet." They felt, as they assessed the situation, that the time was overripe for a fighting stance against Hitler.[27]

Prominent Republicans, notably former President Herbert Hoover and Senator Robert A. Taft, strongly opposed Roosevelt's warlike moves, partly because the opposition party traditionally opposes proposals by the incumbent administration. Undoubtedly some Republicans fought against a genuine shooting war because the sitting President during such a conflict has a better chance of being re-elected. (This electoral advantage was conspicuously evident in the cases of Lincoln and Roosevelt, both of whom profited by the common saying that one should not swap horses while crossing a turbulent stream.)

F.D.R.'s supporters have argued that he was duty bound to issue the limited shoot-on-sight orders. By this formula there would be no real war unless the Germans shot back on a considerable scale, and up to this point they had not been doing much shooting back. The President was sworn to "preserve, protect, and defend the Constitution," which was "to provide for the common defence, promote the general Welfare, and secure the Blessings of Liberty to ourselves and our Posterity." And he foresaw dangers to American liberties that others could not see or even believe possible. In this situation

Roosevelt felt called upon to rise above avowed political principles. He would have to discard platform promises and campaign pledges and do what he thought best for the countless millions of people, born and unborn, entrusted by the electorate to his care.

Lincoln himself rose above the Constitution and the laws in an effort to preserve the Union; Roosevelt rose above platforms, pledges, and campaign oratory in an effort to save the nation from ultimate "Nazi tyranny." Both presidents succeeded, if we assume in the case of Roosevelt that ultimate Nazi domination was a probable prospect. But they succeeded only by resorting to dubious or even high-handed policies.

CHAPTER 13

THE TORPEDOINGS INCREASE

That determination of ours not to take it lying down has been expressed in the orders to the American Navy to shoot on sight. Those orders stand.

Roosevelt's Navy Day address, October 27, 1941

The Sinking of the *Pink Star*

At the presidential press conference of September 23, 1941, twelve days after the shoot-on-sight address, Roosevelt referred to the sinking of the *Pink Star*.[1] This vessel, at one time a Danish freighter, was requisitioned by the U.S. Maritime Commission in July 1941 and then placed under Panamanian registry so as to circumvent the Neutrality Act of 1939 and permit the ship to penetrate combat zones. She had sailed from New York on September 3 with a general cargo and had joined a convoy headed for Iceland. The *Pink Star* was torpedoed and sunk on September 19, even though she was under the protection of Canadian escorts.[2]

Roosevelt himself broached the subject of the *Pink Star*, remarking that he had just received word of the sinking from the Navy Department. But he could not report on what had become of the crew. His only information was that there had been a U-boat attack and that the victim was a part of a Canadian-escorted convoy. One inquisitive newsman then asked whether the President thought that such ships should be provided "with some measures of self-defense." The inquirer obviously was referring to arming these freighters, and he may not have realized that the escorting Canadian warships had been providing protection.[3]

This pointed question gave Roosevelt an excellent opportunity to say what he had on his mind. He responded that by concentrating on the sinking of an isolated freighter, people were overlooking the "main objective, which is national defense." By going into details one was merely dragging a "red herring" across that main objective. The world was facing "the most outrageous movement in history." Certain dictators were "trying to dominate the whole world," and America's supreme obligation was to defend the hemisphere against such "attempted domination."

Roosevelt then obviously referred to the Lend-Lease Act when he stated that Congress had "made it perfectly clear" that the defense of the Americas involved resisting "in every way we can" those dictators who were seeking "domination of the world." The United States was doing all she could, including trying to prevent "the dictators from gaining footholds" that could threaten the American people. That was why American troops were then in Iceland, and why the nation was sending to England munitions and foodstuffs necessary to sustain their resistance.

One brash reporter raised an embarrassing question that Roosevelt had not seen fit to discuss. Would it not be easier to promote the downfall of the dictators by putting guns on American merchant ships than by not doing so? Roosevelt, with surprising candor, replied that he was "probably" heading in that direction and also toward providing arms for the merchant ships of other American nations. He admitted that the *Pink Star*, though of American ownership, was under Panamanian registry and carried a gun.

A reporter then asked the President if it was not true that before the Neutrality Act of 1939 forbade the arming of merchant ships, such armament was "proper under international law." Actually, up to 1914 ordinary commercial ships had been permitted to carry a defensive gun or two to beat off pirates or privateers. No weakly armed merchant vessel would dare tangle with a hostile warship. But the wholesale introduction of the submarine in 1914 undermined this interpretation of international law for the simple reason that one shot from the one gun of a merchant ship could destroy a surfaced submarine.[4] Such a response would change the innocent freighter from a ship that was defensively armed to one that was offensively armed.

Roosevelt responded that it was "absolutely" proper to arm American merchant ships. He referred to the "great many" that had beaten off French privateers (undeclared war, 1798–1800) and British privateers (War of 1812). But he conceded that American freighters could not be legally armed until the existing Neutrality Act was amended, and that this change was then "under consideration" by Congress.

The Armed Merchantmen Issue

A week later, at his regular press conference of September 30, 1941, Roosevelt referred again to the *Pink Star,* which he conceded was a "rather old story for headline artists."[5] He wanted to emphasize the fact that the ship was bound first for Iceland with supplies for the American troops, and then for England with essential supplies for the British. The whole shipment had been lost, and this setback meant that replacement orders would have to be placed, with all that this process involved in delays and priorities.

Most of the *Pink Star*'s cargo was food, which F.D.R. correctly "supposed" was now contraband of war. He specifically referred to the large shipment of cheddar cheese, powdered milk, concentrated orange juice, pork products, and corn. He went into great detail as to the thousands of cows and hogs involved in producing these foodstuffs, and the millions of laborers in British factories who would be sustained thereby for a given time.

Roosevelt then alluded to the loss of a "very small amount" of military supplies for England, including metallic links for machine gun belts, and the machine tools that were to have been used to make aircraft engines. These shipments were intended for the people doing the actual fighting, specifically "for their own preservation" but of nearly equal importance for "the defense of the United States."

Roosevelt emphasized again that the *Pink Star* was "a pretty stale story" but there it was. A few minutes later a newsman went "back to the ship's cargo." He supposed that the President's recitation was "to condition us for something, but I don't know just what." Laughter followed, and the President dismissed the subject with a somewhat irrelevant wisecrack. But it is now clear that he was preparing the people for his message to Congress, nine days in the offing, urging that body to revise the Neutrality Act to permit the arming of merchant ships. It is also evident that the Panamanian *Pink Star,* now a forgotten ship of those dangerous months, became a symbol of some significance in preparing the public mind for the arming of American merchant vessels. The torpedoing of this Panama-registered freighter, steaming in company with Allied warships, thus proved to be another significant milestone in the escalating backdoor war between Roosevelt and Hitler.

The *I. C. White* and Neutrality Revision

While Roosevelt was still pondering the problem of arming American merchant ships, another sinking occurred on September 27, 1941. The victim was the *I. C. White,* an American-owned oil tanker (Standard Oil of New Jersey) operating under Panamanian registry. The vessel had sailed alone from Curaçao, in the Dutch West Indies, on September 14, for Cape Town, South Africa. Like the ill-starred *Robin Moor* of May 1941, she went down far from land, some 600 miles east of Pernambuco, Brazil. This tanker was a neutral ship carrying lend-lease contraband of war in the form of fuel oil to a major unit of the British Commonwealth. Under the ancient practices sanctioned by international law the vessel should have been properly warned before being sunk, and adequate provision should have been made for the safety of passengers and crew. Neither of these requirements was honored.

The *I. C. White* was torpedoed by a U-boat shortly after midnight, with the loss of three lives. The ship was unarmed and lighted. She was also flying the (neutral) Panamanian flag, which, according to the captain, was fully illuminated by a searchlight. The night was clear and the bridge watch could see a light on the U-boat some 300 yards distant from the tanker.[6]

The news of the sinking broke in Rio de Janeiro, Brazil, on October 3, 1941, when an arriving freighter reported having picked up survivors. Shortly thereafter another vessel, due at the same port, radioed that it had rescued others. In all, thirty-four out of thirty-seven were saved. All but three of the crew were Americans, and they had spent about a week in two open lifeboats. The captain of the *I. C. White* stated that he had not radioed for help for fear of attracting other vulnerable ships to the area where the U-boat was operating.

After the inflammatory *Greer* incident and Roosevelt's fiery shoot-on-sight speech, American opinion became increasingly aware of the inconsistency of being hampered by the Neutrality Act. When the warships of one nation shoot at the warships of another without response, there is a warlike act but not war. When the warships of two nations attack and counterattack, as in the case of the *Greer* and the U-boat, they are waging war, although it may be only an isolated incident in an undeclared war. Whatever these clashes might be called, they certainly were not neutrality. "Nonbelligerency" or "quasi-belligerency" were the euphemisms commonly used, as though such contradictions in terms could properly describe belligerent acts.

The Neutrality Act of 1939 forbade American vessels to enter the combat zones designated by the President. But by October 1941, lend-lease aid to Britain would be substantially increased if American merchant ships could sail directly to England without having to transfer their cargoes at Iceland to British or other foreign freighters. American war supplies, such as those on the *Pink Star,* were then being shipped to England through the combat zone on American-owned ships flying the Panamanian flag. This, of course, was both a subterfuge and a privilege then denied United States vessels.

Obviously, American destroyers were protecting the ships they were escorting, whatever their nationality. Then logically these favored freighters, especially those flying the flag of the United States, should assist in their own defense by having a mounted gun or two. At least, this seemed to be the deduction to follow from the decision to escort convoys. Certainly there was little sense in going into a fight with one hand tied behind one's back. The shortsightedness of such self-imposed restrictions had been one of the major reasons, if not the major reason, for Roosevelt's reluctance to sign the original neutrality legislation of 1935 in the first place.

Even before the sinking of the Panama-American *Pink Star* on September 19, 1941, Roosevelt had been thinking seriously of seeking a repeal of at least the more restrictive sections of the Neutrality Act of 1939. He obviously had been trying to prepare the American people for his move by his graphic recitation of the thousands of cows and hogs that had given their all in vain when that Britain-bound ship was torpedoed.

By September 11, 1941, the word was out that Roosevelt had discussed possible repeal with the leaders of Congress. Interventionists were overjoyed. Among numerous journals that gave praise was the *New York Times,* which complained that the restrictions of the Neutrality Act were "worth as much as a thousand submarines to Hitler." The *New York Herald Tribune* declared that the act had "become a stench in the nostrils of anyone for whom two and two still add up to four."[7]

The perplexing question for Roosevelt was whether to ask for total repeal of the act or for a modification of the sections that forbade arming merchant ships or sending them into combat zones. In support of total repeal was a Gallup poll released on October 5 that recorded a 70 percent vote (among those responding) in favor of the proposition that it was more important to defeat Hitler than to keep the country out of war.[8] Yet there was strong opposition in Congress against total repeal, especially in the Senate, where die-hard isolationists like Senator Hiram Johnson of California, a once bitter foe of Woodrow Wilson and the League of Nations, were declaiming against repeal. The certainty of a prolonged and bruising filibuster counted heavily in the administration's decision to seek only partial repeal.

F.D.R.'s Appeal for Repeal

On October 9, 1941, Roosevelt went out on a limb and sent to Congress a ringing message calling for revision of the Neutrality Act, including authority to arm merchant ships.[9] In some respects his clarion call sounded more like a presidential declaration of war against Germany than the shoot-on-sight blast of September 11. He left no doubt as to who the enemy was, for he pointed an accusing finger at the Nazis three times and at Hitler, by name and pronoun, more than twenty times. By now the gloves were off and F.D.R. was pulling no punches.

Roosevelt began his appeal by saying that his original strategy in the war had gone by the board because hostilities could not be contained behind Maginot lines. Many countries had been "conquered and enslaved," victims of Hitler's barbarities. Americans were now aware of what was in store for them if they did not give generous aid to those peoples still resisting "Nazi-Fascist domination." Through lend-lease the United States had adopted the policy of defending herself at long range—not "in Long Island Sound or in San Francisco Bay."

The remedy, Roosevelt insisted, was to maximize American aid by a revamping of the Neutrality Act in a manner essential for the defense of "American rights." Such revision would not call for a declaration of war "any more than the Lend-Lease Act called for a declaration of War." (F.D.R. avoided saying that lend-lease in itself was an informal declaration of economic war on the dictators.)

Roosevelt next reminded the Congress that at the outset of the war the United States had proclaimed danger zones into which American shipping was forbidden to sail. But Hitler had overlapped these vast combat zones with ones of his own; indeed, "he considers the entire world his own battlefield." He had even extended his sinkings of American ships to the zoneless South Atlantic (for example, the *Robin Moor*).

Arming neutral merchant ships for defense, Roosevelt declared, was time-honored and had "never been prohibited by international law." The time had come to arm against "modern pirates of the sea. . . ." Defenseless merchant seamen, in all justice, ought to be allowed to defend "their lives and ships." Placing guns on such vessels would not guarantee safety but in certain circumstances would provide some security.

Roosevelt turned next to the necessity of sending these merchant ships, when armed, into the forbidden combat zones to deliver needed supplies. This was a step that would carry out the plain intent of the Lend-Lease Act, for no Congress was stupid enough to vote such mountainous supplies unless it intended that they should reach the hands of those nations that desperately needed them. The United States should not further endanger the orphaned vessels of the exiled governments of Norway and Holland. Nor should the republic be "forced to masquerade American-owned ships behind the flags of our sister Republics"—an obvious reference to the legal necessity of using Panamanian registry for requisitioned shipping.

Allowing United States ships to enter the combat zones, Roosevelt made clear, had nothing whatever to do with American shippers making more money. He was clearly alluding to the so-called merchants of death who had helped (unwittingly) to inspire the Neutrality Act of 1935. Armed American ships would be allowed to sail only with government approval and "to promote the defense of the United States."

In this stirring presidential message Roosevelt strongly emphasized the dark military outlook then confronting "all of the nations" (including the United States) that were "combating Hitler." The Führer knew that he was "racing against time" and feared "the mounting force of American aid." Shipments must be sent "ever more swiftly" to those nations, including Britain and Russia, that were "fighting slavery." If Hitler succeeded in his scheme of empire the Americans would ultimately have to defend themselves in as bitter a war as that being waged in devastated Russia.

The Führer had flung down a challenge. But Americans would not be driven from their "freedom of the seas" by him or any other foreign power "crazed with a desire to control the world." To that end the restrictions must be removed from United States merchant ships by a revision of the Neutrality Act.

In reading Roosevelt's fighting words today, one would think that the Congress would have been frightened into speedy and resolute action. But this was not to be the case. As we shall note presently, a worrisome period of thirty-nine days elapsed between the submission of the message and the signing of a revised neutrality statute.

The Loss of Two Panamanian Ships

As if to give added emphasis to Roosevelt's provocative message, two American-owned ships were sunk by German U-boats on October 16, 1941, a week after the President's appeal to Congress for revamping the Neutrality Act. Both vessels went down on the same day, though widely separated.

One of the victims was the *W. C. Teagle,* a large tanker owned by the Standard Oil Company of New Jersey.[10] Although sailing under Panamanian registry, she was reportedly flying the British flag and hence unable to claim immunity as a neutral vessel. En route to Great Britain, the *W. C. Teagle* was fatally torpedoed during an attack on her convoy in the North Atlantic, evidently without loss of life to herself.

The *W. C. Teagle,* a vessel of 9,552 tons, had qualified as one of the largest tankers in the world when she was built in 1917. She was capable of carrying 125,000 barrels of oil, a resource badly needed by Britain. Already she had been outmoded and outclassed by tankers with a capacity of 150,000 barrels or more, and these figures convey a concrete idea of the immense amount of war materiel being shipped to England. Estimates were that the destruction of the *W. C. Teagle* brought the total of American-owned ships lost to U-boats to eleven vessels, all sunk within less than a year. Yet we should note that this figure included vessels flying Panamanian flags.

The other "American" steamer sunk on the same day was the *Bold Venture,* a former Danish vessel requisitioned by the U.S. Maritime Commission and placed under Panamanian registry. She had sailed on her first trip from New York to England on September 22, 1941, carrying a cargo of cotton, steel, copper, and other materiel. No citizens of the United States were known to be on board. The vessel, probably a straggler in a convoy, was torpedoed by a U-boat on October 16, some 500 miles south of Iceland. Nineteen of the crew were listed as missing, for the ship had gone down in a short ten minutes. The force of the torpedo blast had wrecked the ship's radio, which consequently could not be used to send out an S.O.S. Men on a Canadian escorting corvette evidently saw the smoke, and hastened to pick up the survivors, who had been tossing about in two small boats for two hours. They were brought safely to Reykjavik, Iceland.[11]

The *Kearny* Torpedoed

A more spectacular plunge into the cauldron of an undeclared shooting war with Hitler came on October 17, 1941, when the U.S. destroyer *Kearny* was torpedoed south of Iceland by a German submarine, the *U-568.* Although the ship was only damaged, eleven seamen lost their lives and more than a dozen were wounded. These were the first American fatalities on an American ship before Pearl Harbor.

Further details flesh out the picture. A convoy of some fifty merchant ships had sailed from a Canadian port early in October 1941. On October 15, when about 400 miles from Iceland, the vessels encountered a submarine "wolf pack." Inadequate protection was provided by a group of Canadian escorts—four corvettes and a destroyer. That hellish night three freighters were torpedoed and sunk. An appeal for help was radioed to Iceland, and in response the U.S. Navy rushed to the rescue a division of four destroyers, including the *Kearny.* Also summoned to the scene were a British and a French warship.

By sunset on October 16, 1941, the rescuers had reached the convoy. In the pitch-black darkness that enveloped the turbulent battle area the Nazi wolf pack attacked successfully six times. Not one of the submarines was seen or heard—only the exploding torpedoes as the victims suffered their death blows. In the course of this slam-bang battle the escorting destroyers launched depth bombs blindly and at will, thus adding to the general confusion. Silhouetted against the light of a burning freighter, the *Kearny* received a torpedo on the starboard side. Yet the destroyer managed to limp back to Iceland under her own power, escorted by the now famous destroyer *Greer*. Four merchant vessels and two non-American warships were lost to German torpedoes during the night-long engagement.[12]

The basic facts are clear enough. A prolonged clash had erupted between German U-boats and armed Canadian escorts; help was summoned by radio from Iceland and the surrounding area. American destroyers responded to the call, including the *Kearny*, which for some hours attempted to drive off or to destroy the German U-boats. In short, this was no chance encounter but a deadly and prolonged combat between German submarines and American warships—that is, wholesale undeclared shooting. In the case of the *Greer*'s first encounter with the U-boat off Iceland, there was some question as to who attacked first. In the case of the *Kearny*, the destroyer had rushed about 400 miles to protect an exhausted convoy from the inevitable attacks that night by German submarines.

When word of the *Kearny* incident first reached Washington, Roosevelt refused to issue a detailed statement at his press conference until he had obtained the facts. He evidently had learned something from having commented on the *Greer* episode prematurely. But he did say that the *Kearny* was within the American defensive zone when the torpedoing occurred, and he did concede that he had not changed his orders to hunt down attackers of convoys— orders issued after the *Greer* incident.[13] At his own press conference, Secretary of State Hull condemned German misdeeds as acts of piracy and calculated frightfulness in pursuance of a general design of world conquest. The Nazi press denounced the American version as an "inpudent lie."[14]

On October 19, 1941, two days after the latest torpedoing, the Navy Department released a few details. The *Kearny*, damaged by a torpedo from a submarine that no doubt was German, had reached Iceland unsunk. But eleven seamen were missing (and presumed dead); twenty-four more were injured.[15] The attitude of the State Department was such as to suggest that diplomatic relations with Berlin already had been broken. When Secretary Hull was asked if he had any plans for lodging an official protest, he remarked that "one does not very often send diplomatic notes to an international highwayman."[16]

The *Lehigh:* A Second *Robin Moor*

On October 19, 1941, two days after the *Kearny* was torpedoed south
of Iceland, the American freighter *Lehigh* (4,893 tons) was sunk
without warning, some 5,000 miles to the south, by what was presumed to be a German submarine. The locale was the South Atlantic near the southern end of the West African bulge. The victim was
en route to the African Gold Coast, from Bilbao, neutral Spain,
under charter to the United States Lines.

The stricken steamer was abandoned in twenty minutes and
sank about an hour later, some seventy-five miles off Freetown. Four
persons on board were slightly injured. All of the thirty-nine crew
members were picked up after they had rowed about forty miles toward the coast in lifeboats. The main rescuer was a British destroyer,
whose attention had been attracted by lighted flares.

The *Lehigh* was not a case of an American steamer transporting
lend-lease supplies to England under escort by warships, whether of
American, Canadian, or British nationality. The victim was not carrying a cargo of contraband, only ballast, and it was legitimately
flying the American flag in an area that had not been staked out as a
combat zone by either camp of belligerents. In fact, the *Lehigh*
rather resembled the *Robin Moor*—the only two bona fide U.S. merchant ships to be sunk by the Germans prior to Pearl Harbor. But
we should note that the *Robin Moor* saw the attacking submarine,
and that the passengers and crew were left in open boats hundreds
of miles from land, rather than seventy-five as in the instance of the
Lehigh. This was still a long distance as envisaged by the London
Protocol that Nazi Germany had freely accepted in 1936, and the
ship involved was unwarned, unarmed, and unloaded.

A wrathful Secretary Hull declared for publication that this
most recent sinking was "in harmony with all the definitions of piracy and assassination." The American press reported that this latest
outrage was adding impetus in the Senate for modification of the
Neutrality Act.[17]

In his regular press conference of October 21, 1941, Roosevelt
parried and then answered several questions about the *Lehigh.* He
remarked that she was an empty ship on a trading voyage, down
near the equator, where there was no fighting going on. The President agreed with Secretary Hull, who had branded the sinking "piracy." The fate of the *Lehigh* seemed to mean that ships of any

nation, anywhere on the high seas, could be attacked and sunk without warning. Roosevelt recalled the German expression of World War I, *spurlos versenkt* ("sunk without a trace").[18]

F.D.R. Damns the Torpedoes

On Navy Day, October 27, 1941, ten days after the eleven Americans had died in the *Kearny* battle, Roosevelt appeared before a packed audience in the Grand Ballroom of the Mayflower Hotel in Washington to deliver a memorable address.[19] Whether moved by his love for the navy or by his hatred of the dictators, or both, he let himself go in an unrestrained fighting speech. In some respects this address was even more scorching than his fireside chat, and strengthened the impression with isolationists that he was inevitably heading toward all-out war. Nor did Roosevelt leave any doubt as to the identity of the real foe. In this relatively short speech he mentioned Hitler and Hitlerism twenty-one times and the Nazis six times. The Führer, busy elsewhere with the Russian invasion, could have regarded this speech as a declaration of war if he had been so minded.

Roosevelt began by saying that five months ago to the day he had proclaimed a state of unlimited national emergency. Since then "much has happened." The Americans were now in Iceland, far out in the Atlantic, there defending the western hemisphere, and Hitler had sunk ships relatively close to the Americas in both the North and the South Atlantic (the *Robin Moor* and the *Lehigh*). One American destroyer was attacked on September 4 (the *Greer*). Another destroyer (the *Kearny*) was "attacked and hit" on October 17, and eleven "brave and loyal men of our Navy were killed by the Nazis." (Actually, the *Kearny* had sped some 400 miles to join in the fight against the U-boat attackers.) In reference to these incidents, Roosevelt the politician was telling only partial truths with the obvious intention of shocking the American people into a fuller awareness of their peril and forcing Congress to move.

"We have wished to avoid shooting," Roosevelt continued. "But the shooting has started. And history has recorded who fired the first shot. In the long run, however, all that will matter is who fired the last shot." All America had been attacked, he declared, for the casualties, including the "honored" dead, had come from twelve states, which he named, ranging from New York to California. The purpose of Hitler's attack on the *Kearny* (the Führer had not known what was going on) was to force America off "the high seas" into "a trembling retreat." The United States rejected this "insulting suggestion," out of both self-respect and self-interest.

Hitler had "often protested" that his plans for world conquest did not extend across the Atlantic, but his piratical raiders "prove otherwise," as did his design for a "new world order." Roosevelt had in his possession, so he claimed, a secret Hitlerian map of the "new world order." The Nazis had reshaped all South America and a portion of Central America into five "vassal States." Included was the Republic of Panama, within which lay America's "great life-line canal."

Roosevelt then proceeded to put the fear of God (and Hitler) into his listeners by saying that he possessed another secret document proving that the Nazis planned to "abolish all existing religions" and superimpose an "International Nazi Church." Hitler's *Mein Kampf* would become the "Holy Writ." "And in the place of the cross of Christ will be put two symbols—the swastika and the naked sword." Despite the protestations that Roosevelt said he expected from Hitler's propagandists and a "few" American isolationists, the people of the United States would not voluntarily choose "the kind of world which Hitler and his hordes would impose upon us." He continued:

"The forward march of Hitler and Hitlerism can be stopped—and it will be stopped."

"Very simply and very bluntly—we are pledged to pull our own oar in the destruction of Hitlerism."

"And when we have helped to end the curse of Hitlerism we shall help to establish a new peace. . . ."

To achieve these epochal ends, Roosevelt continued, the United States was shipping lend-lease supplies to those nations that were doing the fighting. The American people did not want these shipments "locked up in American harbors" or "sent to the bottom of the sea." Yet the Hitlerites had been sinking American ships and killing American sailors. "I say," Roosevelt warned, "that we do not propose to take this lying down." Orders had already been issued in response to the *Greer* incident "to shoot on sight. Those orders stand." (Actually F.D.R. had not used this precise phrase in his *Greer* speech.) Referring to the pending revision of the Neutrality Act, the President added, "Our American merchant ships must be armed to defend themselves against the rattlesnakes of the sea." The U.S. Navy would provide additional protection, in the spirit of its Civil War tradition: "Damn the torpedoes; full speed ahead!"

The so-called secret Hitlerian map of the "new world order." *Courtesy of the Franklin D. Roosevelt Library, Hyde Park, New York*

Roosevelt further declared that the United States, if she wished to gird herself for defense against Hitler's hordes, would have to accelerate production, especially of war materials. Management must discard the "business as usual" approach and labor leaders must forget strikes as usual, at a time when industrial disorders were gravely hampering war production. There would have to be "total national defense," whose primary objective was to "stop Hitler." Dictators could stay in power only through "continuing victories and increasing conquests." Russia particularly deserved help in her heroic chewing up of the advancing Nazi aggressors.

F.D.R.'s most bellicose declarations came rather early in his address, so the concluding paragraphs seem somewhat anticlimactic. They were in the nature of a challenge to the American people, who had met and overcome enormous obstacles in the past. Now they had to face up to the menace of Hitler—"the greatest challenge of them all. . . ."

This ringing message evidently did not make as deep an impression as the fireside chat of September 11, 1941, following the German counterattack on the *Greer*. Isolationists like Senators Wheeler of Montana and Taft of Ohio, among many others, evidently distrusted the direction of Roosevelt's leadership and his fears for the future more than they feared Hitler. Three full weeks of debate and delay would have to drag on before the President could affix his signature to the proposed watering down of the Neutrality Act.

The Nazis Brand F.D.R. a Liar

The Nazi-controlled press promptly charged that the *Kearny* incident was invented by President Roosevelt "to bamboozle Congress, with genuine Jewish unscrupulousness," into modifying the Neutrality Act of 1939. The official Nazi party organ (*Völkischer Beobachter*) was disposed to believe, as in other cases, that if there had been a torpedo hit, a British torpedo "did the trick."[20]

Much more significant was a rare public statement from Hitler's field headquarters overlooking the Russian front that reflected the Führer's concern. Ascribing the firing of German torpedoes at the destroyers *Greer* and *Kearny* to "aggression" by American warships, he declared flatly that "the United States has attacked Germany." This was a direct refutation of Roosevelt's assertion that "America has been attacked." At the same time, the official statement branded as "forgeries" the map and the document referred to by Roosevelt as showing German designs on Latin America and on the religions of the world.

These blunt rejoinders from Hitler himself gave rise to intense speculation in the United States. One of the most alarming rumors had Germany preparing to invoke the Tripartite Pact. Berlin would thus notify Italy and Japan of their obligation to enter the war on Germany's side if the Reich should become the object of an "attack" by an unfriendly nation.

At a presidential press conference on October 28, 1941, the day after his sensational Navy Day speech, Roosevelt explained why he had not exhibited the secret map dividing up much of Latin America into Nazi vassal states. Pointing to the basket on his desk containing the alleged document, he reported that it had a number of notations on it. If these were reproduced in the press, they probably would reveal where the map came from. Such a disclosure "might be exceedingly unfair to a number of people." More than that, it "might also dry up the source of future information."[21]

A map of South America, such as F.D.R. described, actually reposes among his papers at Hyde Park, New York. It bears a printed caption in German, as though other copies had been struck, and reveals in the margins some handwritten commentary in German. The map bears a striking resemblance to one published in 1976 in a book on British intelligence during World War II. British agents, who were then working closely with American operatives, may have supplied the map or may even have fabricated it.[22]

The material on the Nazi "church" also may be found in the Franklin D. Roosevelt Library. The file consists primarily of a seven-page cablegram from an agent in Switzerland; the dispatch was evidently regarded as of such importance as to be forwarded to the White House by the State Department. Roosevelt's lurid summation of its contents actually presented a less grim picture than the document itself. The suspicion seems unwarranted that on this occasion the President was trying, as Clare Boothe Luce later charged, "to lie the American people into war."

CHAPTER 14

THE SINKINGS ESCALATE

The epic stand of Britain, of China, and of Russia receives the full support of the free people of the Americas.

Roosevelt's address to delegates of the International Labor Organization November 6, 1941.

The *Salinas* Torpedoed

Hitler's submarines relentlessly continued their deadly hunt in the North Atlantic. On October 30, 1941, the armed tanker *Salinas,* of the U.S. Navy, was hit by two torpedoes, but not sunk, in a North Atlantic convoy westbound from Iceland. Though badly damaged, the victim did not sink, chiefly because she had discharged most of her oil in Iceland and her empty oil tanks filled with salt water. Her propulsion plant was made operable as her crew hurriedly engaged in emergency repairs. The stern gun of the wounded *Salinas* meanwhile opened fire on the submerging U-boat without serious effect, and a battle raged around the tanker as protecting U.S. destroyers dropped their depth charges.

Four days later the wounded oiler limped into a port in Newfoundland, after having proceeded at about one-third speed. Her crew had suffered no serious injuries; and after she was refitted, the

Salinas served usefully throughout the war that was to be formally declared within six weeks.

The *Salinas* incident thus featured a pitched battle between a German U-boat, on one side, and an armed ship of the U.S. Navy and her escorts, on the other. But the near-fatal episode attracted little attention at the time and virtually none later. Yet the ship deserves to be bracketed with the *Greer, Kearny,* and *Reuben James* as one that fought it out with the undeclared German foe. If the *Salinas* had only sunk with loss of life she probably would have attained a measure of immortality.[1]

The *Reuben James* Goes Down

At daybreak of the next day, October 31, 1941, the U.S. destroyer *Reuben James* was torpedoed by a German U-boat. She bears the unenviable distinction of being the first and only American warship to be sunk by Hitler's navy during the so-called neutrality period from September 1939 to December 1941. The victim went down about 600 miles west of Ireland, well within the enlarged security zone as extended east by the United States as early as July 7, 1941.[2]

The *Reuben James* was one of a group of five U.S. destroyers, under Commander R. E. Webb, engaged in escorting a fast convoy of forty-four ships sailing at nearly nine knots. Day was just breaking and the escorted ships were not yet zigzagging. Like other eastbound convoys this one was carrying lend-lease supplies to the British Isles.

As chance would have it, the *Reuben James* was stationed about 2,000 yards on the port beam of the convoy. The time was just before dawn, and probably not all of the destroyers were maintaining their nighttime stations but had just begun their daylight patrol. The *Reuben James* was just beginning a turn to investigate a suspicious direction-finder bearing when she was struck by an exploding torpedo on the port side near the Number 1 stack. So violent was the resulting explosion that it blew off the forward part of the ship, as well as the area aft of the Number 3 stack. American naval investigators judged that the torpedo must have ignited the forward magazine.

The wreckage of the *Reuben James* remained afloat for about five minutes. The vessel then sank, to the accompaniment of several exploding depth charges, which killed some of the survivors in the water. The officers and crew numbered about 160 men, and of these only 45 were rescued by other escorts. No officers survived. A persis-

Fitzpatrick in the St. Louis Post-Dispatch

tent search with sonar was quickly undertaken by the remaining
four destroyers, but they failed to make contact with the attacking
U-boat.

The Blame for the Sinking

The *Reuben James* incident occurred only thirteen days after the
Kearny attack. It came only three days after Roosevelt had dramatically proclaimed "the shooting has started" and had reconfirmed
orders to crush the "rattlesnakes of the sea." These were the anxious

weeks when Hitler, preoccupied with the Russian campaign, was ordering his U-boats not to fight U.S. warships unless first attacked. In the case of the *Reuben James* the American destroyer was obviously preparing to fire and the submarine was presumably defending itself against a possible assailant. All this, of course, was de facto war, whatever label Roosevelt might give it.

In this instance, the Germans undoubtedly had international law on their side, or whatever remained that was being honored by the combatants. The escorted convoys of the belligerents and their escorts could legally be sunk on sight and without warning. Roosevelt might invoke freedom of the seas until red in the face, but that concept never gave wartime immunity to the escorts of convoys or to their charges, whether armed or not, whether belligerent or not.

The sinking of the *Reuben James* evidently did not arouse Hitler unduly. In a sense, the U-boat may have acted in self-defense because, in the parlance of western gunmen, the U.S. destroyer drew first by moving to strike. These circumstances may explain why later, in his war-declaring speech, Hitler listed the *Greer* and the *Kearny*, but not the *Reuben James*, as among his numerous grievances against the United States. Nor did he mention the tanker *Salinas*, possibly because she had been fighting back defensively and ineffectually. At all events, the Führer continued to expand the radius of U-boat activity in the North Atlantic, with temporarily disappointing results from the standpoint of the Nazis.

Soft-pedaling the *Reuben James*

Roosevelt met the press on October 31, 1941, at a regularly scheduled conference, later on the day of the *Reuben James* sinking. At the outset he referred to the announcement of the torpedoing from the Navy Department, and noted that he had not yet received any details. Surprisingly, the President next turned to the resignation of Josephus Daniels as Ambassador to Mexico, perhaps to head off embarrassing questions about this most recent sinking. He may have felt that one of the more inquisitive reporters might ask if he was going to continue to try to put his money where his mouth was.

In a short time one of the newsmen wanted to know if "there is any possibility of a severance of diplomatic relations with Germany as a result of these sinkings?" Roosevelt replied that he had not heard "anything about it until you asked the question." The next inquirer asked if, in view of the sinking of a U.S. warship there was "any difference in our international situation?" The President answered, "I don't think so. Carrying out the duty assigned."

After some talk about expanding arms production, one reporter asked the President if he had "any information that German submarines had been sunk," or any other relevant information he could reveal. Roosevelt shot back that if he had, he would not give it out. He then recited a lengthy incident from World War I to prove that enemy morale suffered every time a submarine disappeared mysteriously. In short, he would give out news of the sinking of the *Reuben James* but he would not talk about sunken German submarines. Let the Germans worry.

A curious and persistent journalist then asked if Germany had "any reason to wonder about some of the submarines that have been in contact with our—[Laughter]." Roosevelt then broke in, "Go to a good psychologist."

This press conference revealed so little of substance about the issues discussed that it is not included in the tenth volume of Roosevelt's public pronouncements published in 1950 but is presented in the unabridged public press conferences.[3] There seems to have been nothing in it for Roosevelt to want to cover up; in fact, the essence was published in the press, including the flippant reference to a psychologist. Charles A. Beard, a savage critic of the administration, suggested that Roosevelt declined to make a big issue of the *Reuben James* sinking because he had already "exhausted the possibilities" of "seeking war in the Atlantic by exploiting German 'attacks.' "[4]

A more charitable interpretation is that Roosevelt was aware of the tensions with Japan then building up. Without "enough navy to go round," he was willing to let affairs rock along. His immediate objective was to get the lend-lease materials to England, and this he was doing with armed escorts quite successfully. If war came with Japan, the Japanese would certainly attack British outposts in East Asia. Churchill would then have to send more naval support to the Far East, as Roosevelt would need to do for the Pacific, and lend-lease shipments would have to venture out with less protection.

Candidate Roosevelt and his platform had promised the voters to keep out of war, "except in case of attack." Undeniably, attacks had occurred, but in the cases of the *Greer,* the *Kearny,* and the *Reuben James* the U.S. destroyers had been ordered (at F.D.R.'s direction) into combat situations. There they either had to take the initiative in attacking or be torpedoed and possibly sunk. The opposing U-boat commanders had no choice but to strike first if they hoped to carry out their mission and survive. This dilemma was becoming increasingly clear to American public opinion, especially to the vocal isolationists. As a result, the President could not conceivably wring a declaration of war from Congress on the basis of American attacks or counterattacks. In these circumstances he could best help the British, as Commander-in-Chief, by continuing the unneutrality of escorting convoys to England and fighting off German U-boats.

Roosevelt Prefers Undeclared War

The following week, specifically November 3, 1941, Roosevelt made an extraordinary but much-ignored revelation. If it was as sincere as it appears to be, it casts a flood of light on his conduct of the undeclared war during these troubled months. An inquiring reporter at the press conference remarked, "Lots of people who think just as you do on this war issue, also think a continuance of diplomatic relations with Germany is a form of dishonesty. Could you elaborate your thoughts for background."[5]

Roosevelt replied that he would not speak for general "background" but strictly "off the record." His administration had taken the position that it was "actually and truly only acting in defense. That's all. That is literally true on all the oceans, and various other places. There are a great many other things to support that, that haven't come out."

F.D.R. then alluded to a diplomatic dispatch of that morning that exposed an attempt by Germany to establish itself, by infiltration techniques, "in a funny little place called Liberia." To Roosevelt this move was an "attack" on the United States, because it revealed an intention to locate an air base there, "awfully close to South America."* And other "attacks" against America were developing.

Concluding this delicate discussion, the President declared, with startling directness, "We don't want a declared war with Germany because we are acting in defense—self-defense—every action. And to break off diplomatic relations, why, that won't do any good. I really frankly don't know that it would do any good. It might be more useful to keep them [relations] they way they are." F.D.R. added that he thought "the American people understand it [the situation] pretty well."

---

* One of the authors of the present book, Captain Ryan, was with the United States Navy in Liberia in late October 1940, and can testify that German nationals were active there.

These off-the-record comments, with every evidence of candor, reveal in a nutshell Roosevelt's pre–Pearl Harbor thinking. He did not want war with Japan, for that would interfere with helping Britain and thus defending the United States against Hitler. His main purpose in the Atlantic was to safeguard the Americas by getting lend-lease to England. If this meant continued undeclared war with Hitler, he was willing to keep hostilities at this level.

As anyone could see, Hitler was not in a position, involved as he was with the Russian front, to risk inviting or even initiating declared hostilities with the United States. He might yet suffer the fate of Napoleon in 1812, thus unwittingly contributing to the salvation of Britain. Actually, the winter came early that year in Russia. Late in October—Roosevelt was speaking to the newsmen on November 3—the first snow flurries had fallen on the seas of mud produced by the autumnal rains. Early in November the temperature in Russia dropped below the freezing point.[6]

The *Odenwald* under False Colors

On November 6, 1941, an innocent appearing freighter, the unarmed *Odenwald,* burst into public view. This ship was a German steamer that had been finding sanctuary in Japan since September 1939, the outbreak of war. Yet she was flying the American flag and exhibited on her stern in large letters the words "Willmoto, Philadelphia," which happened to be the name of a legally registered American merchant ship. At the time of her capture, the *Odenwald* was carrying a valuable cargo of baled rubber, American tires (casings and inner tubes), and some food—all told worth an estimated several million dollars. She appears to have been headed for Bordeaux, in Vichy France, from which the rubber and other essentials would presumably have been sent to Germany for Hitler's war machine.[7]

The *Odenwald,* when about two months out of Yokohama, was intercepted by a United States cruiser, the *Omaha,* and a destroyer, the *Somers,* roughly halfway between the Brazilian bulge and the African hump. These waters evidently lay within the security zone proclaimed at Panama in 1939 and twice extended. The two U.S. warships were patrolling the area on the lookout for belligerent warships, particularly German submarines and surface raiders. The objective of the Americans was to restrain the activities of these marauders and report their presence by radio to the Chief of Naval

Operations in such a way that nearby British patrol ships could also pick up the messages or be otherwise alerted.

"Neutral" American warships had no belligerent right under international law to seize a bona fide German merchant vessel as a prize, primarily because the United States and Germany at that time had not yet declared war on each other. But an American warship had a perfect right to investigate if the captain suspected that American laws were being violated.* At first sight the *Odenwald* seemed above suspicion. She was clearly displaying American colors, and her name and description roughly squared with relevant information in *Merchant Ships of the World, 1940,* a manual that U.S. Navy vessels routinely carried. But the *Omaha's* executive officer noted that her stern differed from that of the "Hog Island" merchant ships built at Philadelphia during World War I—and the real *Willmoto* was a "Hog Islander." Doubts were further aroused when the *Odenwald* did not respond to a series of flashing signals. When the disguised freighter was finally challenged by megaphone, the shouted responses came back in a thick German accent.

An armed boarding party was sent over from the *Omaha* but before it reached the *Odenwald* the crew was in the process of throwing bundles overboard, lowering lifeboats, abandoning ship, and hoisting the International Code signal meaning "I AM SINKING. SEND BOATS." Meanwhile the Germans were planting or detonating explosive charges as they opened sea cocks in a frenzied effort to scuttle the ship and thus keep both the *Odenwald* and her valuable cargo out of enemy hands.

The American captors than engaged in heroic salvage operations for about twelve hours, at grave risk to themselves. They neutralized bombs, plugged ruptures in the hull through which water was pouring, and sent down divers who were forced to fight off sharks. The rescuers also "persuaded" the recalcitrant German engineers to start the balky diesel engines. The boarding party then headed their prize slowly, and at risk of being torpedoed by some lurking U-boat, toward the friendly British port of Trinidad, where fuel could be taken on. The final stop was the American harbor of San Juan, Puerto Rico, which was reached after eleven days and some 2,700 miles. The *Odenwald's* crew of forty-five, as involuntary immigrants, were interned with other Germans in one of the established prison camps, already containing hundreds of "guests" from

* The Neutrality Act of 1939 forbade foreign ships to use American insignia or markings on pain of exclusion from U.S. ports for three months. This prohibition, however, was not international law. *American Journal of International Law* XXXVI (1942), 98.

German and Italian merchant ships previously sabotaged in American ports.

In Germany, the *Odenwald* incident had a curious sequel. On November 13, 1941, the Commander-in-Chief of the German navy reported to Hitler, then directing the Russian front, that the "rubber transport *Odenwald*" had been accosted by U.S. Navy forces in the mid-Atlantic and scuttled by her own crew. In pursuance of orders, the ship had been flying the American flag, "as this camouflage was the most suitable in view of the situation so far." Arrangements had been made with the Foreign Office not to lodge a protest with Washington, and orders had been issued that other camouflage was to be adopted at once by vessels in the "sea area in question." This change probably involved the colors of some other neutral.[8]

Losing the *Odenwald* in Court

The irony is that if the *Odenwald* had displayed her German name and had flown German colors, the United States, as a nonbelligerent bound by international law, would not have been able to board and seize the vessel as a lawful prize. But if the ship had retained her real identity, she would have risked seizure by British patrols alerted by radio messages from the U.S. Navy. If the Germans had not been scuttling and abandoning their ship, while calling for help before the boarding party arrived, the Americans would have been legally in the wrong. The flying of false colors was a legitimate ruse of war, dating far back to the days when innocent merchant ships had to deceive belligerent warships. Paradoxically, a libel action was brought by the United States government in a federal court in San Juan. The contention was that the American operation was not one of seizing but of salvaging valuable property that would have been completely lost except for the heroic endeavors of the American officers and men.

After the war had ended, the libel action was challenged by the Hamburg-American Line and its Swiss mortgagees. The federal court in San Juan held that the Americans had engaged in a salvage operation, not a seizure. The decision was handed down on April 30, 1947, and substantially upheld by a U.S. Circuit Court of Appeals. In addition, the judge awarded $3,000 to each of the sixty-seven Navy men comprising the boarding and salvaging party. The sum of $30,000 was also allotted to the United States government as owner of the *Omaha* and the *Somers*, plus $42,212 to the United States for expenses. Further, the members of the crew of the *Omaha* and the *Somers* not participating directly in the boarding operation were granted two months' pay and allowances amounting to approximately $124,211. This case is memorable in that the awarding of prize money to officers and men of the United States was rare; in fact, it had not been done since 1839, that is, 102 years earlier.

This salvage decision was belatedly rendered on April 30, 1947, coincidentally two years to the day after Hitler's suicide and cremation. One should note that the Führer, in making his war-declaring speech, had included the *Odenwald* last in the lengthy listing of ship incidents that he regarded as offensive. He noted bitterly that American "forces illegally seized the German steamer, *Odenwald,* and took it to an American port where the crew was taken prisoner."[9]

If the court of last resort had been that of a victorious Germany the judge might well have ruled that the Americans, then actually (undeclared) belligerents, had sent out the boarding party with the clear intent of seizing the suspicious appearing German ship. In these circumstances the Germans had no choice but to scuttle the *Odenwald* to prevent her and her valuable supplies from becoming useful to the enemy. In German eyes the vessel and her cargo were what may be regarded as illegally captured salvage.

The subsequent career of the *Odenwald* is of interest. Her coveted shipment of much-needed rubber was put to good use by the United States in the declared war with Germany that soon erupted. The freighter itself was renamed the *Blenheim* and taken over by the United States Maritime Commission for repairs. Flying the flag of Panama, she served the Allied cause usefully for the duration of the war.

At the same naval conference of November 13, 1941, Hitler approved a new set of orders for German "surface forces." Engagements with U.S. naval or air components were to be "avoided as far as possible." But as soon as the Americans began to take endangering action, including "shadowing," the German commander "in self-defense" must not be "too late in using his weapons. He is to try to destroy the enemy."[10]

CHAPTER 15

EDGING TOWARD
FULL BELLIGERENCY

The people of America ... believe that liberty is worth fighting for. And if they are obliged to fight they will fight eternally to hold it.

Roosevelt's Armistice Day speech,
November 11, 1941

Unneutral Lend-Lease for Stalin

Another turning point in the undeclared naval war between Roosevelt and Hitler occurred on November 7, 1941, a week after the *Reuben James* sinking. On that day Roosevelt sent a formal authorization to Edward R. Stettinius, recently made Lend-Lease administrator. The new appointee was informed that "in accordance with ... the power conferred upon me by the Lend-Lease Act, I have today found the defense of the Union of Soviet Socialist Republics is vital to the defense of the United States." Stettinius was thereupon authorized to "take immediate action to transfer defense supplies" to the U.S.S.R. in accordance with the Lend-Lease Act and Roosevelt's recent letter to Stalin stipulating $1 billion in credit.[1]

The story behind this announcement is complicated, but the essentials are clear enough. We recall that as soon as Hitler attacked

Stalin on June 22, 1941, Roosevelt promised some aid to the U.S.S.R. and declined to apply the neutrality statute to the embattled Russians, although there certainly was a war on—the most gigantic assault thus far in history. Soviet funds in the United States, plus a considerable quantity of war materiel, were to be made available to Russia through loans, various assets, and direct purchases. But the Russians quickly ran into the same problem that had bedeviled Britain when the dollar supply began to run dry.

At the end of July 1941, about five weeks after Hitler's attack, the President sent to Moscow his intimate adviser, Harry Hopkins, who heard at length from Stalin of Soviet strengths and needs. The American emissary returned with enthusiasm for the capacity of the Soviets to halt the Germans—if aid could be sent in time.

Late in September 1941 another conference was held in Moscow, with Lord Beaverbrook representing Britain and W. Averell Harriman representing Roosevelt. The two negotiators, virtually co-belligerents, signed a supply agreement on October 1 known as the First (Moscow) Protocol. The United States agreed to make available war materiel and other supplies valued at about $1 billion. This was but the beginning of a great outflow that reached the figure of some $11 billion and helped the Russians to repulse Hitler and then to crush him.

Legend to the contrary, Roosevelt did not rush into this fray with substantial lend-lease shipments for the U.S.S.R. He waited until he had good reason to believe, by October 1941, that the Russians had the stamina and will to halt Hitler. Further, no strings were attached to American aid, although Stalin was in such desperate shape that he probably would have been willing to promise good behavior after the war—and almost anything else.

One probable reason for not extorting concessions was that promises made under duress can be even more easily repudiated than those made in good faith. And a crafty Stalin had already demonstrated that he was a master of double-dealing. Besides, the British were eager to help the Russians eviscerate the Germans and thus forestall the postponed invasion of the British Isles. They were even quite willing to share a large part of their lend-lease shipments from America with the Russians, and they did.

When Roosevelt finally associated himself with belligerent Britain to send great quantities of lend-lease aid to the Russians, he was waging undeclared war against Hitler by proxy on a newer and wider front. We are somewhat surprised to find that the Führer, in his war-declaring speech of December 11, 1941, did not complain of lend-lease to Russia, although he did mention Britain specifically and other countries that Roosevelt had deemed essential to the defense of the United States. A part of the explanation may be that only a trickle of war supplies had been shipped in the five weeks or so following the President's public announcement that Russia had qualified for American lend-lease aid.

Roosevelt's association with atheistic Russia as a worthy recipient of lend-lease largesse did not go down well in America, particularly with the large and vocal body of Roman Catholics and isolationists. They also remembered the faithlessness and barbarism of Stalin. We recall that when the Lend-Lease Act was making its way through Congress an amendment had been offered to bar the U.S.S.R. from the list of possible beneficiaries. The proposal had lost in the Senate by a vote of fifty-six to thirty-five.[2] Ex-President Hoover and many others thought it folly not to permit the two bloody-handed dictators to fight to mutual exhaustion, rather than to replace Hitler with Stalin as the world's greatest menace. Hoover favored shunning Russia and sending continuing aid to Britain and China; Colonel Lindbergh preferred an alliance with Britain or even Germany.

Churchill and Roosevelt both believed that the sounder strategy was to take on one menace at a time, and the most dangerous one first. There was still no guarantee that Stalin would not surrender. If his allies did not send lend-lease and mount a diversionary second front, he might be goaded into making a separate peace with Hitler, that is, if a collapse or even a bloody stalemate should eventuate. Some observers have argued, including George F. Kennan, that the United States should have throttled down lend-lease during or before the summer of 1944, when the Russian steamroller began to gain a strong westward momentum. But such a withdrawal, followed by a stalemate, might have resulted in a new Nazi-Communist pact or peace, reminiscent of the short-lived, double-dealing Nazi-Soviet Nonaggression Pact of August 1939. Fears of such a deal, not altogether groundless, persisted during much of the war and played a large part in inspiring the controversial and questionable "unconditional surrender" policy jointly announced by Roosevelt and Churchill at Casablanca in January 1942.

At all events, supplying lend-lease to Soviet Russia before Pearl Harbor supports the truism that war and politics make strange bedfellows. And Roosevelt of his own volition got gingerly into bed with Stalin. Other relevant principles were "any stick to beat a dog" and "the enemy of my enemy is my friend"—that is, a co-belligerent.

Debating Weaker Neutrality

Roosevelt's earlier message of October 9, 1941, urging the arming of American ships and the abolition of the combat zones, meant that he was intending to send American vessels into areas, probably in convoys, in which they would have to shoot or be sunk, possibly both. Many worried Americans did not realize that the nation was already in a de facto war with Hitler's Germany. The German chargé d'affaires in Washington reported that the United States did not have enough guns or gun crews. He added, with what turned out to be remarkable foresight, that Roosevelt sought to limit himself to an undeclared war, leaving a declared war to Germany.[3]

Numerous congressmen were distressed because F.D.R. had harsher words for the dictators overseas than he had for the labor leaders at home, some of whom were seriously hampering, if not crippling, America's needed production of war supplies. "Get John L. Lewis first—then Hitler" was a common sentiment. As a result of all these discontents, the revised Neutrality Act underwent a slow and stormy voyage through Congress, especially the clause lifting the ban on merchant ships entering combat zones.

While the repeal resolution was making some progress, the *Kearny* was torpedoed, with the loss of 11 lives, and the *Reuben James* was sunk, with the loss of about 115 lives. A few senators favored an outright declaration of war; others were vehemently opposed. Senator Brooks of Illinois, a Republican and a war hero, declaimed, "You cannot shoot your way a little bit into war any more than you can go a little bit over Niagara Falls."

Finally, on November 7, 1941, the Senate approved repeal by the reasonably comfortable margin of fifty to thirty-seven. This was a measure sponsored by a Democratic administration, so only six Republican senators voted aye, whereas twenty-one voted nay.[4] The margin of victory was smaller than it had been on any other major proposal involving foreign policy since the outbreak of war in 1939. The vote indicated, among other drawbacks, that partisanship was still deeply embedded in foreign policy and that any attempt to get a declaration of war against Hitler would either fail or reveal to the world a dangerously divided country.

The House of Representatives was even more of a hurdle. It bitterly resented the attempt of the President to pull the strongest teeth out of the Neutrality Act, and it continued to be greatly annoyed by Roosevelt's velvet-glove approach to the labor leaders. Strikes were snarling up America's lagging production efforts at a time when an all-out effort was needed, not only for the home front but also for the British. Many nervous citizens felt that Roosevelt, reneging on his campaign promises, was striving to drag the United States, screaming and kicking, into a war for which she was shamefully unprepared. Others believed that the British were scheming to have the Americans do their fighting for them, while refusing to launch a second front that would pull German divisions off Stalin's back.

Many noninterventionists were unwilling to concede that the British—bruised, battered, and fighting alone until Hitler attacked Stalin—were unable to open a second front across the English Channel. Representative Charles L. South of Texas declared in Congress that the United States should tell England that the Americans are "sorry for you" and will continue to send help, but "get in there and fight like hell yourselves for a while and then we will see, what, if anything else, ought to be done."[5]

F.D.R. Promotes Repeal

Roosevelt may well have had in mind giving a boost to the languishing revision in Congress of the Neutrality Act when he spoke at Arlington National Cemetery at a ceremony commemorating Armistice Day, November 11, 1941. His general theme was that in World War I the United States had fought to save the world from German autocracy. The Allies had won, and consequently the present generation had no real remembrance of the dangers it had escaped. But Americans now understood better because they could see what had happened when human freedoms were engulfed by the new Nazi tyranny. Specifically, there were the enslaved peoples of France, Czechoslovakia, Poland, Denmark, Holland, Serbia, Belgium, and Greece. (He might have said that the much-cursed German Kaiser, when compared with Hitler, was an upstanding Christian gentleman.)

Roosevelt then declared that the men who had died in World War I had not sacrificed their lives to make the world safe for democracy and decency "for five years or ten or maybe twenty." It was now America's responsibility, as it was theirs, to make sure, in Lincoln's words, "that these dead shall not have died in vain." Liberty, freedom, and democracy were "prizes awarded only to those peoples

who fight to win them and keep fighting eternally to hold them."
Americans of 1941 believed that "liberty is worth fighting for. And if
they are obliged to fight they will fight eternally to hold it." This
was a duty that the American people owed not to themselves alone,
"but to the many dead who died to gain our freedom for us. . . ."[6]

The thrust of Roosevelt's message was that the liberties Americans had fought for and won would have to be "eternally" fought
for, as the American people were then doing with their current undeclared hostilities. The United States might even have to do so
again, although the President was not that blunt, in a declared war
with Hitler's Germany.

But the neutrality revision continued to be stalemated in Congress. On the evening of November 12, 1941, Speaker Sam Rayburn
and House Majority Leader John W. McCormack addressed a letter
to Roosevelt saying that some members of the House had asked
what effect a failure to pass the neutrality revision would have on
the nation's relations abroad, "especially in Germany."

Roosevelt's answer by letter was to the point. As for arming
American merchant ships, this precaution was necessary because of
"the continued sinking of American flag ships in many parts of the
ocean."* As for entering the combat zones (under convoy), time and
money could be saved by not having to transship cargoes to other
carriers, thus increasing the quantity of supplies being sent to "those
nations fighting Hitlerism." Moreover, the Congress and the President had together taken action (through lend-lease) to strengthen
the supply lines "of those who are today keeping Hitlerism far from
the Americas."[7]

If the proposed revision of the Neutrality Act should fail, Roosevelt declared, the position of the British, Chinese, and Russians
would be weakened with regard to "food and munitions." Such a
failure would "cause rejoicing in the Axis nations" and encourage
aggressions by Germany and other "aggressor" nations "under the
leadership of Hitler." The three Axis powers could only applaud this
evidence of the disunity in the United States that "they have so
often prophesied." The nation's "struggle against aggression" would
be "definitely weakened" not only in the dictator nations but among
the sister republics of the Americas. Friends and enemies alike would
misinterpret America's "mind and purpose."

Roosevelt ended his letter by announcing that the next day he
would hold a conference in the hope that "strikes and stoppages of

* The sunken U.S. merchant ships legitimately flying the American flag were three:
Steel Seafarer, Robin Moor, and *Lehigh.*

work," especially among John L. Lewis's coal miners, would be reduced. Such obstruction by labor, combined with Roosevelt's failure to take aggressive action, had generated much bitterness in Congress, some of which was directed at the revision of the Neutrality Act.

A Victory for Unneutrality

Later on the same day that Roosevelt wrote this letter, November 13, 1941, Speaker Rayburn laid aside his gavel to plead with the House of Representatives for affirmative action. During the course of his remarks he read the response that he had requested of the President. A few minutes later the House voted to remove the remaining major restraints in the existing Neutrality Act, notably the arming of merchantmen and the honoring of combat areas. The date, one should note, was three weeks before Pearl Harbor.

The roll call in the House was uncomfortably close, 212 to 194. Partisanship was blatant, with 137 Republicans opposing the modification and only 22 approving it. Alarmingly, not as many Democrats voted affirmatively as had supported the Lend-Lease Act. But if one may judge from the public opinion polls, the head count in Congress did not faithfully represent public sentiment.* The real issue on Capitol Hill was badly fuzzed by discontent with Roosevelt's allegedly soft-handed treatment of labor disruptions. These in turn were related to the fear that the United States might be plunged into war before she had her economic house in order and before she had increased production to meet American and Allied need.[8]

Despite the closeness of the vote, the significance of the repeal was widely recognized. The *New York Times* regarded this action by Congress as the most important decision "made in this country since the beginning of the war." The *London Times* welcomed "the greatest contribution to the defeat of Hitlerism since the passing of the Lend-Lease Act."[9] Friends of the revision hailed the reversal as a return to the traditional policy of "freedom of the seas." To a degree this was so, but freedom of the seas in the days of Presidents Madi-

---

* A Gallup poll (November 5, 1941) showed that of those with opinions 81 percent favored arming American merchant ships and 14 percent opposed. Similarly, the carrying of war materiel into the danger zones to Britain was approved 61 percent to 31 percent. *Public Opinion Quarterly* VI, 162, 170.

son and Wilson did not involve arming "neutral" ships to fire at belligerent warships approaching to ascertain the victim's identity. Nor
did freedom of the seas authorize armed merchantmen to join convoys that were being escorted by warships of the United States or
declared belligerents.

The earlier and quieter administrative decision to escort both
American and belligerent shipping was more alarming than the repeal legislation in what it portended for a shooting war on the high
seas. This escorting of convoys would inevitably lead to shooting incidents, as it already had in the cases of the *Greer,* the *Kearny,* the *Salinas,* and the *Reuben James.* Roosevelt seemed to be saying, "We'll
have peace even if we have to fight for it—without a formal declaration of war."

Yet the American people could not have been altogether blind,
including not only those who had supported repeal but also the narrow majority in Congress who had passed it. Many citizens must
have known or strongly suspected that modifying the Neutrality Act
would inevitably lead to more numerous shooting incidents in the
undeclared war. If the vote in Congress on a deneutralized neutrality act could be this close, how could that body ever pass a declaration of war against Hitler's Germany, even though an undeclared
war had been going on almost from the beginning? Fortunately for a
united United States, the Führer would react to American provocations with a declared war when it suited his purposes to do so—and
no sooner.

This view was confirmed by the government-controlled Nazi
press and by Hitler himself. After the *Kearny* torpedoing, October 17,
1941, the Nazi press accused Roosevelt of having rigged a "clumsy
swindle" to promote the passage through Congress of the proposed
revision of the Neutrality Act. On October 3, 1941, a month after
the *Greer* incident, Hitler delivered a lengthy speech on the war
against the Soviet Union, and made only tangential references to the
United States. On October 18, the day following the Senate vote on
revising the Neutrality Act, he publicly confirmed secret orders
when he shouted, "President Roosevelt has ordered his ships to
shoot as soon as they sight German ships. And I have ordered German ships, upon sighting American vessels, not to shoot but to defend themselves as soon as attacked. . . . If, therefore, an American
ship shoots . . . it will do so at its own peril. The German ship will
defend itself, and our torpedoes will find their mark."[10] This they
had already done during the engagements with the *Kearny, Salinas,*
and *Reuben James.*

Halting Hitler in Dutch Guiana

Roosevelt's last major defensive-offensive thrust at the Führer before the Pearl Harbor assault was his announcement from the White House, on November 24, 1941, that American armed forces would be sent to Surinam, better known as Dutch Guiana. This tropical area, adjoining Brazil, would need about 3,000 American soldiers to hold it.

Dutch Guiana was valued then, as today, for its priceless deposits of bauxite, a strategically important ore from which aluminum is made. In 1941 this area was supporting about 50 percent of the American aluminum industry, including some 65 percent of the requirements of the wartime aircraft industry that was aimed at Germany. American military leaders, notably General George C. Marshall, greatly feared that these South American bauxite mines would be crippled by sabotage or by Hitlerian raids of some kind. Ruinous attacks by land, sea, or air on this defenseless colony were envisaged by American military planners, and there were rumors of airstrips being prepared by Nazis or Nazi sympathizers in nearby Brazilian jungles. As the White House correctly stated, this supply of bauxite was "vital for the defense of the United States, the Western Hemisphere, and the nations actively resisting aggression [by Hitler]."[11]

The occupation of Dutch Guiana by American troops involved complications, as had that of Greenland and Iceland. When the Nazis overran the Netherlands, Queen Wilhelmina had fled to England, where she had established a government-in-exile, complete with a cabinet. Her initial reactions favored Roosevelt's cablegramed overture suggesting a joint occupation of Dutch Guiana. But she stipulated that Dutch sovereignty be properly respected and that the U.S. forces be promptly withdrawn when the war ended. The Dutch cabinet in exile raised a number of objections, including possible reprisals at home by the Nazis against the already mistreated people of the occupied Netherlands. For various reasons, the cabinet also objected to the American proposal that Brazilian troops be invited to participate. After considerable delay, a compromise was reached by which Brazil would safeguard her side of the border of Dutch Guiana, while sending only a liaison mission into the colony.

The official joint announcement of agreement on all sides came on November 24, 1941. The partial inclusion of Brazil was a clever sop to the Latin Americans, who harbored painful memories of the repeated and protracted landings by United States Marines in the so-called banana republics. The official release concluded by saying that Washington "has notified the governments of the American Republics of the foregoing arrangements which have been reached in the interests of all."[12] Such assurances were in the spirit of the Pan-American conferences at Panama in 1939 and especially Havana in 1940.

Reactions in Latin America to the Yankee occupation of a part of Dutch Guiana were characterized by "calm realism," according to an analysis made on December 5, 1941, by the State Department.[13] Mostly there was silent consent, not to say indifference, together with some expressions of satisfaction. Surprisingly little criticism was voiced by those nations of Latin America, such as Argentina and Brazil, in which the influence of German and Italian immigrants was strong. Evidently the spirit of Havana, buttressed by Hitler's aggressions, had taken deep roots, strengthened as it was by the knowledge that Uncle Sam had long played the role under the Monroe Doctrine of a hemispheric watchdog barring further intrusions by European powers.

By contrast, the American chargé in Berlin reported that the agreement regarding Dutch Guiana had provoked much front-page commentary in the German press. This coup was described variously and lengthily as "Roosevelt's military aggression against South America"; as the springboard for an American seizure of Dakar on the western bulge of Africa; as a violation of the Atlantic Charter; and as a flouting of the Havana agreement with the Latin American republics. This "seizure" of the bauxite mines was but one step in America's new course of "aggressive imperialism." The Brazilian guards near the border, in the view of one German writer, were there to protect Brazil, not Dutch Guiana, from further "Yankee penetration."[14] There can be little doubt that the Nazi press interpreted the Dutch-American agreement as a military-diplomatic setback for Hitler, and this was what Roosevelt intended.

Exposing America's Secret War Plans

On December 4, 1941, three days before Pearl Harbor, the rabidly isolationist *Chicago Tribune* published the confidential war plans of the United States. The headlines—the largest thus far used by the *Tribune*—blared "F.D.R.'s WAR PLANS!" Below in smaller letters were the words, "Goal Is 10 Million Armed Men; Half to Fight in the AEF" (American Expeditionary Forces). This "scoop" has been called one of "the most famous in the history of American journalism."[15]

All major military powers, as well as some minor ones, draw up "contingency plans," that is, precise procedures to be followed in the event of war with some likely foe or combination of foes. Such exercises rank high among the preoccupations of military staffs and war colleges. They serve roughly the role of fire extinguishers in buildings. Otherwise one would have to improvise half-baked plans if war should come, and this starting from scratch would impose damaging if not insuperable burdens. As an angry Secretary of War Stimson asked, "What would you think of an American General Staff which in the present condition of the world did not investigate . . . every conceivable type of emergency which may confront this country . . . ?"[16]

The war plans were undoubtedly authentic. They had been drawn up in response to an order from Roosevelt, dated July 9, 1941, to explore "at once the over-all production requirements required to defeat our potential enemies." The resulting proposal envisaged the drafting of over ten million men into the armed forces, and a joint American-British invasion of the European continent, on July 1, 1943, with a force of some five million men. Now, for the first time, the public learned of the fruition of the Plan Dog scheme, secretly worked out in the United States with the British military leaders early in 1941, and this policy was reaffirmed in the leaked secret plans of defeating Germany first "while holding Japan in check." The conclusion was reached in this sensational document that Britain and Russia together could not defeat Germany, and that an American expeditionary force of huge dimensions was needed to accomplish that task.

Secretary of War Stimson questioned "the patriotism of a man or a newspaper that would take those confidential studies and make them public to the enemies of this country." This information doubtless "would be a gratification to our potential enemies." Secretary of the Interior Ickes believed that charges of treason should be brought against Colonel McCormick, owner and publisher of the *Chicago Tribune*. Attorney General Biddle stated that this isolationist newspaper had violated the Espionage Act, while Secretary Stimson urged vigorous prosecution. But nothing was done because Pearl

2 CENTS
PAY NO MORE!

F★★INAL

THIS PAPER CONSISTS OF
THREE SECTIONS—SECTION ONE

Chicago Daily Tribune

THE WORLD'S GREATEST NEWSPAPER

VOLUME C—NO. 290 C

THURSDAY, DECEMBER 4, 1941.—46 PAGES

PRICE TWO CENTS

IN CHICAGO
AND SUBURBS

1899 U.S PAT OFFICE COPYRIGHT 1941
BY THE CHICAGO TRIBUNE

F. D. R.'S WAR PLANS!

GOAL IS 10 MILLION ARMED MEN; HALF TO FIGHT IN AEF

Proposes Land Drive by July 1, 1943, to Smash Nazis; President Told of Equipment Shortage.

BY CHESLY MANLY.
[Chicago Tribune Press Service.]
Washington, D. C., Dec. 3.—A confidential report prepared by the chief of staff and more hack [illegible]

THE STRONGHOLD OF PEACE

THE MIDDLE WEST

REDS BEGIN NEW DRIVE TO BREAK VISE ON MOSCOW

Strike at Nazi Line South of Leningrad.

BULLETIN.
Berne, Switzerland, Dec. 4 (Thursday)—A special bulletin from Moscow early today announced present [illegible]

LEIBER TRADED TO GIANTS; CUBS GET BOWMAN

The Chicago Cubs early this morning traded Hank Leiber, the Chicago outfielder, to the New York Giants for Bob Bowman [illegible]

HOUSE ADOPTS DRASTIC BILL TO BLOCK STRIKES

Goes to Senate on 252-136 Vote.

BY WILLIAM STRAND.
[Chicago Tribune Press Service.]
Washington, D. C., Dec. 3.—The house of representatives, by a vote of 252 to 136, to [illegible]

NEWS SUMMARY
of The Tribune

[Details on sports pages.]

Harbor came three days later and blasted the isolationists into silence. Not until twenty-one years after the event did Senator Burton
K. Wheeler, probably the most vituperative and influential isolationist in the Senate, reveal in his autobiography that he had leaked
the War Department's secret plans to the press.[17]

Colonel McCormick's unauthorized publication of the nation's
top secrets was only a short-lived sensation, but these imaginative
plans made their publisher look downright treasonable. The leakage
revealed the lengths to which the isolationists were prepared to go in
those tense December days to avert a formal clash with Germany. If
Hitler had not declared war first, there is little doubt that the isolationist senators would have made a desperate effort to block a war
resolution in Congress. Senator Wheeler undoubtedly would have
been among the foremost in opposition.

Stalemate in the Atlantic

Critics of Roosevelt who charge that he was eager to plunge into all-
out war at the time of Pearl Harbor overlook one essential fact. He
was already deeply involved in an undeclared shooting war with
Hitler that had featured pitched battles between four U.S. Navy
vessels, on the one hand, and at least four different German U-boats,
on the other. He was willing to let the informal fighting in the North
Atlantic drag out indefinitely in this informal fashion without a formal declaration of war on either side.

Roosevelt was thus achieving his main goal, which was to protect the flow of lend-lease supplies to Hitler's enemies, primarily
Britain and secondarily Russia. He could tangle with no more submarines on the North Atlantic route than he then was doing, even if
there had been a declared war. Hitler was bent on interrupting the
shipping of supplies and Roosevelt was equally determined to block
such interference. The task of getting materiel to Hitler's enemies
was proceeding without intolerable losses, in fact no heavier than
Hitler's slowly expanding fleet of U-boats was then capable of inflicting, declared war or no declared war. Only after the conflict
broke out into the open did the toll taken by German submarines
become truly frightening, including the wholesale destruction of
American coastal vessels.

At the time of Pearl Harbor, as earlier noted, the United States
armed forces were woefully unprepared for effective operations
against Hitler by means other than the escorting of lend-lease car-

goes. A declaration of war would require the diversion of supplies from American needs to those of the British and the Russians. In fact, some military experts, both American and British, reasoned that the United States could best help the embattled Allies by remaining nominally neutral. The Americans could continue to send military supplies then being manufactured at home for an army that had not yet been drafted, trained, and prepared for transportation to Europe.

CHAPTER 16

THE PACIFIC BACK DOOR
TO WAR

Yesterday, December 7, 1941—a date which will live in infamy—the United States of America was suddenly and deliberately attacked by naval and air forces of the Empire of Japan.

Roosevelt's war message,
December 8, 1941

Sons of the Rising Sun

One of the strangest features of Hitler's war—a war of epochal contradictions and surprises—is that the big blowup did not occur in the North Atlantic, where naval warfare was being desperately fought between destroyers and U-boats. Instead, the explosion came in the faraway Pacific, most spectacularly at Pearl Harbor. Here the Japanese burst onto the scene as undisguised foes, thus enabling the United States to throw off the mask of "neutrality" or "nonbelligerency."

Germany, Italy, and Japan were then categorized in the democratic world as have-not aggressor nations, all needing or claiming to need "living space." The heavily populated German Reich had been divided, mutilated, and truncated by the Treaty of Versailles in 1919. As for the overpopulated homeland Japanese islands, they presented the prime example in East Asia of a have-not nation on the rise. In 1914 Japan had honored her alliance with Britain and had declared war on Germany. Fighting primarily in her own interest, she had seized German holdings in the Shantung peninsula of China and had taken over Germany's scattered but strategic islands in the Pacific.

The Japanese, like the Italians, were bitterly disappointed by the partitioning of territorial spoils at Paris, where President Wilson had not been unduly friendly to their aspirations. They were finally dislodged from Shantung in December 1922, and they never received outright the German Pacific islands that they had captured. Instead they were forced to accept the outposts as a mandate of the League of Nations, while binding themselves not to fortify their booty. Yet in the 1930s Tokyo clamped tight security regulations on the mandated islands, thus triggering accusations of having erected clandestine fortifications. In any event, United States troops certainly encountered fortified resistance in their bloody assaults on these outposts after the Pearl Harbor attack.

Birds of a feather roost together, and thus the three major have-not powers—Germany, Italy, and Japan—formally joined hands in the Tripartite Alliance on September 27, 1940. The compact was scheduled to last ten years, and it bound each member to come to the aid of the other two should one of them be "attacked by a power [U.S.A.?] at present not engaged in the European war or in the Sino-Japanese conflict."[1] Not only were these three Axis powers in the have-not category, but they were all expansionist, militaristic, and ruled by dictators or, in the case of Japan, by a military clique that dominated the Emperor's government. These were the three nations that President Roosevelt repeatedly castigated as "the dictator powers" in his public addresses and fireside chats.

In some respects, Japan surpassed Hitler's Germany as an aggressor nation, as a flouter of treaties and international law, and as a general bad example. In 1931 the Japanese militarists had quickly overrun China's resource-rich province of Manchuria, and then had turned it into the puppet state of Manchukuo. This coup was in flagrant violation of the Covenant of the League of Nations, of the Four Power Treaty of 1921, of the Nine Power Treaty of 1922, and of the Kellogg-Briand Pact of 1928. The toothless League of Nations, by trying to force Japan out of Manchuria, merely succeeded in forcing her out of the League of Nations in March 1933—a precedent that was not lost on Hitler. The fast-rising Führer became Chancellor in January 1933 and then proceeded to outdo his Oriental exemplars as a breaker of treaties and a violator of international law.

The Dictators Draw Together

In 1932, the year after the Manchuria coup, the Japanese warlords launched a savage attack on China's Shanghai. Five years later came Japan's full-scale assault on the Chinese (declarations of war were now going out of style) and this bloody but futile attempt at conquest dragged on for four long years. The Sino-Japanese conflict then merged with the larger declared war that followed the assault on Pearl Harbor and other far-flung outposts.

As this complex clash developed during the 1930s in the Far East, several basic facts stood out like Mount Fuji. To the Japanese, Russia was a hereditary foe that had voracious designs on the same Manchurian territory that Japan had recently wrested from China. In 1938 and 1939 major Russo-Japanese battles were fought on the Manchurian frontier, as a result of which the Japanese were soundly beaten.[2] The lesson was driven home to the Japanese warlords that an invasion of bottomless Soviet Siberia would not be easy pickings.

Not only was Stalin a thwarter of Japanese aspirations but he was joined in this troublesome role by Uncle Sam. The background reaches far into the past, but one turning point was in 1931, when the United States joined the other powers in exerting pressure on Japan to pull out of Manchuria. American sympathy instinctively went out to China, an oversized underdog, but still an underdog. After the full-fledged Chinese war erupted in 1937, invading Japanese soldiers destroyed American missionary property and abused American men and women in "strip and slap" incidents.

Most spectacularly, on December 12, 1937, Japanese aircraft bombed and sank the U.S.S. *Panay,* a gunboat of the Yangtse patrol. This vessel, gaudily marked with American colors, was attacked near Nanking in broad daylight. For good measure, the assailants also machine-gunned the fleeing survivors; two Americans were killed and some thirty were wounded during the melee.[3]

Significantly, the *Panay* was the first U.S. Navy ship to be sunk in the decade before Pearl Harbor. It was destroyed not by German submarines but by Japanese aviators. The explanation appears to be that the Japanese military, as in Manchuria in 1931, took the bit in their teeth and acted without authorization from the government in Tokyo. As everyone could see, the militarists were gradually forcing themselves into the saddle. The shocked nominal government of Japan promptly apologized, offered hollow excuses, and paid an indemnity of $2,214,000. As a consequence, the American public, never greatly aroused, quickly cooled off.

Roosevelt, it seems, was not far from the mark when he branded Germany, Italy, and Japan (but not Soviet Russia after Hitler's incursion) as the "dictator powers." This characterization seemed especially apt after the Big Three bound themselves together in the ten-year Tripartite Alliance. As far as Roosevelt was concerned, both China and Hitler-assailed Russia were deserving of American lend-lease and other aid in their fight against the Axis aggressors. In both cases the President stubbornly declined to proclaim the existence of a war. By this dodge he avoided an application of the Neutrality Act of 1939, and thus was able to provide financial assistance and military supplies to the two greatest nations that were resisting the Axis powers.

Honor may exist among thieves, but there was precious little among the Axis dictators. The Berlin-Tokyo relationship was never close. When Hitler made his sensational deal with Stalin in August 1939—the curtain raiser for World War II—the Japanese were even more appalled than the Americans, and they lost much face. The Russians now would have a freer hand to attack the Japanese in Manchuria or elsewhere in East Asia. The Japanese were deeply offended because they felt that the Hitler-Stalin bargain undercut the anti-Russian, anti-Comintern pact that Hitler had already negotiated with Tokyo in November 1936. But much was forgiven when the Japanese, amid popping champagne corks in Berlin, formally allied themselves with Germany and Italy in the Tripartite Alliance on September 27, 1940.

The Japanese finally got sweet revenge for the Hitler-Stalin sellout of August 1939 when, on April 13, 1941, they negotiated with Stalin (behind Hitler's back) a five-year neutrality pact. Each party solemnly agreed to respect the "territorial inviolability" of the other and to remain neutral if the other were attacked by a third power. The signing took place on the eve of Hitler's stupendous assault on Russia, at a time when Stalin was obviously seeking to safeguard his rear against Japan in the face of the widely predicted invasion of

Russia by the Nazis. For their part, the Japanese would now have less to fear from an attack on their Manchurian flank by Stalin. They would also have some insurance against a bombing of the highly flammable Nipponese cities from the Russian base at Vladivostok, to say nothing of Soviet submarine activity in Japanese waters. We may again note in passing that Stalin never violated this formal compact; he merely gave legal notice of its termination, April 5, 1945, preparatory to launching his overwhelming attack on the weakened Japanese forces in Manchuria and Korea on August 8, 1945.[4]

Prelude to Pearl Harbor

We recall that the Tripartite Alliance of 1940 became operative only when one of its three members suffered from aggression by a fourth power. If Stalin had launched the massive attack of June 22, 1941, on Hitler, instead of the other way around, Germany doubtless would have called upon the other members of the alliance to honor their obligation. Mussolini joined Hitler anyhow, but Japan, the third partner, felt no call to tangle with the Russians, especially since Tokyo was then placing considerable reliance on the Russo-Japanese Neutrality Pact. As an indication of the self-serving nature of the Tripartite Pact, the Japanese were kept completely in the dark regarding Hitler's plan for an all-out assault on Russia.

In the showdown negotiations before Pearl Harbor between Secretary of State Hull and the two Japanese envoys, the Tripartite Alliance of 1940 was a major bone of contention. As Hull reveals at length in his memoirs, and as the official documents confirm, the United States was especially eager to induce the Japanese to promise that they would not help Hitler by honoring the Axis alliance. If a declared war with the Nazis should erupt, the Americans feared that the Japanese would regard the United States as the aggressor. In fact, Japan would not have required much logic chopping to reach that conclusion if she had wanted to. The destroyers-bases deal and the Lend-Lease Act, among other flagrant violations of neutrality, could easily be interpreted as prior acts of aggression.

On the eve of Pearl Harbor the Tripartite Alliance occupied a prominent place in the minds of the American negotiators, along with the demand that the Japanese pull their troops out of China, while abandoning their incursion into French Indochina. But the best that Secretary Hull could extract from Ambassador Nomura was that Japan would interpret the treaty in the light of what she regarded as her best interests.[5] She ultimately did just that.

In Tokyo the Japanese military clique could not bear to lose face by pulling out of China after prolonged, costly, bloody, and stalemated warfare. The Mikado's minions had conquered and occupied an enormous expanse in the coastal region of China. But they were now bogged down and were having to contend with guerrilla resistance in the areas nominally conquered. In 1937 Nationalist China had relocated her capital deep in western China at Chunking, and was receiving a trickle of American lend-lease aid over the famous but hazardous road from British Burma. Understandably, Generalissimo Chiang Kai-shek was bitterly disappointed by the smattering of outside assistance that he was receiving.

At one point in November 1941, Washington was preparing to offer the Japanese a three-month's modus vivendi (Roosevelt preferred six months) that would more or less preserve the status quo pending further negotiations. But Chiang Kai-shek, getting wind of the scheme, raised such a fuss that Winston Churchill deplored the "thin diet" China was getting. The whole project was then dropped, partly in the belief that it would damage American prestige and morale, and partly out of fear that a spurned China might patch up peace with the Japanese. The Western democracies wanted the Chinese to keep on pinning down as much of Japan's military strength as possible.

There is, moreover, little reason to think that Tokyo would have been willing to accept the proposed modus vivendi, primarily because of the delay involved. Time was not on Japan's side. If the Japanese militarists were going to fight the United States with any real hope of success, they reckoned that they would have to strike on or before December 7, 1941, and the most recent American offer, an unacceptable one, was dated November 26 (Tokyo time), the day the Japanese task force left its rendezvous for Pearl Harbor. Further delay would have meant the onset of the worst winter weather, and the limited oil supply was sinking by the day, owing to Washington's "big freeze" of July 25, 1941, accompanied by British and Dutch embargoes. Why not destroy the American fleet at Pearl Harbor and thus prevent it from interfering with Japan's southward expansion until such time as the Japanese had conquered as much of East Asia as they wanted? Then they could dig in behind their fortifications (including those on the mandated Pacific islands) until such time as American public opinion decided that the foreseeable results were not worth the cost of further fighting. (This is about what happened when a war-weary United States pulled out of Vietnam in 1973.)

The Puzzle of Pearl Harbor

The dropping oil gauge and the ticking time bomb finally drove the Japanese warlords to the madness of Pearl Harbor. The U.S. Pacific Fleet was crippled by a diabolically clever tactical stroke that succeeded beyond all reasonable expectations, although at that critical time the three priceless aircraft carriers happened to be absent on operational missions.

The authorities in Washington had broken Tokyo's principal secret code, and they knew that a strike was imminent somewhere, obviously in Southeast Asia. American officials were also receiving reports of large numbers of Japanese troop transports moving from French Indochina down the southeastern coast of Asia, headed presumably for British Malaya or Thailand, possibly both.[6]

Putting two and two together, Washington came to the eminently logical conclusion that a blow was going to fall somewhere in Southeast Asia. So confident were the American leaders of the impregnability of Pearl Harbor—their "Gibraltar of the Pacific"—that they judged the Japanese incapable of mounting so devastating an attack with efficiency and secrecy over such a vast expanse of water. Certainly the Americans did not dream that the reputedly clever Nipponese would be stupid enough to do the one thing above all others that would unite the isolationist-divided American people against them—and the other dictators.

Some of the more extreme postwar revisionists, notably Charles A. Beard, have strongly implied, if not actually stated, that Roosevelt deliberately and temptingly exposed the Pacific Fleet at Pearl Harbor. The President allegedly hoped and expected that the Japanese would fall into this bloody trap and enable him to go before Congress and ask for a declaration of war that otherwise could not be passed.

There is no credible evidence to support this conspiracy thesis, and there is much remorseless logic to refute it. We have noted that American military and naval intelligence did not believe that the Japanese, either technologically or physically, were capable of pulling off such a surprise attack over such a distance. And one does not bait and set a trap for polar bears in the Sahara desert. Roosevelt loved ships, and he had a special fondness for the doomed vessels bombed on December 7, 1941—some of them had been built under his watchful eye while he was Assistant Secretary of the Navy from 1913 to 1920.

If an all-out shooting war had to come, in the Atlantic or the Pacific, Roosevelt wanted the onus to fall on the enemy for having struck first. Secretary of War Stimson, a close presidential adviser, wondered how the United States could "maneuver" the Japanese into "firing the first shot without allowing too much danger to ourselves."[7] But Stimson certainly did not have Pearl Harbor in mind; perhaps he envisioned something like another *Panay* incident. Roosevelt's course actually presents an interesting parallel to what Lincoln had done on the eve of the firing on Fort Sumter, and this similarity Stimson also noted in his diary. Lincoln, like F.D.R., did not want a real shooting war, but he was determined that if one came, the Southerners should bear the onus of having fired the first shot. Roosevelt's purpose was put bluntly in the official war warning radioed to General MacArthur in the Philippines (November 27, 1941): "If hostilities cannot comma repeat cannot comma be avoided the United States desires that Japan commit the first overt act. . . ."[8]

Roosevelt did not welcome war with Japan, primarily because such a conflict would hamper his program of supplying and escorting lend-lease materiel to Hitler's foes—his major objective during those eventful months. He had already detached about one-fifth of the Pacific Fleet for inadequate patrols or escort duty in the Atlantic, and he complained that he did not have "enough Navy to go round." Actually, in the months before Pearl Harbor the Pacific Fleet was left with fewer ships *in every combat category* than the Japanese navy. If a shooting showdown had to come, F.D.R. certainly did not want it to erupt before he had managed to build up a formidable force of long-range bombers in the Philippines as a threat to vulnerable Japanese cities. General Marshall was then rushing more B–17s to their base at Clark Field on Luzon.

Roosevelt was neither a wholesale murderer nor a lunatic—and over 3,400 American men died or were wounded at Pearl Harbor. He was keenly aware that he would go down in history—and he did not relish the thought of going way down. If a President schemes to lure his enemies into a trap, he will want to win, not lose, the ensuing conflict. And how does one win a war against a powerful enemy navy by arranging to have one's weakened Pacific fleet substantially destroyed on the very first day of that war?

Provoking American Wrath

At the time of the Pearl Harbor assault in 1941, the country, as in 1861, was still badly disunited. The isolationist pack was in full cry. About 80 percent of the American people, as the polls repeatedly showed, wanted to keep out of a full-dress war, although a somewhat smaller majority favored aid to the victims of the dictators, even at the risk of war.[9] Neither the Germans nor the Japanese, both Axis

RISING AS ONE MAN: The day of Pearl Harbor. *Orr in the* Chicago Tribune, *1941. Reprinted, courtesy of the* Chicago Tribune.

allies, could conceivably have done anything that would better have united a disunited nation than to bomb Pearl Harbor. "The only thing now to do," growled the bitter-end isolationist, Senator Wheeler, "is to lick hell out of them."

The Japanese succeeded so spectacularly in arousing the American people by their "sneak attack" that attention was diverted from the Hitlerian menace. A cry went up to "get Hirohito first," together with all other treacherous "Japs." They had hit below the belt, without a warning declaration of war, as sanctioned by international law, and while they were deliberately dragging out diplomatic negotiations in Washington as a smokescreen.

Oddly enough, the Japanese, after having run roughshod over international law and treaty obligations as early as 1931, had been making an attempt to observe the conventional procedures. Their formal negative answer to the last American note was to have been presented to Secretary Hull in Washington at 1 P.M., only a short time before the scheduled assault (7:50 A.M. Honolulu time). There would then have been no opportunity to send an adequate warning to the defenders of Pearl Harbor.

As events turned out, the Japanese Ambassador in Washington arrived for his appointment more than an hour late because of the slowness of his staff in decoding a lengthy dispatch from Tokyo. The presentation of the final Japanese diplomatic response came only a few minutes after Secretary Hull learned of the attack in Hawaii, and Japan lost what little credit she may have gained by trying to abide by at least the spirit of international law. There in his office Hull berated the two Japanese envoys for their treachery, bad faith, and double-dealing, ironically while their intercepted and decoded dispatch lay before him.[10] The Emperor formally declared war on the United States several hours after the attack began.

Germany Joins Japan

The Führer, unaware in advance of the secret Japanese blow, may have been more surprised by the Pearl Harbor bombing than Roosevelt himself. The American President at least knew that something big and unpleasant was about to burst, presumably in Southeastern Asia. At all events, Hitler was delighted by the humiliation of the "Jewish tainted" Americans—the worst naval defeat in their glorious history. He was also pleased by the prospect, which was partially realized, of seeing American military and naval strength diverted to the Pacific. One immediate result was that Roosevelt would be able to deploy fewer warships to the Atlantic for anti-submarine warfare. Likewise, much potential lend-lease materiel would have to be retained in America and channeled into the dangerously belated preparedness program.

Technically, Hitler was not bound by the defensive Tripartite Alliance of 1940 to come into this war on the side of the Japanese, for they had obviously struck the first blow at Pearl Harbor. But Tokyo did not have to make excuses because Hitler—not renowned as a man of honor—chose to honor his new and expanded Tripartite commitment.

Secret German documents, now declassified, reveal that the Führer, as early as April 4, 1941, some eight months before the Pearl Harbor attack, engaged in a secret and lengthy conversation with Foreign Minister Matsuoka of Japan. The interchange took place in Berlin. An official record of the conversation reveals that "the Fuehrer declared that if Japan got into a conflict with the United States, Germany on her part would take the necessary steps at once. It makes no difference with whom the United States first came into conflict, whether it was with Germany or Japan. . . . Therefore Germany would . . . promptly take part in case of a conflict between Japan and America, for the strength of the allies in the Tripartite Alliance lay in their acting in common. Their weakness would be in allowing themselves to be defeated separately."[11]

In the early days of December 1941, the attackers of Pearl Harbor were already steaming toward Hawaii. The Japanese ambassadors in Berlin and Rome, acting under urgent instructions from their superiors in Tokyo, frantically sought to persuade the unsuspecting German and Italian foreign offices to honor the Tripartite Alliance, even if Japan struck first. The Japanese cleverly pointed out in these conversations, with more than a hint of blackmail, that Washington was bringing great pressure to bear on them, as was true, to abandon the Axis alliance.

The German Foreign Office, unwilling to lose a powerful ally, was surprisingly agreeable to the Japanese proposal of joint action against the United States. But Foreign Minister Ribbentrop had to wait two days before he could reach Hitler and secure his assent. Ribbentrop evidently received it, for on December 5 (two days before the attack at Pearl Harbor) he wired to the German Embassy in Italy the draft of an agreement. It proved to be fully acceptable to Mussolini, the third party. Article 1 read, "In case a state of war should arise between Japan and the United States of America, Germany and Italy for their part will also immediately consider themselves to be in a state of war with the United States and will carry on this war with all of the powers at their command."[12] Japan would be similarly obligated if Germany and Italy should become involved in a war with the United States. When the agreement was flashed to Tokyo, several minor changes in the wording were suggested, but on the day of Pearl Harbor, December 7, the revised pact remained unsigned. Four days later Hitler announced it to the world at the end of his war declaration.

Hitler was no fool, though a fanatic, and he must have realized that he had been tricked by the clever Japanese. They had hastily negotiated a change in the Tripartite Alliance that would drag Germany and Italy into the war against the United States, all the while keeping the two other Axis nations in the dark. Nothing was even hinted about the powerful task force then steaming to blast Pearl Harbor and plunge America into the war. Clearly the Japanese could not be trusted. Yet a duped Hitler overlooked this glaring act of bad faith, probably because he desperately wanted Japan in the war on his side. Among other considerations, the Russian invasion was now proceeding disastrously, and he evidently hoped (in vain) that he could rely on the (unreliable) Japanese to attack the U.S.S.R. from the rear in a two-front war, that is, if he acted generously toward them.

Hitler's faith was badly misplaced, and he probably would have been more skeptical if he had acquired a better knowledge of history. In World War I the Japanese had declared war on Germany and had joined the Allied cause, but most of their "help" consisted of a self-serving conquest of German holdings in China and among the islands of the western Pacific. Any assistance that the Japanese were to give the Allies in western Europe, even if recognizable, was incidental to their own dreams of conquest.

Hitler Declares War

The German chargé d'affaires in Washington had meanwhile been instructed to present the text of a note from Berlin to the Department of State on December 11, 1941, 3:30 P.M. German time (9:30 A.M. Washington time). This communication would precede Hitler's much longer speech that day. The Führer evidently did not want the United States to beat him to the punch by declaring war on Germany first, for the original draft of Berlin's instruction to the chargé read, "We want to avoid absolutely the American government's stealing a march upon us by taking a step of that kind." For some reason or reasons not clear, these warning words were crossed out but the motive that gave voice to them evidently remained.

Berlin's official war-declaring note began by saying that the United States, "having violated in the most flagrant manner and in ever increasing measure all [?] rules of neutrality in favor of the adversaries of Germany . . . has finally resorted to open military acts of aggression."[13] (Ribbentrop did not concede that such violations of neutrality by the United States as had occurred were regarded in America as counterviolations of international law by Hitler.)

The Nazi note then referred to Roosevelt's speech of September 11, 1941 (after the *Greer* affair), in which he had announced that he had given orders in effect "to shoot on sight at any German war vessel." (This speech, which had not used the phrase "shoot on sight," had referred only to Axis raiders in areas "we deem necessary for our defense. . . .") The German indictment further charged that in a subsequent speech, delivered October 27, 1941 (Navy Day), Roosevelt "once more expressly affirmed that this order was in force." (He did say "shoot on sight.")

American warships, the note from Berlin continued, "have systematically attacked German naval forces." The list included the *Greer,* the *Kearny,* and the *Reuben James,* all of which "have opened fire on German submarines according to plan." (In all three of these cases the German submarines were either attacking or counterattacking.)

American warships were next accused of acting under government orders "contrary to international law," for they had "treated and seized German merchant vessels on the high seas as enemy ships." (This grievance probably referred to the *Odenwald,* a German freighter under false American colors, although it may have meant liners like the *Columbus,* which American destroyers had shadowed and identified by radio for nearby British warships.)

Nazi Germany, the Berlin note concluded, had "strictly adhered to the rules of international law in her relations with the United States" (not so in the cases of the *Robin Moor,* the *Lehigh,* and the *City of Flint*). Yet America, starting with violations of neutrality, had "finally proceeded to open acts of war against Germany. It has thereby virtually created a state of war."

Tokyo's Bloody Blunder

At Pearl Harbor the Japanese had gambled heavily—and lost in headlong kamikaze style. Hitler, who joined the Japanese Emperor in a declaration of war on the United States, also gambled and lost.

Japan made the lethal mistake of uniting the United States and silencing the isolationists by the great "victory" at Pearl Harbor. In retrospect, as a triumph it was worse than a defeat—and besides it was needless. Once Tojo and his fellow generals had decided on war, the great problem facing Japan was the dropping oil gauge. Yet the Dutch East Indies had ample oil, and if the Japanese had struck there instead of Pearl Harbor they presumably could have satisfied this need. A declaration of war against Japan could hardly have passed Congress in response to an attack on one of the centuries-old bastions of Dutch imperialism.

The Japanese could better have staged their Pearl Harbor only at Manila in the Philippines. In fact, they did strike there, catching General MacArthur with his bombers down and neatly lined up for destruction. He had already been advised of the attack on Pearl Harbor some eight hours earlier but his subordinates had not taken adequate precautions, so he claimed.[14]

Even an armed invasion of the Philippines by Japanese troops might not have been enough to get a declaration of war through Congress past isolationist hatchets. To Americans, the Philippines had been a bothersome financial liability since 1899. The Filipinos were then in the process of winning their complete independence (finally achieved in 1946) and were more a foreign country than "good old American soil." Many an isolationist would cry, why die for these "little brown brothers" who themselves had killed American soldiers from 1898 to 1902—and even longer sporadically?

The attack on Pearl Harbor, though a smashing success, was a hollow victory for the Japanese. Hawaii should have been left undisturbed, as we assess Japan's interests from the vantage point of hindsight. Superficially, the blow was a master stroke, but two priceless aircraft carriers of the fleet were then out of the harbor on a special mission and a third was in the California area. Left intact were the huge oil tanks, the Navy Yard, drydocks, and the submarines in port—all later indispensable in fighting the Pacific war.* Of

---

* One of the present authors, Captain Paul B. Ryan, a career Navy officer, experienced this attack at first hand.

course, the Japanese strategy was to immobilize the Pacific Fleet so that the conquests in East Asia would not be blocked and the Japanese could dig in and defy the world. But even this strategy was so faulty as to inspire further doubts as to Japanese cleverness.

As far as December 1941 was concerned, the American Pacific Fleet was already partly immobilized by distance, and consequently the backfiring surprise party at Pearl Harbor was completely unnecessary. An axiom in naval circles then held that a battleship fleet, with necessary supply ships, could not operate effectively more than 2,000 or so miles from its base—and Southeast Asia is more than 4,000 miles from Pearl Harbor. The westward route lay past the fortified Pacific islands, with their bomber-based airfields, including the Marshalls, the Marianas, and the Carolines.

Pearl Harbor—A Blessing in Disguise

We recall that at the time of the Pearl Harbor onslaught about one-fifth of the Pacific Fleet had been withdrawn for the Battle of the Atlantic, leaving the remainder second best to the Japanese navy—both on paper and in Japanese waters. We have also noted that Roosevelt complained of not having naval strength "to go round" and that Admiral Stark spoke of "butter spread thin." If the Japanese had not attacked Pearl Harbor and had merely declared war, contenting themselves with an aerial raid on Manila, what would have happened? "On to Tokyo" was the cry that would have burst from the throats of many red-blooded American patriots, and pressure would have mounted to send the American fleet out into deep Japanese home waters. Late in 1934 Japan had renounced the Washington Naval Treaty of 1922 (effective in 1936), which had given her the small end of a 5–5–3 ratio in capital ships, and was busily designing bigger battleships with eighteen-inch guns. In the western Pacific from the Carolines and the Marshalls to Formosa and Indochina, Japanese land-based aircraft patrolled the sea lanes. The forces of the Emperor would have been more than a match for anything that the United States could have sent across the wide Pacific.

The U.S. Navy, lacking adequate combat ships and supply vessels, as well as air cover, was incapable of halting a Japanese invasion of Southeast Asia, even before the losses at Pearl Harbor. Late in 1941 Churchill, we remember, had unwisely sent out two powerful new fighting ships, the *Repulse* and the *Prince of Wales,* which were based at Singapore. Without proper aircraft cover, they were both sunk at sea, with heavy loss of life, three days after Pearl Harbor. This was not Churchill's "finest hour."

In addition to uniting a badly divided America, Japan unintentionally conferred an immense favor on the United States by sinking or damaging the eight U.S. battleships in an area adjacent to a major navy yard rather than in the deep waters of the western Pacific. Six of the eight were patched up or refloated, repaired, and reconditioned. They lived to help carry the war ultimately into Japanese waters.

If the Japanese gambled and lost with their Pearl Harbor strategy, Hitler gambled and lost when he (with Mussolini) rather surprisingly honored his prior commitment to Japan and declared war. The Führer, in a sense, unwisely conferred an immense favor on the United States (as the Japanese had done at Pearl Harbor) by taking the decision out of American hands. The Japanese, German, and Italian declarations of war ended all possible indecisiveness, disunity, and delay, both in Congress and out. If the Axis powers were united in war against the democracies, the United States was even more united and aroused—though far from adequately prepared.

Hitler's Losing Gamble

In weighing the pros and cons of a declaration of war on the United States, Hitler probably found them fairly close to balancing out. His hatred of the "Jewish-sustained" Roosevelt and the "Judaized" United States may even have tipped the scales. At least one suspects as much in reading the lengthy and undiscriminating list of grievances that the Führer piled up against the United States in his accusatory war speech. He was tired of being called names and held up to scorn in the blistering messages and fireside chats of the hated Roosevelt. He resented having had his hands tied by the Russian campaign, now badly bogged down. Yet Stalin might yet be flattened, now that the tricky Japanese were in the war. They could stab the Russians in their Siberian back and siphon off American and British strength.

On December 14, 1941, one week after Pearl Harbor, Hitler was still happy over the turn of affairs. He ceremonially bestowed on General Oshima, the Japanese Ambassador in Berlin, the Order of Merit of the German Eagle, for which distinguished foreigners were eligible. This was the same honor that Colonel Lindbergh had received in 1938, and it was awarded to Oshima in recognition of services rendered "in the achievement of German-Japanese cooperation."[15] Hitler evidently was not yet fully aware that a treacherous Japan had virtually blackmailed him into such cooperation. Nor did he seem to realize that he had made the fatal error of taking on an enemy with unlimited resources for an ally with severely limited resources.

As for future cooperation with Japan, Hitler had gambled and lost. Despite repeated German suggestions, requests, and pleas, the Japanese stubbornly pursued their own aims, which, as in World War I, differed sharply from those of their allies. To tackle Russian armies in chilly Manchuria was not appealing, especially in view of previous humiliating border clashes. Much more alluring were the richer and warmer pickings to the south, especially in oil-blessed Indonesia.

So each of the Three Musketeers of the dictator world—Hitler, Hirohito, and Mussolini—ignored the device of Dumas's three heroes: "All for One, and One for All." Each was looking out for number one, and each went down to defeat by himself. So much for honor among dictators.

CHAPTER 17

THE FÜHRER FIGHTS BACK

Since the beginning of the war the American President, Roosevelt, has been guilty of a series of the worst crimes against international law....

Hitler's war speech to the Reichstag,
December 11, 1941

Congress Declares War

On December 8, 1941, the day after the Pearl Harbor catastrophe, Roosevelt appeared before Congress to deliver his war message against Japan. In marked contrast with President Wilson's lengthy war address in 1917 and with Hitler's long-winded harangue to the German Reichstag three days later, Roosevelt's speech lasted only six and a half minutes, though interrupted by frequent bursts of applause. The upshot of his message was that the United States had been attacked on a wide front, ranging from the Philippines, Guam, Wake Island, and Midway Island to Hawaii. The major blow at Pearl Harbor had come on "a date which will live in infamy," and while peaceful negotiations were going on, "at the solicitation of Japan," without any hint of an attack. In concluding, Roosevelt asked Congress to declare that "since the unprovoked and dastardly attack" a state of war "has existed between the United States and the Japanese Empire."[1]

A realistic Congress, though often lethargic in the past, moved with such speed that it passed the recommended war resolution with only one dissenting vote. The time was exactly thirty-three minutes after the President had ended his address. This resolution declared that because the Imperial Japanese government had "committed unprovoked acts of war" against the United States, the state of war thus "thrust upon the United States is hereby formally declared. . . ."[2]

We should note, in partial defense of the Japanese militarists, that they did not regard their action as unprovoked. By the big economic freeze and embargo of July 25, 1941, the United States, joined by Britain and the Netherlands, had pushed the Japanese to the wall. They would either have to come down off their high horse, bend the knee, and lose face intolerably or "go for broke." They chose to burst out. In doing so they evidently believed that the United States had "thrust" the war on them, rather than the other way around. Yet as far as the Japanese generals were concerned, they were eager to extricate themselves from the quagmire in China by winning easy and glorious victories to the south.[3]

In his fireside chat of December 9, 1941, two days after the Pearl Harbor assault, Roosevelt declared that "the sudden criminal attacks perpetrated by the Japanese . . . provide the climax of a decade of international immorality."[4] He further charged that, "Powerful and resourceful gangsters have banded together to make war upon the whole human race." (This category obviously included Hitler, who took sarcastic note of the President's choice of words in his memorable anti-Roosevelt speech two days later.) The United States, the President proclaimed, was fighting alongside "other free peoples" in an effort "to maintain our right to live among our world neighbors in freedom and in common decency, without fear of assault." The course that Japan had begun in Manchuria in 1931 now "paralleled the course of Hitler and Mussolini in Europe and in Africa."

To fill out the indictment, Roosevelt listed the numerous attacks "without warning" in Europe and North Africa by Hitler and Mussolini. In the case of Hitler, his victims included fourteen countries, ranging from the Führer's occupation of Austria in 1938 to the invasion of Russia in June 1941. The international "gangsters" were involved in conquests "all of one pattern." But during these later years the United States had gained valuable time by building up American war production machinery so that it could be used to help the defense of any nation "resisting Hitler or Japan. . . ." There was no "security" for any country or person "in a world ruled by the principles of gangsterism." War "conducted in the Nazi manner is a dirty business."

Roosevelt continued by saying that "your government" had learned of German pressure on Tokyo to attack the United States; otherwise Japan would not share in the division of the spoils when peace arrived. Hitler had allegedly promised the Japanese that if they "came in" they might have "the complete and perpetual control of the whole of the Pacific area. . . ." Roosevelt was either misinformed or deliberately distorting the truth. Hitler had earlier urged Japan to stab Russia in her Siberian rear, but he had not held out any special inducements to the Japanese warlords to strike American possessions, much less Pearl Harbor. As we have noted, Hitler was as much surprised as Roosevelt, perhaps more so.

Concluding his historic fireside chat, the President soberly told the American people that "Germany and Italy, regardless of any formal declaration of war, consider themselves at war with the United States at this moment just as much as they consider themselves at war with Britain or Russia." (This accusation was coming rather close to an unofficial declaration of war by the President.) Finally, America would fight a war to make the world, not safe for democracy, but "safe for our children." The nation would be ill-served if she eliminated a dangerous Japan and "found that the rest of the world was dominated by Hitler and Mussolini."

Hitler's War Harangue

On December 11, 1941, four days after Pearl Harbor and two days after Roosevelt's accusatory fireside chat, Hitler delivered his virulent war address to his puppet Reichstag in the Kroll Opera House of Berlin. This effort was plainly a one-sided justification of Germany's declaration of war, designed to arouse the anger and support of the German people.[5]

Near the outset of the speech, and throughout it, Hitler spat out his insults at Roosevelt, "the main culprit of this war." The President liked to make his chats from the warm fireside, "while our soldiers are fighting in snow and ice. . . ." Among other sins, Hitler charged, Roosevelt had been responsible for the outbreak of World War II. As questionable documents captured in Warsaw proved to the Fuhrer's satisfaction, this man, "with devilish lack of conscience," had encouraged the Poles to reject a reasonable German proposal for negotiations during the crisis of 1939.

Hitler then undertook to compare Roosevelt with himself, insultingly and to his own advantage. Both leaders had come to power early in the same year, 1933. Roosevelt was committed to the New Deal and Hitler to the new National Socialism. Roosevelt was a child of the rich, such as democracy spawns; Hitler was a child of the poor, and had been forced to fight his way to the top through hard work. (Actually, during several years of his young manhood he was a hungry and penniless vagabond.) When World War I came, Roosevelt had kept his comfortable desk job; Hitler had fought from the outset as a common soldier and had come out of the conflict as poor as when he entered.

After the war, Hitler further charged, Roosevelt had made profits through speculation and inflation, feeding on the miseries of the millions, while Hitler and hundreds of thousands of others had lain on hospital beds. An aristocratic Roosevelt, with all his silver-spoon advantages, had stepped boldly onto the stage of politics, while an unknown Hitler was battling for "the resurrection of his people." When Roosevelt became President, he served as head of "a capitalist party," while the Fuhrer was head of the Socialist Nazi movement that he had himself created. The White House "brain trust" consisted of the very elements that Hitler had fought against. They were the kind of "parasites," Jewish of course, that he had attacked and removed from public office in Germany.

Yet Hitler, as he noted, was a spectacular success and Roosevelt a flat failure, although both had come into high office early in 1933. Chancellor Hitler had rejuvenated Germany by heroically solving her economic problems and ending unemployment, while President Roosevelt had not brought about "the slightest improvement." The New Deal was "the biggest failure ever experienced by one man," partly because the President was a creature of "the Jewish element." He had no choice but to divert attention from his domestic failures by the hoary trick of stirring up wars abroad. He would at the same time interconnect American interests with those of some European belligerent (Great Britain) in such a way as to revive his own economy and bring his nation closer to the conflict.

Roosevelt's attitude toward the Reich, Hitler complained, had become especially hostile in 1937, when in a Chicago speech he urged a "quarantine" of the aggressor nations (including Germany). Further insults had led to the withdrawing of ambassadors from both countries, ultimately leaving only chargés d'affaires. The American President had directed his efforts toward sabotaging appeasement policies in Europe, as the recently captured Polish archives had allegedly revealed. Various maneuvers in Washington had included Roosevelt's "clumsy" and insulting appeal, dated April 15, 1939, urging Hitler and Mussolini to give pledges of nonaggression regarding the listed free countries of Europe.

Roosevelt's Unneutral Sins

Hitler continued by saying that after the invasion of Poland in 1939, Roosevelt had engineered a repeal of the Neutrality Act so that the United States could one-sidedly send arms to the so-called democracies. (Before then the law had unneutrally favored the dictators.) The speaker then berated Roosevelt for having formally recognized the various governments-in-exile, especially that of Poland, after they had fallen victim to the Führer's fury. F.D.R. had given further offense by freezing the assets of these governments, thus snatching their rich treasures from the lawful hands of the Reich. More than that, in August 1940, the President had entered into a joint military arrangement with Canada, an open belligerent in the war against Germany.

Surprisingly, Hitler gave only slight attention to the destroyers-for-bases deal of 1940, and did not brand it, as he might well have done, a gross violation of international law. He also made only scant mention of the epochal Lend-Lease Act, which he regarded as evidence of the President's "hatred for socialist Germany." Soft-pedaling the significant and emphasizing the inconsequential, he listed by name the seven German merchant ships, notably the great liner *Columbus,* most of which had been treacherously shadowed by American warships and then had been forced to scuttle themselves to avoid capture by the enemy. In somewhat the same category Hitler included all (three) German ships in American harbors that had been unneutrally requisitioned by the "neutral" United States government (March 1941).

Hitler then turned to more important grievances, particularly the aggressive naval and military presence of the United States in the North Atlantic, including the takeovers of Iceland and Greenland. He referred rather offhandedly to the "attacks" by the *Greer* and the *Kearny,* but he omitted entirely the more serious sinking of the *Reuben James* by a U-boat.

As for Roosevelt, Hitler declared that he would "pass over the insulting attacks" on himself personally. He would ignore the President's having called him "a gangster"—a term growing out of gangsterism in America, not Germany. He could not "be insulted by Roosevelt, for I consider him mad, just as Wilson was." The American President had incited war with Japan, all the while wrapping himself "in a cloak of Christian hypocrisy." The German people viewed with "deep satisfaction" the daring sneak attack of the Japanese, who had long been mocked by Roosevelt in the prolonged negotiations in Washington with Secretary Hull.

Roosevelt's policy, Hitler further charged, was aimed at "unrestricted world domination and dictatorship." Ever since the beginning of the war the American President had committed a "series of the worst crimes against international law. . . ." Roosevelt had finally ordered the American navy everywhere to attack ships "under the German and Italian flags," and to sink them—in gross violation of international law (which Hitler had so often flouted). The "everywhere" was actually in areas where the German warships were menacing the shipment of American supplies to Europe.

The Führer next referred to the recent exposure by the *Chicago Tribune* of the U.S. War Department's top-secret contingency plans on December 4, 1941, three days before Pearl Harbor. These proved, he charged, that Germany and Italy were to be attacked by invading American troops by 1943, at the latest. By this sensational revelation, Hitler maintained, Roosevelt's schemes had been "frustrated," in spite of unbearable provocations.

In a wildly applauded peroration, Hitler read the terms of the new three-power agreement, supplementing the existing Tripartite Pact and signed that very day in Berlin. The trio of dictator nations agreed to fight "the common war" in the "closest cooperation" and they avowed their "unshakable determination not to lay down arms until the joint war against the United States and England reaches a successful conclusion. . . ." In short, no separate peace.

Hitler Places Trust in Japan

We have previously observed that if a full-dress war had to come, Roosevelt wanted the dictators to declare it. His luck held, for Japan, Germany, and Italy all obliged him by acting first.

On December 8, 1941, the day after Pearl Harbor and Japan's declaration of war on the United States, Congress honored Roosevelt's recommendation and voted a counter-declaration of war. The

tally in the Senate was 82 to 0; in the House, 388 to 1. The one negative vote came from Jeannette Rankin of Montana. As a feminist-
pacifist and a model of consistency, she had voted against war with
Germany in 1917. On December 11, 1941, the same day Germany
and Italy declared war, the House and Senate responded in kind
without a dissenting vote in either chamber. This time Representative Rankin voted "present."

Obviously, if Hitler (and Mussolini and Japan) had not declared war on the United States first, a war resolution could hardly
have passed Congress, at least at that time. If it had, it surely would
have come only after dangerous delay and a divisively partisan debate; it would have fully reflected the vehement views of a large and
militant minority of isolationists. Many members of Congress would
have argued that the United States already had a real war on its
hands, so why take on two more foes? The Japanese were the real
enemy, for they had delivered a smashing blow below the belt at
Pearl Harbor. The Germans and the Italians had not committed a
remotely comparable outrage. The Russians and the British could
now bleed Mussolini and Hitler to death, while the Americans
would have their hands more than full in avenging the disastrous
setback at Pearl Harbor. The most popular slogans of the hour were
"Get Hirohito First" and "Remember Pearl Harbor," even though
most nations like to forget their most humiliating defeats.

Hitler was a consummate gambler, one of the most successful in
history—up to a point. This time he took a chance when he declared
war on a reluctant United States—and lost. We recall that by the
terms of the original Tripartite Pact he had not been obligated to
fight as an ally of Japan if the Japanese were the aggressors. Japan's
frantic renegotiation of this pact, even after the deception of Pearl
Harbor, must have caused Hitler serious misgivings, but he did not
show them or act on them.

As a gambler, Hitler did not enjoy having his hand forced. Previously he had made his daring moves in his own good time, not
Japan's, from the occupation of Austria and Czechoslovakia to the
assault on Russia. He obviously preferred the ups and downs of the
undeclared war against Roosevelt until he actually had Russia by
the throat. He was painfully aware that only a few days before Pearl
Harbor a Soviet counter-offensive had begun to drive his frost-bitten
troops back from the gates of Moscow, thereby foreshadowing an icy
catastrophe.

Yet the clever Japanese bargainers had made one issue clear to
Berlin. The Americans, in laying down terms for a Japanese-Ameri-

can agreement, had urged Tokyo to forsake Hitler and the Tripartite Pact—the very alliance that Hitler had crafted to restrain and
contain the United States. The Japanese, for their part, sought frantically to strengthen the treaty with firmer commitments. Hitler did
not want to lose his Far Eastern ally, whom he was counting on to
attack Russia in the rear. So he consented to the revised treaty and a
declaration of war on the United States—in writing. Better a pre-
mature ally than no ally at all—or so it seemed. Better the United
States as an open enemy than Japan as a lost friend.

Hirohito and Hitler: Strange Bedfellows

Hitler rather liked the Japanese, who had taught the European dictators that the League of Nations and supporting treaties could be
flouted with impunity when the Mikado's troops had crashed into
Manchuria in 1931. The Führer, as well as Mussolini, greatly admired Tokyo's enterprise and daring in plotting and then engineering the sneak attack at Pearl Harbor, especially at a time when
Hitler's troops, now fading before Moscow, badly needed a victory
to boost drooping German morale. What the Japanese had done was
boldly Hitleresque—the kind of foul blow that he liked to strike
with maximum devastation and in disregard of treaty promises and
international law. Roosevelt's "day of infamy" was to the Nazis a
day of jubilation.

The Führer was also eager to have the Japanese continue to
stab bothersome Uncle Sam in the back in the Pacific. With their
powerful army in Manchuria (Manchukuo), they would also
threaten the Soviets in the rear, thereby pinning down Russian divisions in Siberia that were needed to repulse Hitler's forces in frozen
eastern Europe. The rising flood of lend-lease materiel then going to
Great Britain and also to Russia would have to be slowed, because a
Japanese-American war would suck a large part of these supplies
into the Pacific theater.

Similarly, Japan would drain off British strength—in merchant
ships, warships, and manpower—as the Japanese attacked Hong
Kong, British Malaya (Singapore), Burma, India, Australia, and
New Zealand. But all of these prizes the Japanese were probably
going to garner anyhow. Then why should Hitler declare war on the
United States and take Roosevelt off the hook with the noisy
isolationists?

The Führer evidently reasoned that by joining hands with the war-bent Japanese he could more easily obligate them to attack the Russians from the rear, something he had earlier and unsuccessfully attempted to induce them to do. He seems to have hoped that Japan would abandon or at least soft-pedal any contemplated advances southward. As events turned out, the Japanese were deaf to these pleadings and proddings, as they had been to his earlier ones. They fought their own war and ultimately went down to defeat in their own way. Hitler should have suspected as much when they were so secretive about the impending blow at Pearl Harbor while renegotiating the Tripartite Pact. But to Hitler, the gambler, a generous gesture toward Japan was worth a try and, if successful, might enable him to crush the Soviets in a two-front war. The supreme irony is that the Tripartite Pact, which the Führer had designed to keep the United States out of the war was, with his quiet assent, so amended as to bring the United States in.

As an extravagant admirer of Wagner, Hitler had something of a Götterdämmerung complex. He thought big, succeeded big, and then failed big—in the flaming pyre of Berlin. With the three Axis powers standing foursquare against the only remaining major power not officially at war, he felt that he had everything to gain—and to lose. The dignity of great nations required that they strike first, not wait on events, as Roosevelt was obviously doing. As Hitler said in his post–Pearl Harbor speech, he was grateful "to Providence that it entrusted me with the leadership in this heroic struggle," which for the next millennium would be described as "decisive" in world history.[6] He evidently believed or hoped that by standing together like brothers the three Axis powers would gain greater strength and prestige from one another. He might fail, but it was better to go down in history as a Nero than a zero.

Hitler's grandiose fantasies were apparently inflamed by this exalted self-image. He could make 1941 the year in which he proclaimed war to the death with the two archenemies of human survival: international Communism (Soviet Union) and international finance capitalism (the United States). Both of them were the tools of "international Jewry."

The Führer also seems to have been impressed by the current belief that in 3,000 years the Japanese empire had never lost a war. How could the Axis, with Imperial Japan, a loyal member, lose this one? Hitler evidently had not learned that the United States had never really lost a major war—at least not up to this time.

Despite his mercurial temperament, Hitler had shown remarkable forbearance when American warships were attacking or counterattacking his U-boats, but by the time of Pearl Harbor he was
losing patience. His admirals had been urging him persistently to
take off the wraps and end these long months of humiliation and
frustration. At the time of Pearl Harbor the U-boats were supposed
to be torpedoing only American warships that attacked them as escorts of convoys. Following an open declaration of war, the U-boats
were promptly ordered to sink freely and without warning all
American vessels, merchantmen or warships, encountered anywhere
on the high seas. These included the coastal waters of the United
States, where the hunting was fantastic.[7] In short, the Americans
were already aiding the British and the Russians as much as they
could, and a declaration of war would seriously cut back on lend-
lease supplies. There was no point in waiting for the United States to
intervene at her convenience.

Hitler's Blind Bargain

The Führer was not far from the mark in his estimate of Japanese
naval strength as of December 1941. Actually, the Imperial Navy
was much more powerful than the combined Allied fleet in the Pacific—the American, the British, and the Dutch. This arm of
Japan's fighting force was tough, well trained, and to a high degree
ready for combat, especially in Asian waters. Before the end of the
war the Japanese had two of the largest battleships in the world,
both equipped with monstrous eighteen-inch guns. But no navy is
stronger than its high command, and none can succeed in the long
pull without a firm industrial base. These necessary foundations
proved to be weak, especially when compared with those of the
United States, and ineptitude characterized the strategy with which
the Japanese navy was directed, that is, after Pearl Harbor.[8]

Hitler's declaration of war was undoubtedly made more satis-
fying to him by his animosity toward the United States. A month
after Pearl Harbor (January) the Führer told his associates at military headquarters that America was a "decayed country" with
problems of race and "social inequalities." He went on to say that
"my feelings against Americanism are feelings of hatred and deep
repugnance. . . . Everything about the behavior of American society
reveals that it's half Judaized, and the other half negrified. How can

one expect a State like that to hold together ... a country where everything is built on the dollar?"[9]

Chancellor Hitler made the fatal mistake of overrating Japanese strength and underrating that of the United States. He was too much concerned with what he regarded as the lack of discipline and the "Jewish clique" that ran the country. While he was restraining his U-boats in the North Atlantic, he could remember that the Kaiser's Germany had forced an aroused United States into World War I in 1917. He had been a soldier on the Western Front when the flood of American doughboys reached France full of fight, there to help boost the weary Allies to victory. In the afterglow of Pearl Harbor Hitler forgot or brushed aside the lesson he had once learned so painfully in the trenches. Evidently, the catastrophic defeat of the unwary Americans in Hawaii on that Sunday morning had caused him to overestimate Japanese fighting prowess, particularly that of the Imperial Navy.

Hitler, a common foot soldier in World War I, was land-minded. He thought primarily in terms of millions of troops and thousands of tanks, and of fighting fronts hundreds of miles in length. Franklin Roosevelt, former Assistant Secretary of the Navy in World War I, was sea-minded. He thought primarily in terms of ships and seaplanes, of sea lanes and seaborne supply lines, of defensive fighting against submarines—all combined with small-scale amphibious operations, notably the landing of U.S. Marines in Iceland. Fortunately for his "limited war" with Hitler, operations by sea were much more palatable to the American voters than the prospect of again sending "millions" of "boys" to the hell pits of Europe. Roosevelt was thus able to ease throught the back door of a naval war with Hitler without arousing the opposition of a majority of the American people.

Hitler obviously hated Roosevelt, the Hyde Park aristocrat. His personal feud evidently dated back to at least 1937, when Roosevelt, in a "mean" speech in Chicago, urged a "quarantine" of the dictators, including the Führer.[10] Hitler no doubt relished the thought, as an ally of Japan, of humiliating Roosevelt. This happy prospect may have weighed just enough to tip the scales for what appears to have been a disastrous blunder—declaring war on a United States that otherwise would have been torn by disunity and doubt in debating a formal declaration of hostilities.

CHAPTER 18

THE FINAL JUDGMENT

We are now at war. We are fighting in self-defense. We are fighting in defense of our national existence, of our right to be secure, of our right to enjoy the blessings of peace.

Roosevelt's message to Congress on relations with Japan, December 15, 1941

International Banditry

About three years after Hitler perished in the flaming ruins of Berlin, a German student showed up at Stanford University. Clad in the well-worn leather knee pants (lederhosen) so common in Bavarian Germany, he attended a lecture in American diplomatic history relating to the Hitler-Roosevelt confrontation. At the end of the presentation, the visiting German approached the lecturer and complained, "Why didn't you leave us alone? We had nothing against you. We were not attacking you. The affairs of Europe were our affairs, not yours. Why did you butt into something that was none of your business?"

The lecturer patiently responded by using the analogy of the thug who enters a bank brandishing a loaded pistol. He is merely going about his business of robbing banks. All he wants is to be let alone so that he can grab the cashier's money and reach his getaway car without pursuit. To be sure, this is only one bank, but if bandits meet with no resistance or pursuit, all banks will be in jeopardy, including the one in which any innocent bystander may have deposited his money.

Even before Hitler attacked his neighbors and threw non-aggression treaties and international law into the boneyard of history, he had launched outrageous attacks on humanity, which would of course include Americans. On April 1, 1933, two months after Hitler became Chancellor, the new Berlin government began a national boycott of all Jewish businesses and professions. By ugly degrees came the gas-chambered Holocaust and its six million or so Jewish victims, plus about as many more non-Jews.

Hitler was an iron-nerved poker player who began with small stakes but gradually raised the ante to the point where his opponents had to fold their cards and drop out of the game—or fight. He had laid bare his hemispheric ambitions in *Mein Kampf,* but they were so fantastic as to seem to be the ravings of a jailed lunatic, and they gained little credence for "the funny little man with a Charlie Chaplin mustache." The period of so-called appeasement was often likened to a group of survivors on a raft being pursued down a river by a ravenous crocodile. The weaker members were being thrown overboard in the vain hope that they would appease the pursuing monster. Hitler's appetite plainly increased with eating, as he evidently developed an Alexander-the-Great complex.

When the Führer branded as absurd any accusation that he had designs on the United States, American interventionists simply refused to believe him. But his reputation as a liar was too firmly established by his rapacity, preceded by the blueprint for conquest in *Mein Kampf.* When a confirmed glutton swears off engorgement, only the naive will take him at his word.

War by Indirection

There can be little doubt that a bitter personal feud between Hitler and Roosevelt lay behind the open clash. Even before the Führer attacked Poland he had cavalierly brushed aside Roosevelt's repeated appeals for peace. More than that, Hitler had taunted the President and held him up to ridicule, as his German audience rocked with laughter and cheers. The Führer delighted in comparing his upward struggle with Roosevelt's aristocratic upbringing, and in accusing the President of being under the influence of wealthy Jews. Especially galling were Hitler's references to the Great

Depression: he had conquered it and Roosevelt had not (at least not completely by 1939). Nothing hurts quite like the truth, and F.D.R. could hardly have relished these embarrassing comparisons.

To his credit, Roosevelt did not reply in kind to such personal attacks. Born an aristocrat, he had no stomach for getting into the gutter with this guttersnipe. Not until rather late in the so-called neutrality period did Roosevelt even mention Hitler by name in his public speeches, and then usually in the context of the Nazi menace to Western civilization and the democratic way of life.

Hitler's direct attacks on the United States before Pearl Harbor were largely verbal. He plainly did not want to goad the United States into war—at least not at this time. The lengthy record as laid out in the present book is that Hitler had far more specific and serious grievances against the United States than Roosevelt had against him. The destroyers deal and the Lend-Lease Act come readily to mind, plus a dozen or so German merchant ships whose capture or destruction involved the United States government. The three American destroyers—*Greer* (unhurt), *Kearny* (damaged), and *Reuben James* (sunk)—were all involved in operations against German submarines. On the basis of international law as of 1939, Hitler had ample reason (though he never needed reasons) to declare war on the United States after the destroyers deal. Yet rarely did he protest through diplomatic channels; that task was left to the vitriolic Nazi press.[1]

Before Pearl Harbor, Hitler never gave the United States a valid cause for declaring war, at least on narrowly conventional grounds. The *Robin Moor* and the *Lehigh,* both American merchant ships sunk without remorse by U-boats, involved not so much the legality of the sinking as the failure of the U-boat commander to leave the passengers and crew in a position of safety. The most persuasive legal justification of the United States for pursuing an unneutral course against Hitler was that he had in effect abolished international law and pre-1939 neutrality by his barefaced attacks on Western civilization and humanity. From the point of view of the Western world this charge undoubtedly held water; it certainly was invoked by some of Roosevelt's most influential advisers, including Secretary of War Stimson.

The personal nature of the Roosevelt-Hitler feud is highlighted by the deaths of both men, only eighteen days apart. On April 12, 1945, Roosevelt suddenly died at Warm Springs, Georgia, happily knowing that his war against Germany was all but won. Hitler, remaining in beleaguered Berlin, received the news of his foe's death with elation; Foreign Minister Ribbentrop reported that the Führer was "in seventh heaven." Aside from not wishing Roosevelt well, Hitler sensed that his opponent's death was a favorable omen for a last-minute victory. He was reminded that in 1762 the Germanic armies of Frederick the Great were sorely beset by the Russian invaders, who then occupied Berlin, and the great leader was contemplating suicide by poison. Then, as if by a miracle, on January 5, 1762, came the death of the Russian Czarina, Elizabeth. Her successor, Peter III, greatly admired Frederick, so he promptly withdrew the Russian troops, thereby ending the invasion. Perhaps President Truman would prove to be another Peter III—only he did not.[2]

F.D.R. and Hitler: Wary Warriors

One of the greatest paradoxes of this period is that neither Hitler nor Roosevelt really wanted an all-out land war with the other. Both were willing to accept a severely limited naval clash indefinitely, that is, until such time as more direct fighting seemed imperative, if ever. The hands of both were finally forced by the Japanese attack on Pearl Harbor and other outposts.

Hitler was reluctant to provoke Roosevelt unduly, although he did not especially fear the United States as an immediate threat. He knew that the preparedness effort in America had lagged woefully, and that the Americans could not possibly muster a formidable army to invade Fortress Europe before 1943 (actually the year was 1944). Hitler was counting on knocking Russia out of the war long before that, and evidently he nearly did. His full air strength was needed on the vast Russian front. If all of it was used there, rather than diverted to a war with the United States in the Atlantic, the Soviets would presumably collapse that much sooner.

By October 1941 Hitler recognized, despite tremendous victories, that his invasion of Russia was heading into serious trouble. He had to look forward to revitalizing his weary and frost-bitten forces for a renewed assault in the spring of 1942 (and also 1943, although he did not know that). In brief, if Hitler had sound reasons for not provoking the United States into an unlimited war in 1941, some of them were even more valid in 1942 and 1943.

Hitler's primary objective in clashing with the United States at sea was to curtail shipments of lend-lease materiel to England. By the autumn of 1941 considerable quantities of the supplies earmarked for Britain were being transshipped to northern Russia for use by Stalin's armies. Enough may have come in by December to assist appreciably in the last-ditch defense of Moscow, Leningrad, and other Russian danger points.

Did Roosevelt in early December, at the time of Pearl Harbor, want a full-fledged shooting war with Hitler? The answer appears to be an emphatic no. The President was already doing all he could by helping the British with lend-lease, and he was confining American operations to the protection of convoys that were crossing the North Atlantic with war materiel for Britain—and northern Russia. The shooting that was going on from American destroyers was purely defensive and designed to shepherd these cargoes on to their destination. Torpedoings by German U-boats were also defensive from the German point of view, and aimed at keeping these priceless war supplies from reaching the enemy.

On the eve of Pearl Harbor, the undeclared war was confined almost entirely to the North Atlantic shipping lanes. Roosevelt and Hitler, each with differing main objectives, were content at this point to keep hostilities simmering along at the existing level. Both were achieving their ends with this kind of limited war until the Japanese ruined the game. After Pearl Harbor the German U-boats began attacking, with calamitous effects, American coastwise and Caribbean shipping, much of it silhouetted at night against the well-lighted Florida beaches. The new opportunity to sink United States supply ships anywhere without restriction no doubt helped reconcile Hitler to the Japanese surprise at Pearl Harbor.

There was much to be said in support of Roosevelt's basic strategy of keeping Britain alive and the Russian front resisting, while the Fascist and Communist giants fought to mutual exhaustion. Such indeed might have happened if the United States had throttled down lend-lease to Russia in 1943–1944, but by that time Roosevelt was gambling on Stalin's becoming a cooperative ally in establishing a stable postwar Europe under the yet unborn United Nations. Moreover, reducing lend-lease might have forced Stalin to negotiate a peace with Hitler, to the disadvantage of the United States.

Roosevelt's Motivations

A stock charge of the more bitter isolationists was that Roosevelt was determined from an early date to get into a full-scale shooting war with Hitler on behalf of Britain and the other democracies. The isolationists believed that only their noisy protests had held F.D.R. back from the precipice over which he was eager to plunge. They acted as though they were saving the nation from a bloodbath, and their opposition was so rabid that Roosevelt could hardly have hoped, as we repeatedly have seen, to extract a declaration of war from Congress prior to the attack on Pearl Harbor and Hitler's declaration against the United States.

As for an all-out shooting war with the Nazis, Roosevelt evidently did not say much more in private than he did in public. His important and highly confidential interchanges with Churchill have been published, and they reveal much wariness on the subject of full belligerency. His private letters, including those edited by his son, have little or nothing to say on this subject. On the personal side, he had four sons of military age, all of whom subsequently saw action. Mrs. Roosevelt wrote in 1949, "I do not think Franklin ever felt that war was inevitable, and he always said he hoped we could avoid it. . . ." She herself feared otherwise.[3]

As for his severely limited naval war with Hitler, the President was clearly determined to take whatever defensive steps seemed necessary to protect lend-lease and other shipments to the hard-pressed British. We know that he wanted to get the needed materiel to Britain even at the price of some shooting en route, but this is not to say that his major aim was to plunge into an unrestricted land-and-sea war with Germany and Italy. If it had been, why did he resist for so long the hawkish pressure of "the belligerent old men" in his Cabinet, particularly Secretary of War Stimson?[4] Why did he tell his press conference on November 3, 1941, slightly more than a month before Pearl Harbor, that his major purpose in helping the Allies would best be served by keeping the undeclared naval war at its existing level?[5] And why had he spoken to Harry Hopkins, only hours after the Pearl Harbor attack, of his "earnest desire to complete his administration without [declared] war"—a desire that was dashed because the Japanese "had made the decision for him"?[6] His words squared with his deeds.

Roosevelt's Dilemmas

Some doubts will continue to exist as to whether Roosevelt really wanted an unrestricted war with Hitler. But the evidence is overwhelming that he did not desire a shoot-out with Japan, at least not in December 1941. We must never forget that his primary goal up to that point was to defend America by keeping Britain afloat. This objective was repeatedly proclaimed, with evident sincerity, prior to the destroyers-for-bases deal and the Lend-Lease Act. Clearly Roosevelt could not help the British by prodding Japan into the war. Such a conflagration would certainly result in the draining off of British naval strength to East Asia, to say nothing of forcing an embattled Churchill to defend such faraway imperial outposts as Hong Kong, Singapore, India, Australia, and New Zealand. Australian and New Zealand troops would have to be brought home from North Africa and the Middle East to defend their native soil, as indeed they were. All these responsibilities would undoubtedly weaken operations against Hitler, the main foe, as they did.

Roosevelt fully realized that the objective of aiding Britain would be undercut by forcing Japan into the war. To the very end, after years of "appeasing" Japan so as to help China, he was attempting to negotiate a settlement with the Japanese that would cause them to draw back from their offensive operations in China and Indochina in return for economic concessions. Yet he well knew that he lacked sufficient naval strength, particularly after he had detached about 20 percent of the Pacific Fleet for operations against Hitler in the Atlantic.

The day before Pearl Harbor (Washington time) and while the Japanese carriers were sailing swiftly eastward toward Hawaii, Roosevelt went so far as to cable a personal plea for peace to the Japanese Emperor. The length and earnestness of this appeal (about 900 words) indicate that F.D.R. had not abandoned all hope of compromise but believed, as the Japanese had requested, that negotiations would continue.[7] The devastating answer came the next day (Washington time) to the accompaniment of the bombs that pounded Pearl Harbor.

When December 7, 1941, dawned peacefully in Washington, Roosevelt had no reason to suspect that Japan was about to attack Hawaii, although the Philippines were within the realm of possibility. He clearly did not want a full-dress shooting war with the Japanese. The impending attack would almost certainly hit nearby British or Dutch possessions, and F.D.R. must have been aware of the futility of going to Congress to ask for a war declaration on behalf of British and Dutch imperialism in East Asia. He seemed to

Mrs. Roosevelt to be relieved when the news arrived of the crushing blow in Hawaii, but his sense of relief appears to have been of the kind that comes with the ending of prolonged suspense.[8] The other shoe had finally dropped.

Abused Presidential Powers?

Revisionist critics of Roosevelt, notably Charles A. Beard, have accused him of having abused his presidential powers by dragging the United States into an all-out war with Hitler. We have already observed that the President was content with hostilities that were limited, defensive, and maritime. Hitler, responding to Japan's outburst, was the one who opted for a declared, unlimited war. But had Roosevelt overstepped his lawful powers up to that point?

Beyond question the Constitution stipulates that Congress, and only Congress, can declare war, although the President normally signs the joint resolution. That body was forced to respond as expected after Japan, Germany, and Italy had first declared war on the United States. But the Constitution also permits the President, as Commander-in-Chief, to make war, even without a formal declaration of war by Congress.

Roosevelt recognized the distinction between the war-making powers of the President and the war-declaring powers of the Congress, and he was keenly aware of the impeachment process. The President may order the armed forces, without a declaration of war, to go anywhere in the world he chooses to send them. The record reveals that as of 1970 there have been about 160 such landings, some followed by shooting, mostly in the so-called banana republics of the Caribbean.[9] In 1926–1927 President Coolidge had a "private war" going against "bandit forces" in Nicaragua that involved over 5,000 United States troops. We should also remember that American participation in the Korean war (157,000 casualties) and in the Vietnam war (361,000 casualties) was never sanctified by a formal declaration of hostilities.

Roosevelt realized that under the Constitution previous presidents had invoked their powers as Commander-in-Chief to wage protracted but undeclared wars. In press conferences during the pre–Pearl Harbor days he repeatedly referred to the undeclared war with France (1798–1800) and to the armed actions against the

Barbary pirates, under both President Jefferson and President
Madison.

F.D.R. was especially fond of referring to the fracas with France
(1798–1800) because it presented interesting parallels to the clashes
with Hitler's submarines.* It involved the greatest of the European
powers; it was fought on the high seas for about two and one-half
years; it never escalated into an all-out land and sea war; and it was
settled amicably by a treaty with France in 1800. Similarly, Roosevelt may have thought that the undeclared naval war with Hitler, if
luck held, might drag out for several years, end in a negotiated
peace, and then fade into history.

In the Franklin D. Roosevelt Library at Hyde Park there reposes a highly interesting, fourteen-page memorandum. It is ini-
tialed by Green H. Hackworth, the legal adviser of the Department
of State, and is entitled "Extent to which the President May Use the
Navy in the Protection of American Interests." The memorandum
states that in more than 100 instances the President had used the
army and navy "for purposes short of war and without involving us
in war." The conclusion was that, "The President may use the Navy
in any manner that to him seems proper." On the outside of the document appear the words: "Put in Middle Drawer of the President's
Desk in the Office."

The date of the Hackworth memorandum is August 21, 1941,
seven days after the Atlantic Charter was issued. We recall that
Roosevelt and Churchill had entered into discussions regarding the
escorting by the United States of convoys carrying lend-lease materiel to Britain. The Hackworth memorandum deals at some length
with international law relating to convoys, and we may reasonably
assume that this document was prepared at the request of Roosevelt,
or someone in his office, either after or shortly before the historic
conference off the shores of Newfoundland.

"He Lied Us into War"

Even granted that Roosevelt acted within his constitutional authority, many of his isolationist critics claimed that he acted deceit-

---

* The Quasi-War with France is not completely analogous because Congress
(March 28, 1798) formally authorized the President to direct commanders of U.S. war-
ships to seize armed French vessels attacking American merchant ships. Also, in 1802
Congress officially recognized the declaration of war by Tripoli in 1801.

fully. This belief persisted even in 1944, when in a campaign speech Republican Congresswoman Clare Boothe Luce declared that Roosevelt "lied us into a war because he did not have the political courage to lead us into it."[10] She probably had in mind, for example, Roosevelt's precipitate misrepresentation of the counterattack by the German U-boat on the U.S. destroyer *Greer*. F.D.R., we recall, had not made clear that the *Greer* had provoked the attack. Then, as at other times, he was uncandid, but deception is the tribute that politicians traditionally pay to hostile public opinion.

One of Roosevelt's principal biographers, James M. Burns, entitled the first of his two volumes *Roosevelt: The Lion and the Fox*. As a leader of public opinion, the President would act sometimes with boldness, at other times with craft. On October 5, 1937, he delivered his memorable Quarantine Speech in Chicago, in which he daringly declared that the dictators were getting out of hand and the time had come for the democracies to "quarantine" them. The angry uproar from the isolationists taught him the prudence of moving by indirection, if possible. He did so when he engineered the destroyers-for-bases deal of September 2, 1940, by an executive agreement, without the previous sanction of Congress. He also downplayed the issue of escorting convoys, and avoided the subject of lend-lease by not bringing it up until he was safely re-elected in November 1940. To the very day of Pearl Harbor, the isolationists were a well-organized and vocal minority that had to be reckoned with, particularly in regard to congressional legislation. If Roosevelt had asked Congress for permission to escort convoys, he might have been turned down cold—with his leadership gravely weakened and the alternative of independent action thrown away. So he quietly and inconspicuously began escort operations, as lay within his power as Commander-in-Chief of the U.S. Navy. This indirection his critics referred to as "father knows best" or "doing good by stealth."* Roosevelt himself virtually said at his press conference of September 5, 1941, "Teacher knows best."

Some cynic has remarked that the American people do not prepare for war until they feel "the hot breath of the approaching enemy." This witticism is a gross exaggeration, but it makes the

---

* Thomas A. Bailey wrote in *The Man in the Street* (New York, 1948), p. 13, that because the masses are "notoriously shortsighted . . . our statesmen are forced to deceive them into an awareness of their own long-run interests. This is clearly what Roosevelt [felt he] had to do, and who shall say that posterity will not thank him for it?" The bracketed words were not included through inadvertence, and the result was a flareback from isolationist critics and shocked students of American democracy.

point. Roosevelt experienced great difficulty in persuading the American people that the dictators presented a menace against which adequate military preparedness was vital. We recall that a renewal of the Selective Service Act passed by a margin of only one vote in the House of Representatives, August 18, 1941, some *four months before Pearl Harbor,* although labor politics was also involved. Little wonder that Roosevelt should undertake to defend the United States, not by raising a huge army, but by sending lend-lease to the British, who could sacrifice their own "boys" in fighting the menace of Hitler. England would not be permitted "to fight to the last American."

Politicians and Principles

Presidents are politicians or they would not be presidents. Few politicians get very far by blurting out disagreeable truths that the public would rather not hear. Most presidents have sought power, presumably so that they can use it for the public good. They are fully aware that they cannot do maximum good (or bad) unless they manage to get elected and re-elected. Few presidential aspirants have ever achieved great success at the polls unless they have refrained from taking unpopular and positive stands on unpopular issues, or have dealt in half-truths, or have made campaign promises that they probably could not keep or did not really intend to keep. Roosevelt saw more clearly than did the isolationist voters that the dictators, conspicuously Hitler, were a potential menace to the United States. In what F.D.R. conceived to be the national interest, he fought the Führer by indirection and by adopting courses that ran counter to concepts of neutrality before the new-style dictators burst onto the scene.

Where Roosevelt could, he gained his ends by avoiding bitter clashes with the isolationist-riddled Congress, notably in the destroyers-deal executive agreement and in the Atlantic Charter. Where he could not avoid Congress, as in the Lend-Lease Act and in the modification of the revised Neutrality Act in November 1941, he applied heavy pressure. In the latter case he won a narrow victory. In all these critical instances, the public opinion polls revealed a strong majority in his favor.

The opposition in Congress was not all isolationist. Much of it was Republican, primarily for the reason that the opposition party—sometimes the "disloyal opposition"—often does not support legislation recommended by the party in power. Why present it with legislative laurels that could be used in a campaign for re-election? Why not continue to play pragmatic politics while the world was falling to pieces?

Some critics have advanced the thesis that Roosevelt was trying desperately to involve the United States in an all-out war because the production of war supplies was lagging perilously. There was too much "business as usual," especially in manufacturing private automobiles. Hostilities formally declared would supposedly end labor disputes and rally the masses behind a supreme production of war materials.

This superficially appealing theory is undermined by grave weaknesses. First, there is no solid evidence that Roosevelt really wanted to get into an all-out war or was trying to do so before the attack on Pearl Harbor. Moreover, the formal declarations of war did not end labor problems in America any more than they did in England. Much of the lagging production had resulted from such bottlenecks as shortages of designers, machine tools, machines, essential materials, and technicians, none of which could be produced overnight under the prod of patriotic frenzy. Even so, the manufacturing of aircraft in 1941 rose from 3,797 to 19,290; of tanks, from 280 to 3,900.[11] Furthermore, much of the needed output would have to go to building up and equipping the U.S. Army and Navy, at the cost of such supplies for the Allies.

There was also the drag of the die-hard isolationists, as there had been of the die-hard Federalists in 1812. At that time President Madison thrust forward the flag in the form of a declaration of war against England in the hope of rallying the country behind him. Because the United States was the official attacker, the Federalists were content to let the Stars and Stripes lie in the mud. Roosevelt, perhaps remembering this painful lesson of history, played the waiting game of supplying Britain until the Axis powers pushed the United States into a declared war, with Pearl Harbor as the curtain raiser. The isolationists then fell silent as a united nation rallied behind its Democratic President.

An additional lesson could be drawn from the War of 1812. The vote for formal hostilities in the House was 79 to 49; in the Senate, a close 19 to 13. The disunity thus proclaimed resulted in America's worst fought war. As Roosevelt no doubt knew, getting a formal declaration was not so much the problem as amassing the whopping majority that was not possible until after Pearl Harbor. Without such a support the chances of winning the war would be gravely reduced.

Democracy or Dictatorship?

The United States is a democracy within a republic. The silent majority is supposed to rule, but if the noisy minority does, we have the "tyranny of the minority" rather than the more common "tyranny of the majority." In 1940–1941 the isolationist minority, with burning intensity, came close to thwarting the will of the majority. Yet the public opinion polls consistently showed that the American people favored massive aid to England—even at the risk of war.

Colonel Lindbergh and his fellow isolationists of the "America First" organization were confident that Germany could not be beaten, and that Hitler would never challenge or otherwise menace the United States. So why waste money by sending lend-lease to an imperial Britain that was doomed to die?

The first assumption, that Germany could not be beaten, especially in the air, proved false. The second one, regarding a Nazi assault on the Americas, is unprovable because Germany lost. But one can reasonably argue that Stalin would have been beaten without American lend-lease. Hitler then would have been free to turn against Roosevelt, whom he evidently hated, and America, which he despised as Jewish dominated. On occasion he would deny that he had designs on the United States, and at other times he indicated otherwise. Yet Hitler was one of the greatest liars in history, if not the greatest, and no one could safely predict who would be next on his lengthening grab list. A scholar who has carefully researched this aspect of Hitler's makeup concludes that "inflated by success and drawn along by a certain momentum of conquest, Hitler would not have indefinitely confined himself to Europe."[12] The hundreds of thousands of Germans in South America, notably Brazil and Argentina, had already been partially Nazified.*

After the war, the Nazi military archives yielded no secret plans for invading the Americas. But their absence proves nothing because an impulsive and impatient Hitler was prone to play by ear. When France fell in 1940, he had no plans for invading either England or Russia but he managed to whip some together. In 1978 Albert

---

* A *Fortune* poll (August 1941) found that 72 percent of the respondents felt that Hitler would not be satisfied until he had tried to conquer everything, including the Americas. *Public Opinion Quarterly* V, 677.

THE ONLY "PAN-AMERICAN RAT HOLE." *Bishop in the* St. Louis Star-Times, *1943*

Speer, Hitler's confidant and talented minister for armaments, wrote in his newspaper memoirs that the Führer definitely planned to conquer America after crushing Europe.[13]

Churchill had promised never to surrender the British fleet, but suppose that successfully invading Germans had threatened to burn every British city unless the escaping warships were returned. The French fleet itself might yet be wrested from the Vichy government. In July 1940, the Germans were planning to construct a mighty fleet of battleships after England suffered defeat, but against whom if not the Yankees?

Isolationists argued that if America helped Stalin defeat Hitler, the result would be a more menacing dictatorship in the Führer's place. In the long run, this prediction proved correct, for both the

Soviet Union and the United States for a decade or so have been capable of mutual incineration with nuclear weapons.

As events turned out, the Soviet Union, with its lagging technology, did not develop the atomic bomb until 1949. A victorious Germany almost certainly would have done better because German scientists had made great progress in atomic research before the invasion of Russia. More than that, they were achieving advances in rocketry, including the forerunners of the intercontinental ballistic missile. All this further suggests that Hitler (or a Nazi successor) might not have been content to rest on his laurels after prostrating Russia and invading Britain. A victorious Germany with long-range rockets and atomic bombs was not within the power of the American isolationists to envisage in 1941.

A Fox in the White House

Roosevelt was no rank amateur as a global strategist, especially in naval warfare. He had received some seven years of on-the-job training as Assistant Secretary of the Navy. He had available a flood of top-secret information from sources such as the diplomatic corps and military and naval intelligence. He certainly was in a better position than anyone else in the country to assess the perils to the United States posed by the new breed of dictators. F.D.R.'s efforts to alert his countrymen to their peril generally brought disturbing results because the American people, comfortably removed from the battlefields by their ocean moats, traditionally have been short-sighted, whether the danger was a foreign foe or a domestic petroleum shortage.

No doubt Roosevelt would have preferred to lead public opinion. But to have leadership one must have followership—and before Pearl Harbor the masses conspicuously lacked that inclination. F.D.R. was well aware that if he got too far out in front he would be shot at from the rear. He was shot at anyhow—but less lethally. Even so, he was often astonishingly frank in his press conferences.

Confronted with this perilous situation, Roosevelt acted because he recognized his obligation under his constitutional oath to promote what he conceived to be the "common defence." He did even less than he felt needed to be done in the national interest, for he felt compelled to play the role of both the lion and the fox. But isolationist and Republican critics did not like him in either role. As a fox, on occasion Roosevelt tried to educate the American people, even deceive them, so that they would become more fully aware of what he considered to be their peril. He evidently thought of himself as a doctor, more than a teacher, who feels that he must tell white lies for the patient's own good. This is not the ideal way to lead a democracy, but democracy is not an ideal form of government, only better, Winston Churchill remarked in 1947, than all "other forms that have been tried from time to time."

Expediency vs. Legality

Presidents other than Roosevelt, even recent ones, have taken controversial steps in the national interest, or what they have conceived to be the national interest. F.D.R., unlike Lincoln, appears to have been guilty of no clear-cut violations of the Constitution. The destroyers-for-bases deal was a valid executive agreement; the Lend-Lease Act was approved by Congress; the deployment of destroyers against U-boats was within Roosevelt's authority as Commander-in-Chief. Yet these were all unneutral acts, as neutrality was defined in September 1939.

In 1848 President Polk had shamelessly deceived Congress and the American public when he did not confess that he had goaded the Mexicans into the initial attack in 1846. He no doubt felt that he was acting in the national interest—and he probably was, because the United States added vastly and richly to its domain.

Lincoln, often rated as the greatest President, provoked the Confederates into attacking Fort Sumter, and then proceeded to ride roughshod over the Constitution that guaranteed civil liberties. This course he felt was in the national interest, as indeed it was if his goal was the preservation of the Union under the Constitution. If Roosevelt had his isolationists, Lincoln had his Copperheads.

Woodrow Wilson contrived to involve the United States in World War I after having been elected on the strength of the slogan "He Kept Us Out of War." In so doing he took an unrealistic and untenable position regarding human rights and neutral rights, including a rejection of repeated German suggestions of guaranteed safe conduct for American shipping. In 1919, before a Senate committee, Wilson denied that he had known about the notorious secret treaties among the Allies prior to going to Paris. Either he lied deliberately to save the Treaty of Versailles or he had suffered an unaccountable mental lapse.

The President, not the windy body known as Congress, is the final judge of what constitutes the national interest at any given time; historians are the ultimate judges as perspective lengthens and as the wisdom of hindsight deepens. Thus, Lincoln is generally forgiven for his questionable measures against those who were trying to set small fires while the Union was already ablaze.

In 1939–1941 "teacher" Roosevelt proceeded with extreme caution in pursuing what he regarded as the national interest—that is, a defense of his 130 million wards against Hitler and his cohorts. F.D.R. felt that he had to nurse public opinion along, lest he lose contact with it and become powerless. In 1977 former Secretary of State Dean Rusk remarked that a constitutionally elected President is not a statesman but a sheep dog "trying to round up enough people to go in the same direction for a long enough period to have a policy."[14]

As for platform "covenants" and campaign "promises," most politically sophisticated Americans realize that these are in fact aspirations rather than iron-clad pledges. Senator Barry Goldwater, whose campaign "promises" had hurt him as the losing Republican presidential candidate in 1964, reacted realistically but unhappily to President Carter's cancellation of the program for building the costly B-1 bomber in 1977. The Senator conceded that Carter had made such a campaign promise "somewhere," but "I don't think much of a president who puts his campaign promises ahead of the welfare of the country."[15]

With much justification Roosevelt conceived of the dictators, especially Hitler, as an intolerable menace to the Americas—and Western civilization. The events of 1939–1945 tended to confirm the popular judgment that the Führer was a homicidal maniac, burning with bitterness and vengefulness. When American troops reached Germany they were appalled when they actually saw and smelled the blood-bedaubed crematoria in which countless millions of innocent people had been incinerated.

No one knows, or ever will know, what would have happened to the United States if a power-mad Hitler and his Axis accomplices, including Japan, had triumphed. But Roosevelt, supported by his closest advisers and a strong majority of the American people, attempted to control events in the national interest. He would use limited, defensive, and undeclared acts of war to keep the British afloat, even at the risk of all-out shooting. This is not only what he said he was going to do but also what he actually did. He regarded this affirmative course as preferable to sitting back and waiting for the whole world to be engulfed by dictatorial megalomaniacs. What F.D.R. did, even deceptively, he evidently felt he had to do, in accord with his sworn constitutional duty to "preserve, protect, and defend the Constitution of the United States" (Article II, Section 1). The "buck" stops at the lonely White House, and the back-breaking responsibility rested squarely on Roosevelt's shoulders, not on those of his countless critics. He preferred to control events, or try to, rather than leave the nation completely at the mercy of the dictators.

Colonel Lindbergh and other isolationists erroneously assumed that military technology had come near reaching its ultimate point, and that America could safely hunker down behind her ocean moats. These critics of Roosevelt did not take fully into account the following scenario:

In 1942 Hitler defeats Stalin, and then Britain, because of insufficient lend-lease support from Roosevelt. The Führer now has his scientists give full-throttle to the sidetracked program for an atomic bomb. With Germany in possession of this horrendous new weapon, as well as long-range bombers and other sophisticated devices, New York becomes Hiroshima, Philadelphia becomes Nagasaki, and Marshal Goering becomes Gauleiter of America.

Roosevelt may have peered into the future with more perception than he or anyone else realized. The supreme irony is that after his death the bombs he had been preparing for Germany finally fell on Japan. Such was the frightful climax of the confrontation between Hitler and Roosevelt.

REFERENCES AND NOTES

Bibliographical References

Valuable background on the American side, with bibliographies, may be found in the following: Robert A. Divine, *The Reluctant Belligerent: America's Entry into World War II* (New York, 1965); Donald F. Drummond, *The Passing of American Neutrality, 1933–1941* (Ann Arbor, Mi., 1955); W. L. Langer and S. E. Gleason, *The Challenge to Isolation, 1937–1940* (New York, 1952), and *The Undeclared War, 1940–1941* (New York, 1953); Basil Rauch, *Roosevelt: From Munich to Pearl Harbor* (New York, 1950), primarily a rebuttal of Charles A. Beard's anti-Rooseveltian *President Roosevelt and the Coming of the War, 1941* (New Haven, Ct., 1948).

Background on the British side, with bibliographies, may be found in the following: Winston S. Churchill, *The Gathering Storm* (Boston, 1948); *Their Finest Hour* (Boston, 1949); and *The Grand Alliance* (Boston, 1951); Joseph P. Lash, *Roosevelt and Churchill, 1939–1941* (New York, 1976); Francis L. Loewenheim, Harold D. Langley, and Manfred Jonas, eds., *Roosevelt and Churchill: Their Secret Wartime Correspondence* (New York, 1975).

Background on the German side, with bibliographies, may be found in the following: James V. Compton, *The Swastika and the Eagle: Hitler, the United States, and the Origins of World War II* (Boston, 1967); Saul Friedländer, *Prelude to Downfall: Hitler and the United States, 1939–1941* (New York, 1967). Alton Frye, *Nazi Germany and the American Hemisphere, 1933–1941* (New Haven, Ct., 1967); Norman Rich, *Hitler's War Aims* (New York, 1973); William Shirer, *The Rise and Fall of the Third Reich* (New York, 1960); Hans L. Trefousse, *Germany and American Neutrality, 1939–1941* (New

York, 1951); Gerhard L. Weinberg, "Hitler's Image of the United States," *American Historical Review* LXIX (1964), 1,006–1,021.

Background on the Japanese side, with bibliographies, may be found in the following: F. W. Iklé, *German-Japanese Relations, 1936–1940* (New York, 1956); F. C. Jones, *Japan's New Order in East Asia: Its Rise and Fall, 1937–1945* (London, 1954); J. M. Meskill, *Hitler and Japan: The Hollow Alliance* (New York, 1967); E. L. Presseisen, *Germany and Japan: A Study in Totalitarian Diplomacy, 1933–1941* (The Hague, 1958); P. W. Schroeder, *The Axis Alliance and Japanese-American Relations, 1941* (Ithaca, N.Y., 1958).

Documentation

Key to longer titles and their shortened forms:

Brassey's Naval Annual, 1948 (New York, n.d.). Cited as *Fuehrer Conferences, Brassey.*

Complete Presidential Press Conferences of Franklin D. Roosevelt, Volumes XIII–XVIII (New York: Da Capo Press, 1972), photocopies of originals in Roosevelt Library, Hyde Park, New York. Cited as *Presidential Press Conferences.*

Department of State, *Documents on German Foreign Policy,* Series D, 1918–1945, 13 volumes, 1918–1945 (Washington, D.C.). Relevant volumes cited as *Documents on German Foreign Policy.*

Foreign Relations of the United States: Diplomatic Papers. Department of State, Washington, D.C. Volumes, dates, and subtitles as indicated.

Francis L. Loewenheim, Harold D. Langley, and Manfred Jonas, eds., *Roosevelt and Churchill: Their Secret Wartime Correspondence* (New York, 1975). Cited as Loewenheim *et al., Roosevelt and Churchill.*

S. I. Rosenman, comp., *The Public Papers and Addresses of Franklin D. Roosevelt, 1938 Volume* (New York, 1941); *1939 Volume* (New York, 1941); *1940 Volume* (New York, 1941); *1941 Volume* (New York, 1950). Cited as *Roosevelt Public Papers.*

Notes

Chapter 1 (pp. 1–14): The Day of the Dictators

1. John Toland, *Adolf Hitler* (Garden City, N.Y., 1976), p. 67.
2. *Roosevelt Public Papers, 1938 Volume,* p. 289.
3. Gordon W. Prange, ed., *Hitler's Words* (Washington, D.C., 1944), p. 343.
4. *Ibid.,* p. 209.
5. Winston S. Churchill, *The Gathering Storm* (Boston, 1948), pp. 130–131, 133. This work is most useful for the background of the present chapter and some succeeding ones.

6. *Ibid.*, pp. 137–142.

7. *Ibid.*, pp. 212–215, 244–249.

8. Hugh Thomas, *The Spanish Civil War* (New York, 1961), pp. 440–441.

9. *Ibid.*, pp. 419–421.

10. *Ciano's Hidden Diary, 1937–1938* (New York, 1953), p. 8.

Chapter 2 (pp. 15–30): Hitler Launches a Global War

1. Roosevelt's appeal and the responses evoked by it are published fully in *Department of State Press Releases,* XIX, pp. 219–223.

2. *Ibid.*, p. 223.

3. *Roosevelt Public Papers, 1938 Volume,* p. 537.

4. There is still no agreement among scholars as to Stalin's intentions at the time of the Munich crisis. See M. L. Toepfer, "The Soviet Role in the Munich Crisis: An Historiographical Debate," *Diplomatic History* I (1977), 341–357.

5. N. H. Baynes, ed., *The Speeches of Adolf Hitler* (New York, 1969), II, p. 1,526.

6. Winston S. Churchill, *The Gathering Storm* (Boston, 1948), pp. 336–339.

7. The story of "Ultra" is told in William Stevenson, *A Man Called Intrepid* (New York, 1976).

8. John Toland, *Adolf Hitler* (New York, 1976), pp. 502–503.

9. *New York Times,* November 16, 1938.

10. *Foreign Relations of the United States, 1938,* II, p. 451.

11. Text in *Roosevelt Public Papers, 1939 Volume,* pp. 201–205. Other than Hitler's speech, no direct reply to Roosevelt came from either Hitler or Mussolini.

12. Text in Carnegie Endowment for International Peace, *International Conciliation, Documents for the Year 1939* pp. 297–345.

13. W. L. Shirer, *The Rise and Fall of the Third Reich* (New York, 1960), pp. 471–475.

14. See W. L. Langer and S. E. Gleason, *The Challenge to Isolation, 1937–1940* (New York, 1952), pp. 83–90.

15. Churchill, *The Gathering Storm,* p. 362.

16. Gordon W. Prange, ed., *Hitler's Words* (Washington, D.C., 1944), p. 215.

17. Shirer, *The Third Reich,* pp. 518–520.

18. *British Blue Book,* Cmd. 6106, p. 195.

19. R. J. Sontag and J. S. Beddie, eds., *Nazi-Soviet Relations, 1939–1941* (Washington, D.C., 1948), p. 78.

20. *Roosevelt Public Papers, 1939 Volume,* pp. 463–464.

21. *Public Opinion Quarterly* VI, 102.

22. National Opinion Research Center, *Opinion News,* April 3, 1945.

23. S. A. Diamond, *The Nazi Movement in the United States, 1924–1941* (Ithaca, N.Y., 1974).

24. For a summary of the incidents that embittered German-American relations until July 29, 1940, see *Documents on German Foreign Policy,* X, pp. 350–352.

Chapter 3 (pp. 31–47): Roosevelt's Unneutral Neutrality

1. *Roosevelt Public Papers, 1939 Volume*, pp. 473–478.
2. James M. Burns, *Roosevelt: The Lion and the Fox* (New York, 1956), p. 395.
3. *Ibid.*, pp. 395, 531.
4. *Presidential Press Conferences*, XIV, pp. 125–127.
5. *New York Times*, August 29–September 4, 1939; *ibid.*, December 14, 1939.
6. Text of message in *Roosevelt Public Papers, 1939 Volume*, pp. 512–522.
7. *Public Opinion Quarterly* IV, 105–111.
8. *U.S. Statutes at Large*, Vol. 54, Part I, p. 4.
9. *Ibid.*, p. 8.
10. *Foreign Relations of the United States, 1939*, I, pp. 665–667.
11. Winston S. Churchill, *The Gathering Storm* (Boston, 1948), p. 529.
12. T. E. Hachey, ed., *Confidential Dispatches* (Evanston, Il., 1974), p. 19.
13. "Administrative History of U.S. Atlantic Fleet," Vol. I, Part 1, p. 42, from manuscript in U.S. Navy Department Library, Washington, D.C.
14. *Roosevelt Public Papers, 1939 Volume*, pp. 552–553.
15. Saul Friedländer, *Prelude to Downfall: Hitler and the United States, 1939–1941* (New York, 1967), pp. 62–63.
16. *New York Times*, December 21, 1939.
17. *Ibid.*, December 22, 1939.
18. Our account of the *Columbus* is taken substantially from an unpublished article, together with supporting photocopied documents from the British and American naval archives, graciously provided by Paul A. Miller of Milton, Wisconsin.
19. Captain Frank K. B. Wheeler to Captain Paul B. Ryan, January 8, 1977.
20. *New York Times*, December 21, 1939; Abbazia, *Mr. Roosevelt's Navy*, pp. 74–75.
21. *New York Times*, August 20, 1941.
22. Gordon W. Prange, ed., *Hitler's Words* (Washington, D.C., 1944), p. 373.
23. *Ibid.*
24. *New York Times*, November 30; *ibid.*, December 9, 1940.
25. Prange, *Hitler's Words*, p. 373.

Chapter 4 (pp. 48–59): U-Boat Warfare Begins

1. *Fuehrer Conferences, Brassey*, p. 39.
2. Stephen Heald, ed., *Documents on International Affairs, 1936* (London, 1937), p. 633.
3. J. W. Wheeler-Bennett and Stephen Heald, eds., *Documents on International Affairs, 1935* (London, 1936), I, pp. 142–143.
4. ONI (U.S. Office of Naval Intelligence) *Review*, October 1946, p. 29.
5. *Trial of the Major War Criminals before the International Military Tribunal* (Nuremberg, 1949), XL, pp. 88–90.

6. Winston S. Churchill, *The Gathering Storm* (Boston, 1948), p. 439.

7. *Ibid.,* pp. 436–437. For the arming of British merchant ships see S. W. Roskill, *The War at Sea* (London, 1954), I, pp. 20–21.

8. *Department of State Bulletin* I, 651 (U.S. note of December 8, 1939).

9. T. E. Hachey, ed., *Confidential Dispatches* (Evanston, Il., 1974), pp. 18–19.

10. The general facts about the *Athenia* sinking are set forth in great detail in the *New York Times,* September 4, 1939, and dates following as indicated in the *Times* index. The German side is revealed in *Trial of the Major War Criminals* (1947, 1948, 1949), V, pp. 264–269; XIV, pp. 78–80, 277–279, 293–294; XXII, pp. 562–563; and XXXV, pp. 235–236, 525–527. An excellent summation of the *Athenia* incident from the German documents appears in W. L. Shirer, *The Rise and Fall of the Third Reich* (New York, 1960), pp. 636–638.

11. On *Lusitania* parallels see T. A. Bailey and P. B. Ryan, *The Lusitania Disaster* (New York, 1975).

12. *The Memoirs of Cordell Hull* (New York, 1948), I, p. 677.

13. *Trial of the Major War Criminals* (1949), XXXV, pp. 235–236.

14. Bailey and Ryan, *The Lusitania Disaster,* p. 337.

15. *Roosevelt Public Papers, 1939 Volume;* pp. 488–489.

Chapter 5 (pp. 60–71): Scandinavian Sideshows

1. Hull tells the story of the *City of Flint* in some detail in *The Memoirs of Cordell Hull* (New York, 1948), I, pp. 704–705; for extensive documentation see *Foreign Relations of the United States: The Soviet Union, 1933–1939* (Washington, D.C., 1952), pp. 984–1,013.

2. *Foreign Relations: The Soviet Union,* pp. 999, 1,012.

3. Hull, *Memoirs,* p. 705.

4. Affidavit of Captain Gainard, November 6, 1939, in a dispatch from U.S. Consul Dunlap at Bergen, Norway, to the State Department, November 6, 1939, National Archives, Washington, D.C.

5. *Foreign Relations: The Soviet Union,* p. 1,000.

6. See Charles C. Hyde, "The City of Flint," *American Journal of International Law* XXXIV, 89–95.

7. *New York Times,* January 27, 1940.

8. *Fuehrer Conferences, Brassey,* p. 56.

9. The German chargé in Washington so reported. *Documents on German Foreign Policy,* VIII, pp. 370–371.

10. *Roosevelt Public Papers, 1939 Volume,* pp. 587–589.

11. *Ibid., 1940 Volume,* p. 93; Eleanor Roosevelt, *This I Remember* (New York, 1949), p. 201.

12. For the *Altmark* episode see Winston S. Churchill, *The Gathering Storm* (Boston, 1948), pp. 526, 527, 561–564.

13. Hague Convention XIII of 1907, Article 5, in J. B. Scott, ed., *The Hague Conventions and Declarations of 1899 and 1907* (New York, 1915), p. 210.

14. Churchill, *The Gathering Storm,* chaps. XI–XVI, Book Two, tells the story of Norway's plight.

15. *Roosevelt Public Papers, 1940 Volume*, p. 133.

16. A legal defense of freezing appears in the *American Journal of International Law* XXXV, 651 ff.

17. Gordon W. Prange, ed., *Hitler's Words* (Washington, D.C., 1944), pp. 371–372.

18. *Presidential Press Conferences*, XV, p. 280.

19. *Roosevelt Public Papers, 1940 Volume*, pp. 127–129.

Chapter 6 (pp. 72–81): Hitler's Blitz in the West

1. *Documents on German Foreign Policy*, IX, pp. 299–307.

2. Gordon W. Prange, ed., *Hitler's Words* (Washington, D.C., 1944), p. 372.

3. *Roosevelt Public Papers, 1940 Volume*, pp. 198–205.

4. *Ibid.*, pp. 250–253.

5. *Ibid.*, pp. 259–264.

6. Prange, *Hitler's Words*, p. 372.

7. *Department of State Bulletin* II, 681.

8. *Documents on German Foreign Policy*, X, p. 78.

9. S. S. Jones and D. P. Myers, eds., *Documents on American Foreign Relations* (Boston, 1940), II, pp. 93–95; III, pp. 85–97.

10. Prange, *Hitler's Words*, p. 371.

11. *Ibid.*, p. 372.

12. *Ibid.*, p. 371.

13. Winston S. Churchill, *Their Finest Hour* (Boston, 1949), pp. 310–311.

14. T. E. Hachey, ed., *Confidential Dispatches* (Evanston, Il., 1974), p. 20.

15. *U.S. Statutes at Large*, Vol. 40, Part I, p. 43.

16. See T. A. Bailey, *A Diplomatic History of the American People*, 5th ed. (New York, 1955), pp. 768–769.

17. Prange, *Hitler's Words*, p. 372.

Chapter 7 (pp. 82–98): The Destroyers-for-Bases Deal

1. Winston S. Churchill, *Their Finest Hour* (Boston, 1949), p. 34.

2. J. P. Lash, *Roosevelt and Churchill, 1939–1941* (New York, 1976), pp. 130–132.

3. Basic information appears in Churchill, *Their Finest Hour*, pp. 398–417, and Philip Goodhart, *Fifty Ships That Saved the World* (London, 1965). See also Loewenheim *et al.*, *Roosevelt and Churchill*, p. 97, and J. R. Leutze, *Bargaining for Supremacy: Anglo-American Naval Collaboration, 1937–1944* (Chapel Hill, N.C., 1977), pp. 75–87.

4. *Public Opinion Quarterly* IV, 713.

5. *New York Times*, March 28, 1939; *ibid.*, October 15, 1939; *ibid.*, December 3, 1939.

6. Churchill, *Their Finest Hour*, p. 415.

7. *Parliamentary Papers, Great Britain; Debates*, 5th Ser., Vol. 365, col. 39.

8. Churchill, *Their Finest Hour*, p. 404.

9. *American Journal of International Law* XXIV, 499–502, 569, 587, 680–689.

10. See J. B. Scott, ed., *The Hague Conventions and Declarations of 1899 and 1907* (New York, 1915), p. 210.

11. *Ibid.,* pp. 215, 218.

12. *U.S. Statutes at Large,* Vol. 40, Part I, p. 222.

13. *Ibid.,* Vol. 54, Part I, p. 681.

14. Samuel E. Morison, *The Battle of the Atlantic* (Boston, 1947), p. 36. Admiral Stark really wanted to trade for sovereign rights, not leaseholds (p. 119). See also Leutze, *Bargaining for Supremacy,* p. 118.

15. *Roosevelt Public Papers, 1940 Volume,* p. 402.

16. W. L. Langer and S. E. Gleason, *The Challenge to Isolation, 1937–1940* (New York, 1952), p. 773.

17. *American Journal of International Law* XXXV, 357, 358.

18. Elliott Roosevelt, ed., *F.D.R. His Personal Letters* (New York, 1950), II, pp. 1,056–1,057.

19. *Roosevelt Public Papers, 1940 Volume,* pp. 379–380.

20. *Ibid.,* p. 391.

21. Lash, *Roosevelt and Churchill,* p. 220.

22. *Fuehrer Conferences, Brassey,* pp. 134–135; Lash, *Roosevelt and Churchill,* p. 218.

23. Hugh Gibson, ed., *The Ciano Diaries, 1939–1943* (New York, 1946), p. 290.

24. Gordon W. Prange, ed., *Hitler's Words* (Washington, D.C., 1944), p. 372.

25. Alan Bullock, *Hitler: A Study in Tyranny,* rev. ed. (New York, 1962), p. 613.

26. Gibson, *The Ciano Diaries,* p. 293.

27. *Roosevelt Public Papers, 1940 Volume,* p. 594.

28. For the activation of the destroyers and later see Goodhart, *Fifty Ships That Saved the World,* chaps. XIV–XVI.

29. *Ibid.,* p. 202.

30. *Ibid.,* p. 207.

31. Morison, *The Battle of the Atlantic,* p. 36.

Chapter 8 (pp. 99–117): Lend-Leasing a War

1. K. H. Porter and D. B. Johnson, comps., *National Party Platforms, 1840–1956* (Urbana, Il., 1956), p. 382

2. *New York Times,* October 31, 1940.

3. *Roosevelt Public Papers, 1940 Volume,* p. 517.

4. R. E. Sherwood, *Roosevelt and Hopkins* (New York, 1948), p. 191.

5. See *Public Opinion Quarterly* V, 148, 158, 483, 497.

6. *Roosevelt Public Papers, 1940 Volume,* pp. 510–514.

7. Text in Winston S. Churchill, *Their Finest Hour* (Boston, 1949), pp. 558–567.

8. *Ibid.,* p. 563.

9. *New York Times,* December 11, 1940.

10. *Roosevelt Public Papers, 1940 Volume,* pp. 606–608.

11. *Ibid.,* pp. 609, 612.

12. *Ibid.,* pp. 633–644.
13. *New York Times,* December 30–31, 1940; W. L. Langer and S. E. Gleason, *The Undeclared War, 1940–1941* (New York, 1953), pp. 249–250.
14. *Roosevelt Public Papers, 1940 Volume,* pp. 663–672.
15. W. F. Kimball, *The Most Unsordid Act: Lend-Lease, 1939–1941* (Baltimore, Md., 1969), pp. 151–152.
16. *New York Times,* February 10, 1941.
17. *U.S. Statutes at Large,* Vol. 55, Part I, p. 31.
18. *American Journal of International Law* XXXV, 305–314.
19. *Presidential Press Conferences,* XVII, pp. 86–88.
20. Samuel E. Morison, *The Battle of the Atlantic* (Boston, 1947), pp. 78, 84–85.
21. *Presidential Press Conferences,* XVII, pp. 200–201.
22. *Ibid.,* p. 282.
23. Churchill, *Their Finest Hour,* p. 563.
24. U.S. Senate, *Hearings before the Committee on Foreign Relations,* 77th Cong., 1 sess., on S. 275 (Washington, D.C., 1941), p. 309.
25. *U.S. Statutes at Large,* Vol. 55, Part I, p. 32, sec. 3(c).
26. U.S. Senate *Hearings,* p. 316.
27. Wayne S. Cole, *Charles A. Lindbergh and the Battle against American Intervention in World War II* (New York, 1974), pp. 31 ff.
28. See *ibid.,* p. 491.
29. *New York Times,* January 31, 1941.
30. *U.S. Statutes at Large,* Vol. 55, Part I, p. 32; see also Kimball, *The Most Unsordid Act,* p. 198.
31. *Roosevelt Public Papers, 1940 Volume,* pp. 711–712.
32. H. L. Stimson and McGeorge Bundy, *On Active Service in Peace and War* (New York, 1947), pp. 360, 362.
33. Gordon W. Prange, ed., *Hitler's Words* (Washington, D.C., 1944), p. 373.
34. Churchill, *Their Finest Hour,* p. 569.

Chapter 9 (pp. 118–132): The Firing Begins

1. W. L. Langer and S. E. Gleason, *The Undeclared War* (New York, 1953), pp. 285–289; J. R. Leutze, *Bargaining for Supremacy: Anglo-American Naval Collaboration, 1937–1941* (Chapel Hill, N.C., 1977), pp. 178–215.
2. T. A. Bailey, *The Man in the Street* (New York, 1948), pp. 142–143.
3. Winston S. Churchill, *The Gathering Storm* (Boston, 1948), p. 381.
4. R. E. Sherwood, *Roosevelt and Hopkins* (New York, 1948), p. 274.
5. Samuel E. Morison, *The Battle of the Atlantic* (Boston, 1947), pp. 51–55.
6. *Presidential Press Conferences,* XVII, pp. 221–225.
7. William Stevenson, *A Man Called Intrepid* (New York, 1976), p. 461.
8. Gordon W. Prange, ed., *Hitler's Words* (Washington, D.C., 1944), pp. 372–374.
9. *The Memoirs of Cordell Hull* (New York, 1948), II, p. 927.

10. Prange, *Hitler's Words*, p. 373.

11. See *American Journal of International Law* XXXV, 497.

12. *Presidential Press Conferences*, XVII, p. 235.

13. Langer and Gleason, *The Undeclared War*, p. 435; *Roosevelt Public Papers, 1941 Volume*, pp. 110–113.

14. Prange, *Hitler's Words*, p. 373.

15. Winston S. Churchill, *The Grand Alliance* (Boston, 1951), III, p. 89.

16. *Presidential Press Conferences*, XVII, p. 281.

17. *Ibid.*, XVII, pp. 318–319.

18. *Ibid.*, XVII, pp. 247–249.

19. Friedrich Ruge, *Der Seekrieg* (Annapolis, Md., 1957), p. 64.

20. Morison, *The Battle of the Atlantic*, p. 58.

21. *Ibid.*, p. 61; Leutze, *Bargaining for Supremacy*, p. 256.

22. *Memoirs of Cordell Hull*, II, pp. 935–939. For the argument that the occupation of Greenland should have been based on the Monroe Doctrine rather than on an agreement with a recalled minister see *American Journal of International Law* XXXV, 506–513.

23. Prange, *Hitler's Words*, pp. 371, 374.

24. Morison, *The Battle of the Atlantic*, p. 57.

25. This account of the *Niblack* incident is drawn largely from Patrick Abbazia, *Mr. Roosevelt's Navy* (Annapolis, Md., 1975), pp. 191–195 (the best and most detailed account, based on U.S. and German records); W. L. Langer and S. E. Gleason, *The Undeclared War* (New York, 1952), pp. 445, 452, 458, 520–521; *The Secret Diary of Harold L. Ickes* (New York, 1954), III, pp. 539–540; letter of F.D.R. to Ickes, June 16, 1941, Roosevelt Papers, Secretary Ickes's file, PSF 75, Roosevelt Library, Hyde Park, New York.

26. J. P. Lash, *Roosevelt and Churchill* (New York, 1976), p. 340; *Secret Diary of Harold L. Ickes*, III, p. 466.

Chapter 10 (pp. 133–150): Increased Friction and the *Robin Moor*.

1. Roosevelt to Ickes, July 1, 1941, in *The Secret Diary of Harold L. Ickes* (New York, 1954), III, p. 567.

2. Samuel E. Morison, *The Battle of the Atlantic* (Boston, 1947), p. 61.

3. W. L. Langer and S. E. Gleason, *The Undeclared War* (New York, 1953), pp. 444–446, 451.

4. R. E. Sherwood, *Roosevelt and Hopkins* (New York, 1948), p. 291.

5. *Presidential Press Conferences*, XVII, pp. 285–295.

6. Morison, *The Battle of the Atlantic*, p. 78.

7. *Presidential Press Conferences*, XVII, p. 289.

8. *Ibid.*, p. 290.

9. J. P. Lash, *Roosevelt and Churchill* (New York, 1976), p. 315; Walter Karig, *Battle Report: The Atlantic War* (New York, 1946), p. 33.

10. Sherwood, *Roosevelt and Hopkins*, p. 295.

11. *Roosevelt Public Papers, 1941 Volume*, pp. 158–162.

12. S. W. Roskill, *The War at Sea, 1939–1945* (London, 1954), I, p. 381.

13. *Roosevelt Public Papers, 1941 Volume*, pp. 94–95.

14. Details about the *Robin Moor* sinking are taken from the thick file in the National Archives (file 195.7), in Washington, D.C., including affidavits of the survivors and an exceptionally full diary by a British passenger.

15. Before the war ended Jost Metzler published an account of his U-boat exploits in *Sehrohr Sudwarts!* [Periscope southward] (Berlin, 1943), pp. 138–148. He gives details of the *Robin Moor* episode, noting particularly his suspicions. See also *Fuehrer Conferences, Brassey*, p. 230.

16. Stephen Heald, ed., *Documents on International Affairs, 1936* (London, 1937), p. 633.

17. *New York Times,* June 11, 1941.

18. *Ibid.,* June 14, 1941.

19. Sherwood, *Roosevelt and Hopkins*, p. 299.

20. S. I. Rosenman, *Working with Roosevelt* (New York, 1952), p. 289; Ickes wanted war. See *Secret Diary of Harold L. Ickes*, III, p. 552.

21. Langer and Gleason, *The Undeclared War*, p. 519.

22. Rosenman, *Working with Roosevelt*, p. 289.

23. *Ibid.,* p. 299.

24. Text of message and proclamation in *Roosevelt Public Papers, 1941 Volume*, pp. 181–195.

25. *Ibid., 1939 Volume*, pp. 488–489.

26. *Presidential Press Conferences*, XVII, p. 364.

27. *Roosevelt Public Papers, 1941 Volume*, pp. 217–225.

28. *Foreign Relations of the United States, 1941*, II, pp. 628–634; *Documents on German Foreign Policy*, XII, pp. 1,034–1,036.

29. Message and notes, *Roosevelt Public Papers, 1941 Volume*, pp. 227–230.

30. *Department of State Bulletin* V (1941), 363–365.

31. The published diplomatic correspondence regarding the *Robin Moor* is in *Department of State Bulletin* IV (1941), 716–717, 743; *ibid.* V, 363–365; *Documents on German Foreign Policy*, XII, pp. 1,029–1,030, 1,060–1,061; *ibid.*, XIII, pp. 548–549.

32. *Fuehrer Conferences, Brassey*, pp. 219, 220.

33. *Ibid.,* p. 222.

34. *Ibid.,* pp. 232–233.

35. Admiral Doenitz, *Memoirs* (Westport, Ct., 1958), pp. 189–190; *Fuehrer Conferences, Brassey*, p. 219; Patrick Abbazia, *Mr. Roosevelt's Navy* (Annapolis, Md., 1975), pp. 173–176.

36. Doenitz, *Memoirs*, p. 189; *Fuehrer Conferences, Brassey*, pp. 219, 220.

37. Doenitz, *Memoirs*, pp. 190–191.

38. Lash, *Roosevelt and Churchill*, pp. 354–355.

Chapter 11 (pp. 151–167): Quasi-Allies of Stalin

1. R. J. Sontag and J. S. Beddie, eds., *Nazi-Soviet Relations, 1939–1941* (Washington, D.C., 1948), pp. 226–254.
2. *Presidential Press Conferences,* XVII, pp. 408–411.
3. Samuel E. Morison, *The Battle of the Atlantic* (Boston, 1947), p. 61.
4. W. L. Langer and S. E. Gleason, *The Undeclared War* (New York, 1953), pp. 575–576.
5. Morison, *The Battle of the Atlantic,* p. 74.
6. *Roosevelt Public Papers, 1941 Volume,* pp. 255–262.
7. *Presidential Press Conferences,* XVIII, p. 18; *Public Opinion Quarterly,* V, 686.
8. Morison, *The Battle of the Atlantic,* p. 78.
9. *Fuehrer Conferences, Brassey,* p. 221.
10. *Ibid.,* p. 222.
11. Gordon W. Prange, ed., *Hitler's Words* (Washington, D.C., 1944), p. 374.
12. *Ibid.,* p. 374.
13. *The Memoirs of Cordell Hull* (New York, 1948), II, p. 1,019.
14. *Roosevelt Public Papers, 1941 Volume,* pp. 314–315.
15. Winston S. Churchill, *The Grand Alliance* (Boston, 1951), p. 449.
16. Morison, *The Battle of the Atlantic,* p. 78.
17. Churchill, *The Grand Alliance,* p. 444.
18. *Ibid.,* pp. 431–432.
19. *Ibid.,* pp. 618–619.
20. British Public Record Office, War Cabinet Minutes, Cab. 65/19, 84 (41), frames 102–104. Stanford University Microfilm n.s. 1102.
21. Secretary Ickes wrote in his diary (April 20, 1941) that the administration was looking for an incident to jusify "setting up a system of convoying ships to England." *The Secret Diary of Harold L. Ickes* (New York, 1954), III, p. 485.
22. *Documents on German Foreign Policy,* XIII, pp. 291–292.
23. Loewenheim *et al., Roosevelt and Churchill,* pp. 49–53.

Chapter 12 (pp. 168–187): The Disputed *Greer* Affair

1. The best secondary account of the *Greer* incident is in Patrick Abbazia, *Mr. Roosevelt's Navy* (Annapolis, Md., 1975), chap. 20. We have also found the following valuable: "Administrative History of the U.S. Atlantic Fleet in World War II," vol. I, pt. 1, pp. 215–221, unpublished manuscript available from the U.S. Naval Historical Center, Operational Archives Branch, Washington, D.C.; Report of Commander, Destroyer Division 61 (Commander G. W. Johnson) to Commander in Chief, U.S. Atlantic Fleet, September 9, 1941, held at Naval History Division of Navy Department, Washington, D.C.; Report of Commanding Officer, U.S.S. *Greer* (Lt. Comdr. L. H. Frost, USN), to Commander in Chief, Atlantic Fleet, September 9, 1941 available at Naval Historical Center, Washington, D.C.; captured war diary of *U-652,* section on *Greer* incident (in translation) provided by National Archives and Record Service, Washington, D.C.; Vice Admiral L. H. Frost to Paul B. Ryan, De-

cember 27, 1976, and February 14, 1977; Report of Admiral H. R. Stark (September 20, 1941) to Senate Naval Affairs Committee and Stark's reply to questions, *Congressional Record,* 77th Cong., 1 sess., vol. 87, pp. 8,314–8,315.

2. Abbazia, *Mr. Roosevelt's Navy,* p. 228; "Administrative History of the U.S. Atlantic Fleet."

3. Personal information in letters from the late Vice Admiral Laurence Frost to Paul B. Ryan, December 27, 1976, and February 14, 1977. Admiral Frost died May 23, 1977.

4. *New York Times,* September 5, 1941.

5. *Ibid.,* September 6, 1941.

6. *Presidential Press Conferences,* XVIII, pp. 140–146.

7. J. P. Lash, *Roosevelt and Churchill* (New York, 1976), pp. 417, 421.

8. *Documents on German Foreign Policy,* XIII, p. 455.

9. *New York Times,* September 7, 1941.

10. *Ibid.*

11. *The Secret Diary of Harold L. Ickes* (New York, 1954), III, p. 567.

12. *Documents on German Foreign Policy,* XIII, pp. 454–456.

13. *Ibid.,* pp. 467–469.

14. *Roosevelt Public Papers, 1941 Volume,* pp. 384–392.

15. L. M. Goodrich *et al.,* eds., *Documents on American Foreign Relations* IV, p. 87; *New York Times,* September 10, 1941.

16. *New York Times,* September 9, 1941; Goodrich *et al., Documents on American Foreign Relations,* IV, p. 87.

17. *Roosevelt Public Papers, 1941 Volume,* pp. 110–113.

18. *New York Times,* September 13, 1941.

19. W. L. Langer and S. E. Gleason, *The Undeclared War* (New York, 1953), p. 746.

20. Edwin Borchard and W. P. Lage, *Neutrality for the United States* (New Haven, Ct., 1937), pp. 224, 229.

21. Samuel E. Morison, *The Battle of the Atlantic* (Boston, 1947), p. 74.

22. *Fuehrer Conference, Brassey,* pp. 232–233.

23. *New York Times,* September 17, 1941.

24. Lash, *Roosevelt and Churchill,* p. 421.

25. Langer and Gleason, *The Undeclared War,* p. 748.

26. Samuel E. Morison, *By Land and by Sea* (New York, 1953), p. 336. This in expanded form is the famous article "History through a Beard," the uncut review of Charles A. Beard's *President Roosevelt and the Coming of the War* (New Haven, Ct., 1947).

27. Langer and Gleason, *The Undeclared War,* p. 747.

Chapter 13 (pp. 188–203): The Torpedoings Increase

1. *Presidential Press Conferences,* XVIII, pp. 174–182.

2. L. M. Goodrich *et al.,* eds. *Documents on American Foreign Relations* (Boston, 1942), IV, p. 87.

3. *Presidential Press Conferences,* XVIII, pp. 174–182.

4. T. A. Bailey and P. B. Ryan, *The Lusitania Diaster* (New York, 1975), pp. 21–23.

5. *Presidential Press Conferences,* XVIII, pp. 183–189.

6. Details in *New York Times,* October 4–5, 1941; *ibid.,* October 8, 1941.

7. Quoted in W. E. Langer and S. E. Gleason, *The Undeclared War* (New York, 1953), p. 751.

8. *Ibid.,* p. 752.

9. *Roosevelt Public Papers, 1941 Volume,* pp. 406–411.

10. Details in the *New York Times,* October 23, 1941.

11. *Ibid.,* October 24, 1941.

12. Samuel E. Morison, *The Battle of the Atlantic* (Boston, 1947), pp. 92–93; Pattrick Abbazia, *Mr. Roosevelt's Navy* (Annapolis, 1975), chap. 24.

13. *Presidential Press Conferences,* XVIII, pp. 229–230, 235.

14. *New York Times,* October 20, 1941; *ibid.,* November 18, 1941.

15. Theodore Roscoe, *United States Destroyer Operations in World War II* (Annapolis, Md., 1953), p. 38.

16. *New York Times,* October 22, 1941.

17. Details on the *Lehigh* case appeared in the *New York Times,* October 22–25, 1941; *ibid.,* November 23, 1941.

18. *Presidential Press Conferences,* XVIII, pp. 239–245.

19. Text in *Roosevelt Public Papers, 1941 Volume,* pp. 438–444.

20. German press reports in *New York Times,* October 20, 1941; *ibid.,* November 2, 1941.

21. *Presidential Press Conferences,* XVIII, pp. 260–261.

22. William Stevenson, *A Man Called Intrepid* (New York, 1976), p. 230.

Chapter 14 (pp. 204–213): The Sinkings Escalate

1. Patrick Abbazia, *Mr. Roosevelt's Navy* (Annapolis, Md., 1975), pp. 283–291.

2. Samuel E. Morison, *The Battle of the Atlantic* (Boston, 1947), p. 94; Abbazia, *Mr. Roosevelt's Navy,* pp. 293–308.

3. *Presidential Press Conferences,* XVIII, pp. 267–275.

4. Charles A. Beard, *President Roosevelt and the Coming of the War* (New Haven, Ct., 1948), p. 149.

5. *Presidential Press Conferences,* XVIII, pp. 278–279; also *Roosevelt Public Papers, 1941 Volume,* pp. 462–463.

6. J. P. Lash, *Roosevelt and Churchill* (New York, 1976), p. 449.

7. For the *Odenwald* incident see *New York Times,* November 17–20, 1941; *ibid.,* November 27, 1941. The awards granted are in *ibid.,* July 13, 1947. A legal analysis is in the *American Journal of International Law* XXXVI, 96–99. The decision of the federal district court at San Juan is published in the *Federal Reporter* (Second Series) Vol. 168, 47–57. A slight modification of the court's decision was made by the Circuit Court of Appeals, First Circuit, on May 10, 1948. The ruling is published in the *American Journal of International Law* XLII,

720. Two articles that describe the incident are Paul B. Ryan, "The 'Peacetime' Capture of the *Odenwald*," *Navy*, March 1968, pp. 20–25, and Edward F. Oliver, "The *Odenwald* Incident," *U.S. Naval Institute Proceedings*, April 1956, pp. 378–384.

8. *Fuehrer Conferences, Brassey*, p. 239.

9. Gordon W. Prange, ed., *Hitler's Words* (Washington, D.C., 1944), p. 374.

10. *Documents on German Foreign Policy*, XIII, p. 779.

Chapter 15 (pp. 214–227): Edging toward Full Belligerency

1. *Roosevelt Public Papers, 1941 Volume*, pp. 481–482.

2. W. F. Kimball, *The Most Unsordid Act: Lend-Lease, 1939–1941* (Baltimore, Md., 1969), p. 216.

3. *Documents on German Foreign Policy*, XIII, pp. 621–623.

4. W. L. Langer and S. E. Gleason, *The Undeclared War* (New York, 1953), p. 757.

5. *Congressional Record*, 77th Cong., 1 sess., vol. 87, part VIII, p. 8,777.

6. *Roosevelt Public Papers, 1941 Volume*, pp. 485–487.

7. *Ibid.*, pp. 488–490.

8. A Gallup poll of October 17, 1941, reported that 76 percent of those with opinions approved Roosevelt's foreign policy; 24 percent disapproved. *Public Opinion Quarterly* VI, 161, 163.

9. Langer and Gleason, *The Undeclared War*, p. 759.

10. *Ibid.*, p. 760.

11. *Roosevelt Public Papers, 1941 Volume*, pp. 495–497.

12. *Ibid.*, p. 496.

13. *Foreign Relations of the United States, 1941*, II, pp. 833–834.

14. *Ibid.*, pp. 831–832.

15. J. E. Edwards, *The Foreign Policy of Col. McCormick's Tribune* (Reno, Nev., 1971), pp. 176–180.

16. *Ibid.*, p. 178.

17. Burton K. Wheeler, *Yankee from the West* (New York, 1962), pp. 32–36.

Chapter 16 (pp. 228–244): The Pacific Back Door to War

1. *Foreign Relations of the United States, Japan, 1931–1941*, II, pp. 165–167.

2. *New York Times*, July 16, 1938–August 11, 1938; *ibid.*, February 5–10, 1939.

3. Samuel E. Morison, *The Rising Sun in the Pacific* (Boston, 1950), pp. 16–17.

4. Adam B. Ulam, *Expansion and Coexistence* (New York, 1968), pp. 308–309, 388.

5. *The Memoirs of Cordell Hull* (New York, 1948), II, pp. 1,059 ff.

6. Morison, *The Rising Sun in the Pacific*, p. 157.

7. Diary entry in E. E. Morison, *Turmoil and Tradition* (Boston, 1960), p. 525.

8. *Hearings before the Joint Committee on the Investigation of the Pearl Harbor Attack*, pt. 14 (Washington, D.C., 1946), p. 1,329.

9. Gallup poll, October 4, 1941, *Public Opinion Quarterly* VI, 164.

10. *Memoirs of Cordell Hull,* II, pp. 1,095–1,096.

11. *Documents on German Foreign Policy,* XII, pp. 455–456.

12. *Ibid.,* XIII, p. 958.

13. *Ibid.,* XIII, pp. 999–1,000, for entire note.

14. Morison, *The Rising Sun in the Pacific,* pp. 169–170.

15. Hans L. Trefousse, *German and American Neutrality, 1939–1941* (New York, 1951), p. 151.

Chapter 17 (pp. 245–255): The Führer Fights Back

1. *Roosevelt Public Papers, 1941 Volume,* pp. 514–515.

2. *Ibid.,* p. 516.

3. Samuel E. Morison, *The Rising Sun in the Pacific* (Boston, 1950), p. 44.

4. *Roosevelt Public Papers, 1941 Volume,* pp. 522–530.

5. The best English translation is in Gordon W. Prange, ed., *Hitler's Words* (Washington, D.C., 1944), pp. 367–377.

6. *Ibid.,* p. 97.

7. *Fuehrer Conferences, Brassey,* p. 245.

8. Morison, *The Rising Sun in the Pacific,* pp. 19–20.

9. Norman Cameron and R. H. Stevens, trans., *Hitler's Secret Conversations, 1941–1944* (New York, 1953), p. 155.

10. Prange, *Hitler's Words,* p. 370.

Chapter 18 (pp. 256–273): The Final Judgment

1. Hans L. Trefousse, *Germany and American Neutrality, 1939–1941* (New York, 1951), pp. 161–162.

2. John Toland, *Adolf Hitler* (New York, 1976), pp. 860–861.

3. Eleanor Roosevelt, *This I Remember* (New York, 1949), p. 207.

4. Secretary H. L. Stimson and McGeorge Bundy, *On Active Service in Peace and War* (New York, 1947), pp. 355–381.

5. *Roosevelt Public Papers, 1941 Volume,* p. 463.

6. R. E. Sherwood, *Roosevelt and Hopkins* (New York, 1948), p. 431.

7. *Roosevelt Public Papers, 1941 Volume,* pp. 511–513.

8. Roosevelt, *This I Remember,* p. 233.

9. "Background Information on the Use of United States Armed Forces in Foreign Countries," Appendix II, U.S. House, Committee on Foreign Affairs, 91st Cong., 2 sess. (Washington, D.C., 1970).

10. *New York Times,* October 14, 1944.

11. J. P. Lash, *Roosevelt and Churchill* (New York, 1976), p. 338.

12. James V. Compton, *The Swastika and the Eagle: Hitler, the United States, and the Origins of World War II* (Boston, 1967), p. 258; this conclusion is backed by Alton Frye, *Nazi Germany and the American Hemisphere, 1933–1941* (New Haven, Ct., 1967), p. 194.

13. United Press dispatch from Bonn, *San Francisco Chronicle,* November 20, 1978, p. 13.
14. *San Francisco Chronicle and Examiner,* July 3, 1977.
15. Radio statement, June 30, 1977.

INDEX

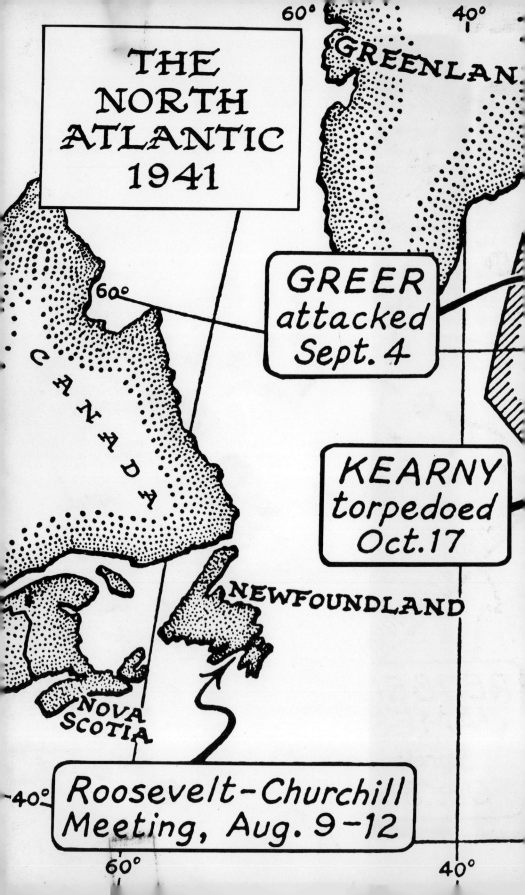